The Big Book of Marine Electronics

The Big Book of Marine Electronics

FREDERICK GRAVES

ILLUSTRATIONS BY ANNIE GRAVES

SEVEN SEAS PRESS · *Newport, R.I.*

Published by Seven Seas Press, Inc.,
Newport, Rhode Island 02840

Library of Congress Cataloging in Publication Data

Graves, Frederick.
    The big book of marine electronics.

    Bibliography: p.
    Includes index.
    1. Ships—Electronic equipment.   2. Boats and
boating—Electronic equipment.   I. Title.
VM480.G73   1986   623.89′3   85-22196
ISBN 0-915160-86-2

1   3   5   7   9   8   6   4   2

Designed by Irving Perkins Associates
Typesetting by American–Stratford Graphic Services, Inc.
Manufactured in the United States of America by
        Maple–Vail Book Manufacturing Group
Edited by James R. Gilbert

Acknowledgments

First, I want to thank my wife, Annie, the finest partner an old man like me could ever hope for. Her excellent illustrations enlivened my text, her patient proof-reading minimized my errors, and her kind encouragement kept me at it.

Second, I want to thank all the others who've helped in this project—especially those who shared the trade secrets and tips they've picked up during years of working with marine electronics on the water, on the service bench, and on the editor's desk.

My sincerest gratitude to Jim Gilbert and Dale Nouse who are two of the most patient and talented editors a writer could want.

The others are too numerous to list, but they include the American Radio Relay League, Battery Council International, Mike Buffington, Central Florida Computer Society, Chesebrough Communications, Embry Marine, Feadship of America, Gilfer Associates, Gulfstar Yacht Corporation, The Harborage at Bayboro, IMI Southwest, Jim Johnston, Rufus Lattimer, King Marine Radio Corporation, Miracle Radio Company, Si-Tex Marine Electronics, Tampa Bay Pilots Association, Tate Enterprises, United States Department of Commerce, United States Coast Guard, United States Navy, Williams Communications, Forrest Wood, Zimmerman Electronics, and many other friends who've helped me in one way or another to mess around in boats.

To David Curtis Graves, my Dad, W8LRT, a pioneer in radio who sparked my interest in electronics and taught me how things work and what to do when they quit working. I can't remember anything my Dad couldn't fix. His common sense and good humor have been an inspiration to me. I want to thank him for taking the time to teach a young boy how to make a good solder joint, how to read code, and how to dive right in and tackle any problem with the certainty that it can be done.

Contents

Prologue: How to Use This Book

This book is aimed at you, the marine electronics user.

It will show you how to get the most from your electronic gear, how to use it more effectively, how to keep it working, and what to do when it quits—before packing it in to the shop for expensive repairs.

It is not a book for electronics technicians. It is designed for you, the everyday boatowner.

Every type of marine electronic gear is explained, and each area of marine electronics is examined, including installation, emergency use, preventive maintenance, troubleshooting, and more.

This book will help you understand the theory and operation of any particular type of marine instrument or gadget. It also is intended as a general information reference source to keep your entire marine electronics installation operating at its peak.

The book is divided into six basic sections. The section on navigation gear includes chapters on Loran-C, satellite navigation equipment, radio direction finders and radar.

The section on communications equipment includes chapters on VHF coastal radio, single-si-deband high-seas radio, amateur radio communications, and the various licensing requirements for shipboard radio use.

Depth instruments are the topic of the next section. Starting with simple sounders, this section explains the use and theory of flashing sounders, digital sounders, depth recorders, and the latest color sounding devices.

A miscellany section includes such gear as emergency position indicating radiobeacons (EPIRB's), autopilots, speed/distance logs, and wind instruments.

The next section is an overview of electronic circuit theory, the lead-acid storage battery, installation guidelines, and a chapter on elementary troubleshooting, including instruction on using a multimeter and what to do to prevent electrolysis.

At book's end is a relatively complete appendix with reference information you need to understand how your marine electronics equipment works and what you can do to keep it working. Included are tables, charts and graphs for finding wire sizes and resistances, battery voltage and electrolyte specific gravity levels, electrical power consumption, radio propagation limits, speed of sound in water, and many other useful values.

In each section, essential principles and electronic laws are discussed in everyday language with an emphasis on the common sense needed to use electronic equipment more effectively and to deal with electronic problems as they arise—if not *before*.

Each chapter is designed to be studied as needed. Whenever necessary, cross-references will detail ancillary sources of information in other chapters. Use the book as a tool. Keep a copy on your boat. Recommend the more important chapters to your crew.

Electronics needn't be a mystery.

Introduction

Marine electronics is changing rapidly. Manufacturers keep advancing the art—new gadgets, more bells and whistles. Today the emphasis is on microcomputer chips, integrated circuits and satellite telemetry. Positions are pin-pointed with an accuracy undreamed of twenty years ago. Best of all, prices continue to plummet as exploding technologies compete in the marketplace. Never have there been more reasonably-priced devices available to small boat sailors to make their boating safer and more enjoyable.

Owners of small craft now can afford luxuries once available only on ocean-going ships or world-class yachts. Automatic steering is controlled by computers receiving information from a satellite 10,000 miles away. Wind instruments interfaced to electronic compasses and sensitive speed logs compute velocity made good toward your destination and the anticipated time before arrival. Depth sounders call out feet or fathoms in spoken words, freeing the helmsman to concentrate on the rocks and markers.

An exciting device now in development promises to dispense with the need to fumble with navigation charts. An on-board computer, pre-programmed with digitized chart informa-

Things are changing!

tion, displays a full-color chart on the radar screen or separate television screen. Visible at a glance are course lines, waypoints, distances and hazards to be avoided. The next step, industry leaders claim, will be circuits to update these programmed charts via satellite. No longer will tired crews have to search in vain for an extinguished flasher or changed or malfunctioning navigation aids.

Imagine it—and the marine electronics industry will find a way to make it happen.

Electronics, as perhaps no other business, continues to offer us more for less. Complexity and precision increase while prices decrease. A simple general-coverage shortwave radio, for example, costs far less today in adjusted dollars than it did twenty or even thirty years ago. Meanwhile the improved performance staggers the imagination—especially of those old-timers who can remember going to sea with spark-gap transmitters and three-tube receivers. Prices will continue to fall—while the number of features and increased precision will continue to rise and amaze us all.

However, with all the complexity and convenience of today's marine electronics offerings—perhaps because of it—some are left wondering, "Why do I need it?" The answers to that question are safety, convenience, pleasure.

Most of us use our boats for pleasure. Why drudge laboriously with a manual leadline when a flip of the switch (and a couple of hundred dollars at most) will provide you with accurate and reliable readings of the water's depth. Of course, if you like to swing a leadline, by all means do so! But, when it's cold and raining on deck, isn't it nicer to stay in the wheelhouse or under the dodger?

Or, when the fog rolls in thick as Maine chowder, do you really want to reduce speed to a crawl or drop anchor and wait for the soup to lift? Isn't it easier to turn on the electronic eye of a compact radar unit and keep on truckin'?

And, do you really want to ring that consarned bell or blow the fog whistle all day long? Isn't it be better—and safer—to throw a switch and let the genie do it?

Finally, when one of your crew complains of increasing pain in the abdomen, lower right side, becomes slightly nauseous, runs a moderate fever, and tells you she has never had an operation of any kind, do you really want to attempt an impromptu appendectomy using the galley cutlery? Isn't the saner alternative to grab a microphone off its hook and call for professional assistance?

Electronic chart system—a promise of things to come!

This book assumes you have chosen the more modern options. I have explained each type of gear in everyday terms and outlined some practical tips on how to use each individual device to its maximum potential. I've examined the theories of operation in sufficient detail to help you understand the limitations as well as the potential utility of each device. Finally, I've included some pointers on proper installation, maintenance, and emergency repair.

I hope my book will be as useful to you as it has been a pleasure for me to compile.

Happy sailing!

PART II

Navigation

CHAPTER 1

LORAN-C

With almost magical precision, Loran-C provides navigators with pin-point positioning, permitting them to find their way in any kind of weather, day or night. It is neither expensive nor difficult to use, and its reliability is excellent.

The word, "LORAN", derives from *LO*ng *RA*nge *N*avigation, and that's precisely what loran provides. Distances out to 1200 miles from the shore-based transmitter sites are covered by the system. Ships beyond 1200 miles continue to receive navigation data, but at reduced accuracy. Shore-based transmitter sites are placed so vessels can receive high-precision Loran-C transmissions along nearly all high-traffic coastal areas in the northern hemisphere. Less accurate information is available almost everywhere north of the equator. We will examine the causes of accuracy limitations—and what you can do about them—later in this chapter.

Loran has been around since World War II, when it was developed for military use. The first application was not Loran-C but its less accurate cousin, Loran-A. The equipment was unwieldy, unreliable, and difficult to tune. Of course, this was long before microprocessors and the inexpensive memory chip. But, even into the 1970's,

Compact full-function Loran-C. Note four lines of display. (*King Marine Electronics*)

Loran-A operation required complex adjustment of at least a dozen knobs and dials, the visual alignment of two oscilloscope patterns on a cathode ray tube (CRT), and tedious interpolation of the lines of position (LOPs) indicated by strings of numbers that appeared on thumbwheel dials or in tiny windows on the receiver's face.

In 1970, the "National Plan For Navigation" was published by the U.S. Department of Transportation (DOT). In this report, the DOT delineated all waters up to 50 miles offshore or out to the 100 fathom curve, whichever is greater, as the Coastal Confluence Zone or CCZ. The report suggested a system of electronic navigation be devised for ships operating in the CCZ. Proposals included Loran-C, Omega, and the Navy's transit satellite systems. The Coast Guard, after careful review of the needs of yachtsmen and commercial fishermen as well as the imperatives of large shipping interests, selected Loran-C. The choice reflected findings of the Sea Grant Program and the needs of 50,000 users of the older Loran-A system.

Today, Loran-C navigation is possible far beyond our CCZ.

Loran-C is automatic. The better machines require only to be turned on. After a moment of internal calculations, the LOPs appear on the display. When the boat moves, the numbers change in response to your new position—all automatically.

And the numbers are precise! If you know the Loran-C numbers (time difference coordinates or "TDs") of a popular fishing hole, trap buoy, or windward mark in a sailing course, you can navigate to within 50 feet of that spot every time (within certain limits which will be discussed later). A chart with Loran-C overlays can be used in newly explored waters to put you as close as 500 feet from your charted position (again within limits to be discussed).

The latest Loran-C receivers with built-in microcomputers perform internal calculations on the position data received from the Loran-C transmitters. These computers convert LOPs to latitude and longitude, displaying earth coordinates instead of Loran-C coordinates. If waypoints are entered into the computer's memory, the range and great-circle bearing of those waypoints can be displayed on the unit. An audible alarm can be set to sound as the boat approaches within a specified distance of the programmed waypoint. Cross-track error, or your distance from the great-circle route between two points, also can be displayed. Some units even tell the helmsman which way to steer so he can hold the boat on its best course, automatically accounting for constantly changing effects of current set and drift or displacement due to leeway.

Interfaces will connect Loran-C computers to other on-board navigational gear. Loran-C data can be sent to the autopilot, for example, to optimize steering efficiency. Position updates sent to satellite navigation equipment will provide constant fix information between transits. Plotters can be connected to the Loran-C to record the course made good over the bottom (valuable for search and rescue work, fishing, or surveying).

Manufacturers are now developing the electronic chart, the latest word in marine electronics. Digitized chart information is electrically stored in a read-only memory device (ROM). The ROM is then plugged into a microcomputer circuit that displays the bottom contours and coastal features in vivid colors on a CRT screen. The Loran-C interface not only tells the electronic chart where you are, it draws a line to show where you've been!

System Fundamentals

Loran-C (and Loran-A, its extinct forerunner) operates by combining hyperbolic geometry with radio and computer technology. A hyperbola is a curved line whose shape and location bears a fixed mathematical relationship to two distinct points. In Loran-C, the two points are the locations of a pair of Loran-C transmitters. At any position along a hyperbolic line, the difference between the distances to the two points is constant. In the diagram that follows, each position along the hyperbola is exactly one mile farther from point A than from point B. At position P_1, point A is five miles away, while point B is four miles away. At position P_2, point A is four miles away, while point B is three miles distant. At all positions on the hyperbola, the difference is one mile. In other words, a hyperbola is a line whose geometric shape is such that at any position on the hyperbola, the following equation is true:

$$PA - PB = K$$

where PA is the distance from position P to point A, PB is the distance from P to point B, and K is a constant value.

The following example illustrates how the

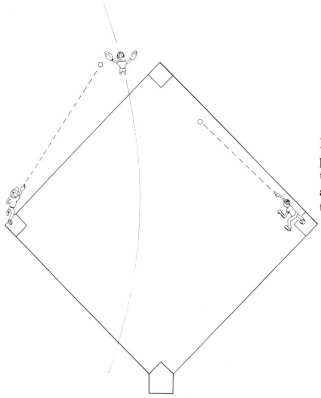

If the first and third basemen pitch to the shortstop at precisely the same instant, the time delay (TD) between the arrival of the two balls will be the same anywhere along the curved line (assuming the two players throw the balls at the same speed).

Loran-C system uses time delays (TDs) to define the hyperbola's position.

Suppose you are playing shortstop for the Loran Dodgers. The coach sends you out to practice with the first and third basemen.

The object of this practice is to improve your reflexes. The first and third basemen both pitch to you at once (both throwing at the same speed). No matter where you stand (other than on the line from home plate through second base to the middle of the centerfield wall) there will be a measurable time difference (TD) between the arrivals of each of the two balls. If you're far enough to one side or the other of the centerline, you should be able to catch one of the balls before the other gets to you. If you're closer to third, for example, you should be able to catch the third baseman's throw in time to turn and catch the ball from first.

In fact, if first and third basemen pitch at precisely the same instant, you can tell how much closer you are to one than the other by measuring the TD between arrival of the two balls. If the third baseman's throw arrives exactly one-half

second before the throw from first, you must be closer to third and, if you know the velocity of each pitch, you can compute from the one-half second TD to find just how much closer you are to third.

Notice, however, that anywhere you stand along a curved line from left field through the infield to the dugout, the third baseman's ball will arrive one-half second before the first baseman's toss. As long as the TD is constant, you know you are somewhere on that line of position (LOP). That curved line is called a hyperbola.

Of course, in the world of Loran-C the players at first and third are really high-powered transmitters located hundreds of miles away. But, the principle remains the same. The TD between reception of the two signals from those distant transmitters can only be measured along a hyperbolic LOP. If another transmitter is added to the scheme, a second hyperbolic LOP is established. By crossing the two LOPs, we can obtain a navigational fix.

One of the differences between Loran-C and the baseball example is that the pairs of Loran-C transmitters don't transmit their pulses at the same instant, but transmit at staggeringly precise time delay intervals devised so the hyperbolic lines on our charts will be situated where they will be most useful. The pulses are not particles like bullets but timed bursts of radio energy traveling at a constant velocity nearly equal to the speed of light (300 million meters per second or 2.99792458×10^8 meters/sec to be more precise). Finally, Loran-C transmitters send continuous trains of pulses, one after another, day and night, around the clock. Each train of pulses is coded so receiving equipment can identify the transmitters from which the signals originated. The time delays for Loran-C are measured in microseconds (millionths of seconds or μsecs) and fractions of microseconds .

The Loran-C receiver aboard your boat receives signals from more than a dozen shore-based transmitters, times the intervals between the arrival of pulses from one transmitter and pulses arriving from another transmitter, and displays this interval or time difference (TD) on the front of the unit. Any TD for a pair of Loran-C stations corresponds to a specific line of position (LOP) in the real world. How to navigate from TDs is explained in detail later.

Loran-C operates at 100 KHz where radio propagation is good, static noise is limited, and interference from foreign broadcast stations is virtually non-existent. Loran-A, the forerunner of Loran-C, operated near 2 MHz, a frequency limited to a few hundred miles at best and plagued by intolerable atmospheric noise and interference from foreign broadcast stations.

But there's another reason for choosing 100 KHz. Individual waves of Loran-C energy are 3000 meters long (about 2 miles) and take 10 microseconds to pass over your boat. Loran-C receiving equipment times the arrival of each pulse of energy by counting waves. Longer waves are easier to count.

Every Loran-C pulse has a distinct shape, as shown in the following figure. Rather than measure the time difference between the arrival of complete pulses (wave trains), the Loran-C receiver looks for the third wave or cycle in the pulse and locks on it. By comparing the arrival times of the third cycle from each pair of pulses,

much more precise timing is possible. The older Loran-A measured the time intervals between arrival of complete pulses, a less accurate procedure.

Loran theory is not difficult to understand. Having a basic idea how the sytem works can improve your use of the aid.

The Loran receiver on your boat is far more than a simple radio receiver. It is a high precision clock and a high-speed computer as well. The receiver listens for pulses of radio energy at 100 KHz. The clock times their arrival. The computer checks each code for possible transmission errors and determines which station transmitted the pulses, Then it determines which pairs of stations are best for local navigation and displays the TD's for the selected pairs. In addition, most sets today convert TDs to latitude/longitude coordinates, display course and distance to programmed waypoints, compute the amount of set and drift due to current, correct for errors in steering, and perform other complex navigational tasks. Despite this complexity, an individual Loran-C unit is usually called a "receiver".

Remember: Loran requires two pairs of transmitting stations, usually separated by hundreds of miles, to provide an accurate navigation fix.

Loran-C transmitters are organized in groups called chains. Each chain consists of from three to five stations—one master (M) and two or more slaves (W, X, Y, and Z). Transmitters in each chain send groups of pulses rather than a continuous string of pulses, and stations in each chain repeat their groups of pulses at unique intervals

Full-function Loran-C receiver. (*Si-Tex*)

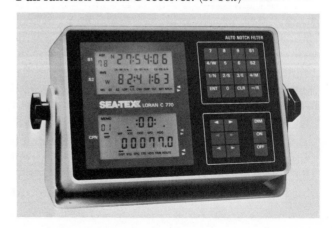

that identify the chain in a way your Loran-C receiver can understand. The group repetition interval (GRI) that identifies the chain is given as a four-digit number between 4000 and 9999. These numbers represent the group repetition interval in microseconds/10.

Each chain of transmitters is positioned to provide the best possible coverage of TD hyperbolas (LOPs). Thus, a chain that works well in the Gulf of Maine won't work at all off the coast of San Diego. A table of active Loran-C chains and their GRI numbers follows.

TABLE 1-1
LORAN-C CHAIN IDENTIFIERS BY REGION

Northwest Pacific	GRI 9970
Central Pacific	GRI 4990
North Pacific	GRI 9990
Gulf of Alaska	GRI 7960
Canadian West Coast	GRI 5990
U.S. West Coast	GRI 9940
Southeast U.S.	GRI 7980
Northeast U.S.	GRI 9960
Great Lakes	GRI 8970
Canadian East Coast	GRI 5930
North Atlantic	GRI 7930
Norwegian Sea	GRI 7970
Mediterranean	GRI 7990

Some receivers require the operator to select a chain GRI and then determine which station pairs within the chain will give the best fix. Many modern Loran-C receivers automatically select the best available chain. The Loran's built-in computer examines all received chains and locks onto the strongest chain. If the chain has more than two slaves so more than two sets of TDs are available, the computer selects the pairs that produce the best navigational fix. However, automatic receivers should provide some means to override the computer so a different chain or a different set of station pairs can be selected if needed. More on this later.

The following charts show coverages of active Loran-C chains worldwide.

A three-station chain produces only two sets of LOPs—one for each master-slave pair. If four stations are operational in a chain, three master-

Loran-C region charts.

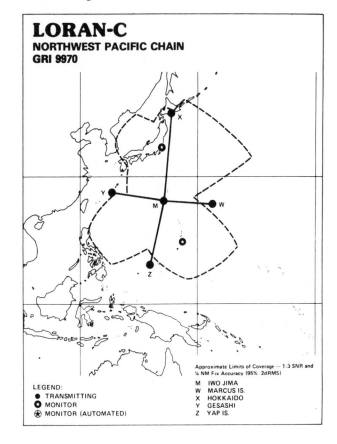

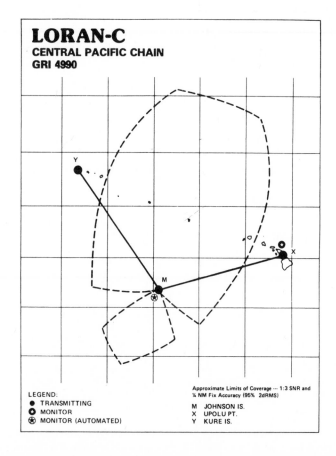

LORAN-C
NORTH PACIFIC CHAIN
GRI 9990

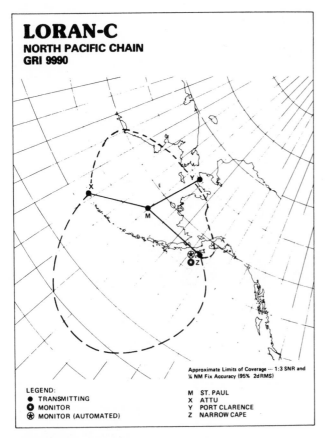

Approximate Limits of Coverage --- 1:3 SNR and
¼ NM Fix Accuracy (95% 2dRMS)

LEGEND:
● TRANSMITTING
◉ MONITOR
✪ MONITOR (AUTOMATED)

M ST. PAUL
X ATTU
Y PORT CLARENCE
Z NARROW CAPE

LORAN-C
CANADIAN WEST COAST CHAIN
GRI 5990

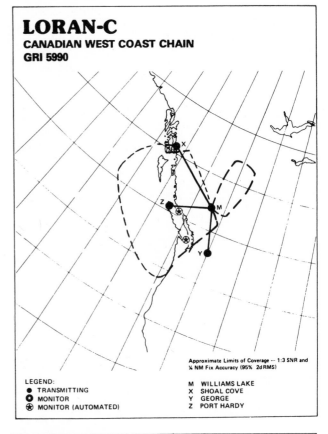

Approximate Limits of Coverage --- 1:3 SNR and
¼ NM Fix Accuracy (95% 2dRMS)

LEGEND:
● TRANSMITTING
◉ MONITOR
✪ MONITOR (AUTOMATED)

M WILLIAMS LAKE
X SHOAL COVE
Y GEORGE
Z PORT HARDY

LORAN-C
GULF OF ALASKA CHAIN
GRI 7960

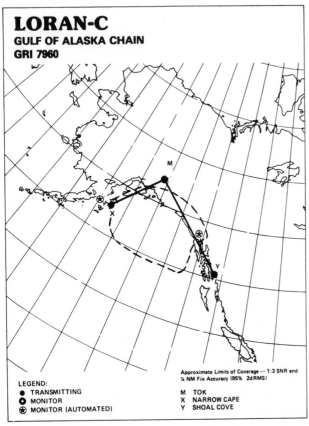

Approximate Limits of Coverage --- 1:3 SNR and
¼ NM Fix Accuracy (95% 2dRMS)

LEGEND:
● TRANSMITTING
◉ MONITOR
✪ MONITOR (AUTOMATED)

M TOK
X NARROW CAPE
Y SHOAL COVE

LORAN-C
U.S. WEST COAST CHAIN
GRI 9940

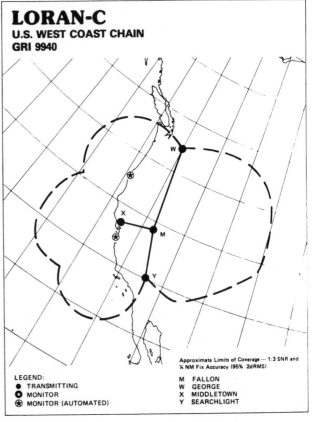

Approximate Limits of Coverage --- 1:3 SNR and
¼ NM Fix Accuracy (95% 2dRMS)

LEGEND:
● TRANSMITTING
◉ MONITOR
✪ MONITOR (AUTOMATED)

M FALLON
W GEORGE
X MIDDLETOWN
Y SEARCHLIGHT

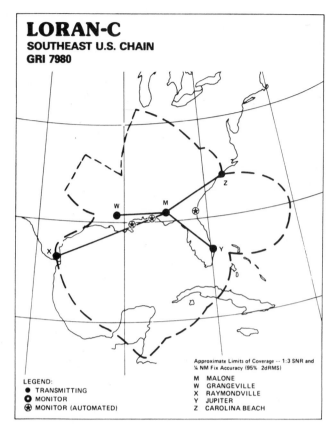

LORAN-C
SOUTHEAST U.S. CHAIN
GRI 7980

Approximate Limits of Coverage --- 1:3 SNR and
¼ NM Fix Accuracy (95% 2dRMS)

LEGEND:
● TRANSMITTING
◉ MONITOR
✴ MONITOR (AUTOMATED)

M MALONE
W GRANGEVILLE
X RAYMONDVILLE
Y JUPITER
Z CAROLINA BEACH

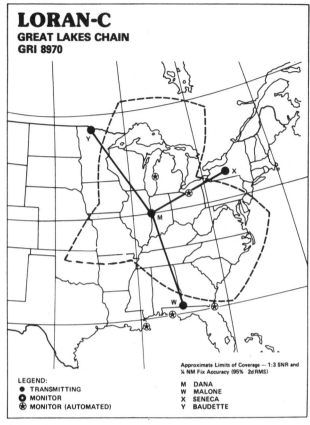

LORAN-C
GREAT LAKES CHAIN
GRI 8970

Approximate Limits of Coverage --- 1:3 SNR and
¼ NM Fix Accuracy (95% 2dRMS)

LEGEND:
● TRANSMITTING
◉ MONITOR
✴ MONITOR (AUTOMATED)

M DANA
W MALONE
X SENECA
Y BAUDETTE

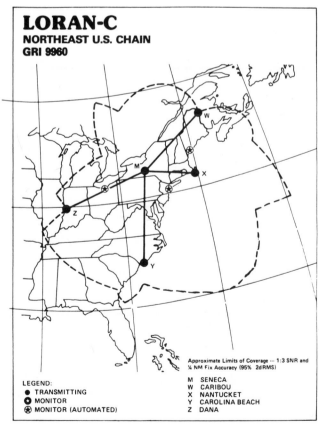

LORAN-C
NORTHEAST U.S. CHAIN
GRI 9960

Approximate Limits of Coverage --- 1:3 SNR and
¼ NM Fix Accuracy (95% 2dRMS)

LEGEND:
● TRANSMITTING
◉ MONITOR
✴ MONITOR (AUTOMATED)

M SENECA
W CARIBOU
X NANTUCKET
Y CAROLINA BEACH
Z DANA

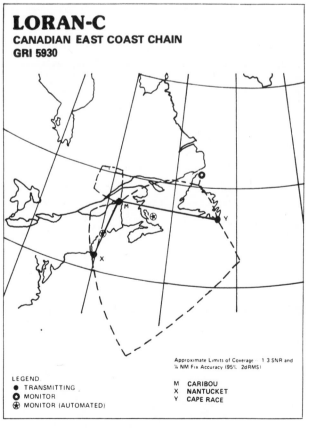

LORAN-C
CANADIAN EAST COAST CHAIN
GRI 5930

Approximate Limits of Coverage 1 3 SNR and
¼ NM Fix Accuracy (95% 2dRMS)

LEGEND
● TRANSMITTING
◉ MONITOR
✴ MONITOR (AUTOMATED)

M CARIBOU
X NANTUCKET
Y CAPE RACE

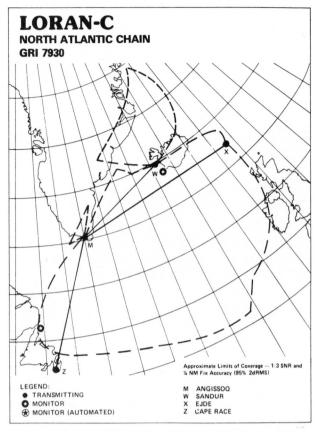

LORAN-C
NORTH ATLANTIC CHAIN
GRI 7930

Approximate Limits of Coverage --- 1:3 SNR and
¼ NM Fix Accuracy (95% 2dRMS)

LEGEND:
● TRANSMITTING
◉ MONITOR
✪ MONITOR (AUTOMATED)

M ANGISSOQ
W SANDUR
X EJDE
Z CAPE RACE

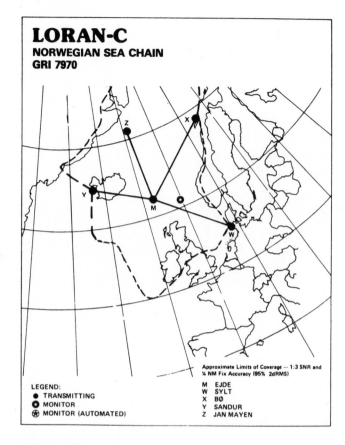

LORAN-C
NORWEGIAN SEA CHAIN
GRI 7970

Approximate Limits of Coverage --- 1:3 SNR and
¼ NM Fix Accuracy (95% 2dRMS)

LEGEND:
● TRANSMITTING
◉ MONITOR
✪ MONITOR (AUTOMATED)

M EJDE
W SYLT
X BØ
Y SANDUR
Z JAN MAYEN

slave pairs are available. Chains with five stations provide four master-slave pairs. Each pair of stations provides a different set of TD hyperbolas for LOPs.

Station pairs are identified by a letter: W, X, Y, or Z. The code 7980X, therefore, identifies the M-X pair of the Southeast U.S. Chain.

In the early days of Loran-C, sets displayed TDs from only one pair of stations at a time. In order to get a fix (by crossing two TD position lines) the operator had to switch to another master-slave pair by pressing buttons or turning knobs until the new set of numbers appeared on the display. Equipment built today can keep track of several pairs of stations at once, displaying any two master-slave pairs so the operator can take one look at the Loran-C receiver and go directly to his chart.

TD readouts are in microseconds. Equipment should be capable of displaying the TDs to the nearest ¹⁄₁₀ microsecond, such as 13374.8 or 34569.2, for full use of the precision available from the Loran-C system.

Limits of Accuracy

Many factors affect Loran-C's accuracy. Advertisements that promise accuracy to one or two boatlengths do not tell all. There are limits. Understanding these limits is imperative. You should never assume too much from Loran-C.

Always compare Loran-C positions to positions derived by other means—radar, visual bearings, soundings. Murphy's law is applicable to Loran-C: "Anything that can go wrong, will go wrong."

It doesn't happen often, but Loran-C transmitting stations do go off the air from time to time—for scheduled maintenance or due to sudden failures. The tight synchronization between station pairs may exceed tolerances now and then. Pulse timing or other critical factors can go whacko. When problems are detected at the transmitters, a special code called "blink" is transmitted to alert operators that position accuracy may be temporarily in question. Loran-C receivers are equipped to detect the blink code and display the error condition by flashing the display, beeping or

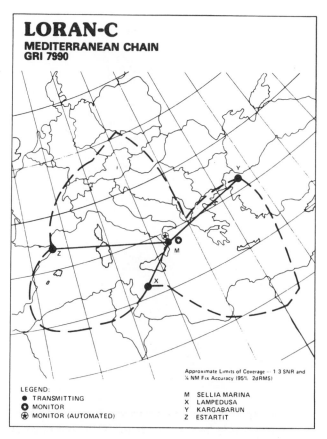

LORAN-C
MEDITERRANEAN CHAIN
GRI 7990

Approximate Limits of Coverage — 1 3 SNR and
¼ NM Fix Accuracy (95% 2dRMS)

LEGEND:
● TRANSMITTING
○ MONITOR
✪ MONITOR (AUTOMATED)

M SELLIA MARINA
X LAMPEDUSA
Y KARGABARUN
Z ESTARTIT

notifying the operator some other way that the readings may be in error. But, what if the blink code isn't transmitted for some reason . . . or your receiver doesn't detect the error? Positions indicated by the receiver can be dangerously in error—and you may not know about it! Always double-check with other piloting information: radar displays, soundings, visual bearings.

Scheduled service interruptions are announced by Coast Guard radio broadcasts and published in the *Local Notice to Mariners.*

Signal quality can deteriorate and render Loran-C positions unreliable. Decreased transmitter power, atmospheric conditions, or interference from man-made or natural causes can lessen the ability of your receiver to detect the Loran-C signals and time the incoming pulses. Interference from skywaves on the fringe of the Loran-C coverage area can cause errors in accuracy that may not be detected by even the most cautious operator.

The Coast Guard makes no guarantees.

Accuracy of charted positions averages ⅒ to ¼

nautical mile. Charts with Loran-C overlays show the approximate positions of Loran-C lines of position. Some of the latest charts are better than earlier versions, but never rely on a plotted Loran-C LOP being closer than ¼ mile (barring local knowledge or precise visual or radar bearings).

The accuracy of positions found by plotting Loran-C LOPs on a chart is called "absolute accuracy". Never rely on a plotted Loran-C fix to be better than +/− ⅒ mile. You should consider the possibility that absolute accuracy may be worse than +/− ¼ mile. Absolute accuracy limits are important when you haven't been able to fix your position by visual or radar bearings—as is the case when you're offshore and approaching an unfamiliar coastline for the first time. For example, to rely on Loran-C to find the sea buoy in pea-soup fog—without the aid of radar or depth readings to confirm what the Loran-C reports—is highly irresponsible and egregiously hazardous. The charted TD lines just aren't accurate enough.

On the other hand, the actual position in the real world out there on the water, where a particular line of position can be measured by a Loran-C receiver, is far more consistently accurate than its counterpart representative printed on the chart. The propagation characteristics of Loran-C pulses are fairly consistent. If you measure TDs at the sea buoy on your way out to sea in the morning, you can be relatively certain that those same TDs will be measured again when you return to the same spot on your way back to the dock in the evening—rain or shine. This is called "repeatable accuracy".

The TDs you measure at the sea buoy may not agree closely with the lines printed on your chart. Chartmakers use computers and complex equations to predict TD positions when printing their charts—not direct measurements of TDs at every little buoy on the chart. If you measure a particular TD at the sea buoy in the morning, and the Loran-C system doesn't go haywire during the day, you'll be able to measure that same TD in the afternoon. In some areas, repeatable accuracy may be as good as +/− 50 feet!

Whether we're talking about repeatable or absolute accuracy, three factors affect the quality of

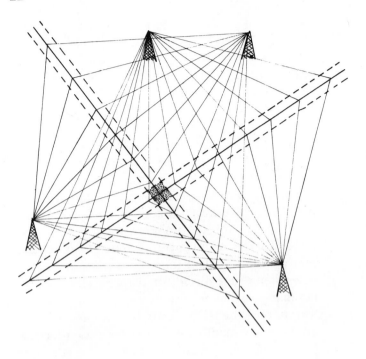

Crossing angles and fix accuracy. Perpendicular LOPs provide better fixes than LOPs that cross at more acute angles.

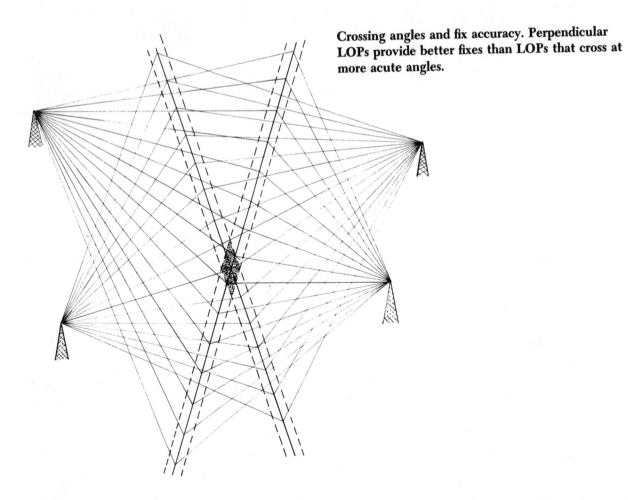

a Loran-C fix—crossing angle, gradient, and signal quality.

Crossing angle is just what its name suggests, the angle at which two LOPs cross. If the lines intersect at a right angle, the intersection is highly defined, and the point where they cross is precisely located. Each crossing line marks the position on the other line where the fix must be. If the lines cross at an acute angle, the position of the intersection is less distinct and the fix is subject to greater error. The figure that follows shows why LOPs should be selected that cross at angles of at least 30°. The smaller the angle, the less accurate is the fix—regardless of how sharp your pencil is!

Every measurement is subject to some error. If the plotted TDs are subject to an error of +/− 100 feet, the actual positions of the LOPs corresponding to the TDs can be 100 feet either side of the plotted line. We've drawn the plotted LOPs as solid lines in the figure above. We've also drawn dotted lines to represent the possible actual positions of the LOPs due to the accuracy limit of +/− 100 feet. Notice the shaded area for both fixes. Because the LOPs can be in error by 100 feet in either direction, the fix can not be a single point. You can not cross two LOPs, point to their intersection, and proclaim, "We are here!"

Your actual position may be anywhere within the shaded area, and even that depends upon the *actual* errors being the same as the *predicted* errors—a condition that often will not exist!

If actual error is no greater than predicted error, then you're located somewhere in the shaded area. Notice that the area defined by LOPs intersecting near right angles is smaller than the region where the LOPs intersect at a more acute angle.

Crossing angles should be as near 90° as possible. It is important to select chains and pairs that give proper crossing angles for accurate fixes. Some of the latest receivers can pick the best pairs for optimum crossing angles automatically—other receivers can't. Moreover, a receiver that converts to lat/lon coordinates may display an Earth coordinate fix derived from pairs with poor crossing angles, and the operator may not know that the fix is no good. We'll get back to this problem later.

Another factor affecting accuracy of Loran-C positions is the TD gradient, i.e., how rapidly a TD changes as you move from place to place. If a TD changes 20 microseconds over a distance of 1 mile the gradient is 20 microseconds per mile. In this case, a Loran-C TD difference of 1 microsecond represents a distance of 1/20 mile. If a TD changes only 4 microseconds in 1 mile, the gradient is 4 microseconds per mile, and a Loran-C reading difference of 1 microsecond represents a distance of 1/4 mile. Thus, TD readings where the gradient is 20 microseconds per mile are five times more accurate than TD readings where the gradient is 4 microseconds per mile. The following figure shows the effect of gradient on fix accuracy.

We've depicted two fixes—one where the gradient is 20 microseconds per mile, the other where the gradient is 4 microseconds per mile. Both crossing angles are the same. For simplicity, let's assume a TD accuracy no better than +/− 1 microsecond. Therefore, one fix is a square only 1/10 mile on a side. The other fix is a square 1/2 mile across. When picking a chain and pairs, select those with the closest TD gradient.

The best fix accuracy results from crossing angles near 90° and tight gradients where TDs are closely packed. This is true for both repeatable and absolute modes of Loran-C use.

If you know the TD coordinates of a particular location, say a sunken wreck where hungry fish are known to swim about, you can find your way to that spot by changing your course and running until those numbers appear on your Loran-C receiver's display. If the TD coordinates were originally measured by you on *your* receiver, the accuracy of your return is limited only by the accuracy of your receiver, the crossing angles, the gradient and, of course, the adjustment of the Loran-C transmitters. However, if you got the numbers from a local fisherman who measured the TDs on *his* receiver, there may be some slight differences due to inaccuracies between the receivers' internal timing references.

Quite large differences are possible, however, when one attempts to return to a location by lat/lon coordinates. Suppose a friendly fisherman finds a hole where giant grouper congregate. Instead of measuring the Loran-C TDs at that loca-

Gradient and fix accuracy.

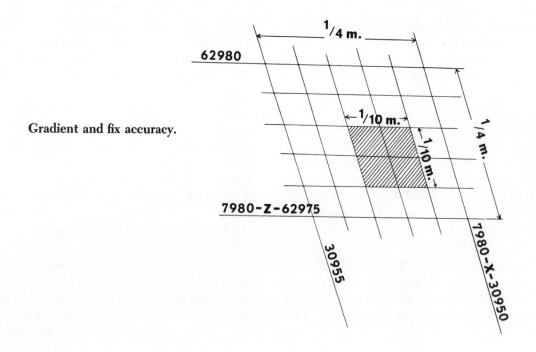

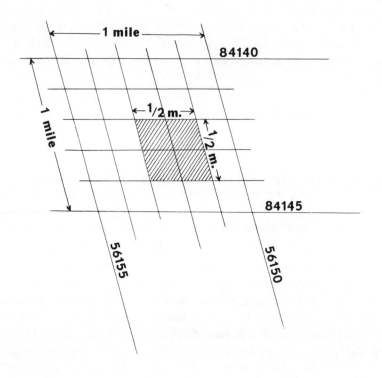

tion, he reads the latitude and longitude from his receiver instead and reports these to you. You head off in your boat to find the same lat/lon coordinates, drop anchor, and begin to fish. If your receiver and your friend's receiver are the same model and built by the same company, you might catch a grouper. If not, chances are you may be several hundred yards away from the desired location—and possibly much farther.

The explanation for this discrepancy is twofold. First, the algorithm (computer solution) that converts Loran-C TDs to lat/lon coordinates varies from manufacturer to manufacturer, and from receiver model to receiver model. If the same solution process isn't used to make the conversion, the same answer is not likely. If you want to share Loran-C coordinates with others, use TDs instead of lat/lon readings.

Causes of Error

The most common cause of Loran-C inaccuracy is the effect land and water masses have on the speed of radio waves as they travel from the shore-based transmitting stations to the antenna on your boat.

Radio waves travel in two modes: groundwave and skywave. Loran-C pulses travel primarily along the surface of the earth to a distance of about 1200 miles—groundwave. Beyond 1200 miles, pulses propagate by reflecting from the ionosphere—skywave.

Skywaves travel at predictable speeds but over unknown paths because every reflection or "hop" increases the total distance that a pulse must travel from the transmitter to your boat. Moreover, skywave paths depend on ionospheric height. When the ionosphere is high, skywave paths are long, and pulse arrival times are delayed. When the ionosphere is low, skywave paths are shorter, and arrival of pulses may be sooner than expected. Loran-C skywaves can be used to fix your location when you are beyond groundwave distances, and no other means of navigation is available, but the results should be regarded as highly questionable. Positions can be in error by several miles or more.

Groundwave arrival times vary, too, but more predictably. The groundwaves leaving a Loran-C transmitter follow the curvature of the earth, so propagation distances remain fairly constant. But groundwave speeds vary with the conductivity of the earth's surface beneath them. Groundwaves moving over water travel slightly faster than those moving over land, especially dry desert land.

Computer predictions used by government agencies to prepare the early Loran-C charts used algorithms that assumed a totally wet planet completely blanketed by a sea of constant depth. Those early equations predicted arrival times of radio pulses based on a speed of radio over saltwater—no dry deserts, no snow-capped mountain peaks, no dense forests, no electrically noisy cities. The predictions of TD positions did not account for factors that affect the speed of radio pulses as they travel over land. Charts were reasonably accurate, but serious errors existed in certain areas.

The latest charts also are printed from computerized predictions of Loran-C TD locations, but charting agencies now send survey vessels to measure precise TDs at reference points within the areas charted. These reference measurements are fed to the computers, and the machines adjust the position of TDs accordingly. The newer charts are more precise.

But errors remain. There are millions of square miles within the range of Loran-C coverage. Making direct Loran-C measurements everywhere is impractical, so a few sampling measurements are taken for the purpose of adjusting the positions of TDs to account for differences in the speed of Loran-C pulses traveling over land. These corrections improve the charts, but they do not make them perfect.

The computer inside your Loran-C receiver is similarly affected by the timing error caused by variations in the speed of radio waves traveling over land paths between the transmitting stations and your boat. Early Loran-C receivers, just like early chart-printing computers, did not account adequately for the time differences caused by the land path propagation. This created particularly nasty problems for the user who relied on lat/lon conversions provided by an older receiver.

Note here that when we speak of an "older" Loran-C receiver, we aren't talking about World War II surplus! A receiver built in 1977 may be ancient. A unit built in 1982 may be antiquated. A receiver built last year already may be obsolete when compared to today's latest model. Loran-C technology advances rapidly. New ideas are constantly implemented to add convenience or improve accuracy. Industry competition is as keen as competition can be. There are hundreds of thousands of boats without Loran-C—each a potential sale awaiting added features, simpler operation, or reduced price. If you're using an older receiver, be aware that its accuracy may be limited—especially in the lat/lon mode.

State-of-the-art Loran-C receivers permit adjustment of TDs for land path error. The time delay adjustment due to land path propagation is called "additional secondary phase factor" (ASF for short). When ASF is not considered, TDs may be inaccurate, and substantial errors in lat/lon conversions may appear because your receiver's built-computer may assume an average phase factor that may produce an inadequate correction in many areas.

ASF can be "plugged into" the Loran-C receiver's computer directly or indirectly. In the direct mode, you must know how much ASF applies to TDs for a particular station pair in your area. This number is the difference, in microseconds, between what a TD should measure at a given location in your area and what actually measures. Input methods differ from unit to unit. Consult the manufacturer's literature for actual procedure.

Probably easier for most of us (but not possible with all receivers) is the indirect method of ASF calibration. In the indirect mode, the operator simply navigates to a known location, notes the charted TDs or lat/lon coordinates of that location, and tells the Loran-C receiver where it is. The computer compares what the receiver "sees" with what you "plugged in", and computes the amount of ASF for each station pair automatically. It then uses those ASF corrections to update *all* displayed information.

Now, depending on the precision of the receiver's algorithm, you have increased the accuracy of its navigational information. However, a few problems may still arise.

For example, if you input ASF directly or indirectly using charted TD coordinates, the TDs may be more precise, but they may not agree with TDs reported by other navigators who did not apply the ASF corrections. If you want to exchange Loran-C positions for the purpose of assisting someone else to locate the excellent fishing spot you found last weekend, use uncorrected TD values and tell your friend to use his receiver without ASF.

Do not use lat/lon coordinates. Even if you plug in the ASF correction indirectly using lat/lon coordinates, calibration will be accurate over a limited range. Unless the other boat uses the same make and model Loran-C unit and calibrates for ASF at the same location you did, it's unlikely the two of you will be able to find the same spot using lat/lon. The lat/lon conversion introduces too many variables.

Oh, yes! Do not rely on buoys or other floating aids to fix your position when calibrating the ASF. And remember: the amount of ASF to apply varies with location. If you travel fifty miles in one direction, you may need to plug in a new ASF correction.

The value of applying ASF corrections indirectly by calibrating on a known lat/lon position is in piloting. For example, if you're sailing in unfamiliar waters and want to do some marker-hopping through the fog, you can switch to lat/lon mode on your Loran-C receiver and calibrate the ASF with a daybeacon's precise lat/lon coordinates as you sail by. If your unit has waypoint steering, you can enter the lat/lon coordinates of the next daybeacon and let the Loran-C display tell you which direction to steer, how far you have to go, how much the current or leeway is setting you off course. When you get within a preset distance of the next beacon, the Loran-C can be programmed to alert you with a beep—and you can send someone forward to the bow pulpit to peer into the haze.

This type of piloting can be done in the TD mode, but the process of finding the lat/lon coordinate of a charted location is somewhat easier than the process of finding its TD coordinates.

Either way, TD or lat/lon, you can make the job easier by calculating the charted positions before you shove off, noting the coordinates of waypoints in your log or marking them directly on the chart in waterproof ink.

Another source of error comes with signal deterioration. Any interference to a Loran-C signal reduces the system's ability to provide accurate navigational measurements. Fortunately, 100 KHz is not plagued by atmospheric noise as much as other frequencies, but there are sources of man-made interference that can severely degrade Loran-C operation. Depending on location, various sources of man-made interference compete with Loran-C signals on nearby frequencies. Radio filters can eliminate these sources of interference. These filters may be factory-set to eliminate interference at known frequencies, they may be user-tunable, or they may be tuned automatically by the microcomputer in the Loran-C receiver. Fixed filters are, of course, the least expensive—and these are included in all receivers. Filters you tune yourself or filters the Loran-C computer tunes automatically may be standard equipment or options available at extra cost. The point here is that some filtering is necessary. If you intend to travel great distances, you may need tunable filters to eliminate interference in faraway ports. A receiver tuned to eliminate interference in one area may not work well in another area. Ask your dealer to advise you, and read the manufacturers' specifications sheets before you buy.

Plotting

Plotting your positions with Loran-C is easy once you learn how. If the coordinates are in lat/lon, the principles are the same as with any other plotting problem. Measure in the proper direction, keep the LOPs parallel to the lines of latitude and longitude, and label the fix position with the time.

Plotting TD coordinates is only a bit more difficult.

Because the TDs are constantly changing as your boat moves, jot down the time and the values of the TD coordinates in the log or on a piece of scrap paper. Note the chain and which station pairs are being timed. A typical notation of Loran-C coordinates may be as follows:

7980-X   30923.4
7980-Y   44703.8

Both coordinates are in GRI 7980, the Southeast U.S. Chain. The first TD is measured from the 7980-X master-slave pair, the second TD is measured from the 7980-Y master-slave pair. The master station in this chain is located in the Florida panhandle, the X-slave is on the Texas Gulf Coast, and the Y-slave is near West Palm Beach.

We've used these two coordinates to plot a fix on the chart section depicted below.

Notice that two plots are depicted in the chart. Plot #1 has an excellent crossing angle very near 90°. Plot #2 is not acceptable because of acute crossing angles.

As you can see, there are many parallel lines crossing the chart from border to border, meeting each other at various angles. These lines may seem confusing at first, but notice that there are actually only four sets of parallel lines. Look closely and you'll see that many of these lines have labels. Look once again and you'll notice that some of these labels are longer than the others. One of these is circled in the upper-left-most corner of the chart; it reads "7980-W-14175". Another is "7980-X-30950", and next to it is "7980-Y-44750". Finally, near the lower left edge of the chart is "7980-Z-63000".

These are all Loran-C LOPs. Each line represents all the positions where a computer predicted you could measure the designated TD with a Loran-C receiver on board tuned to receive pulses from the Southeast U.S. Chain, GRI 7980. Each TD line is produced by a different master-slave pair. In reality, this chart is reproduced in color, and the 7980-W lines are blue, the 7980-X lines are magenta, the 7980-Y lines are grey, and the 7980-Z lines are green.

Look at plot #1. One line runs roughly SE-NW and is parallel to the 7980-X lines. The exact value of this line is 30923.4, and it is located be-

Plotting a Loran-C fix.

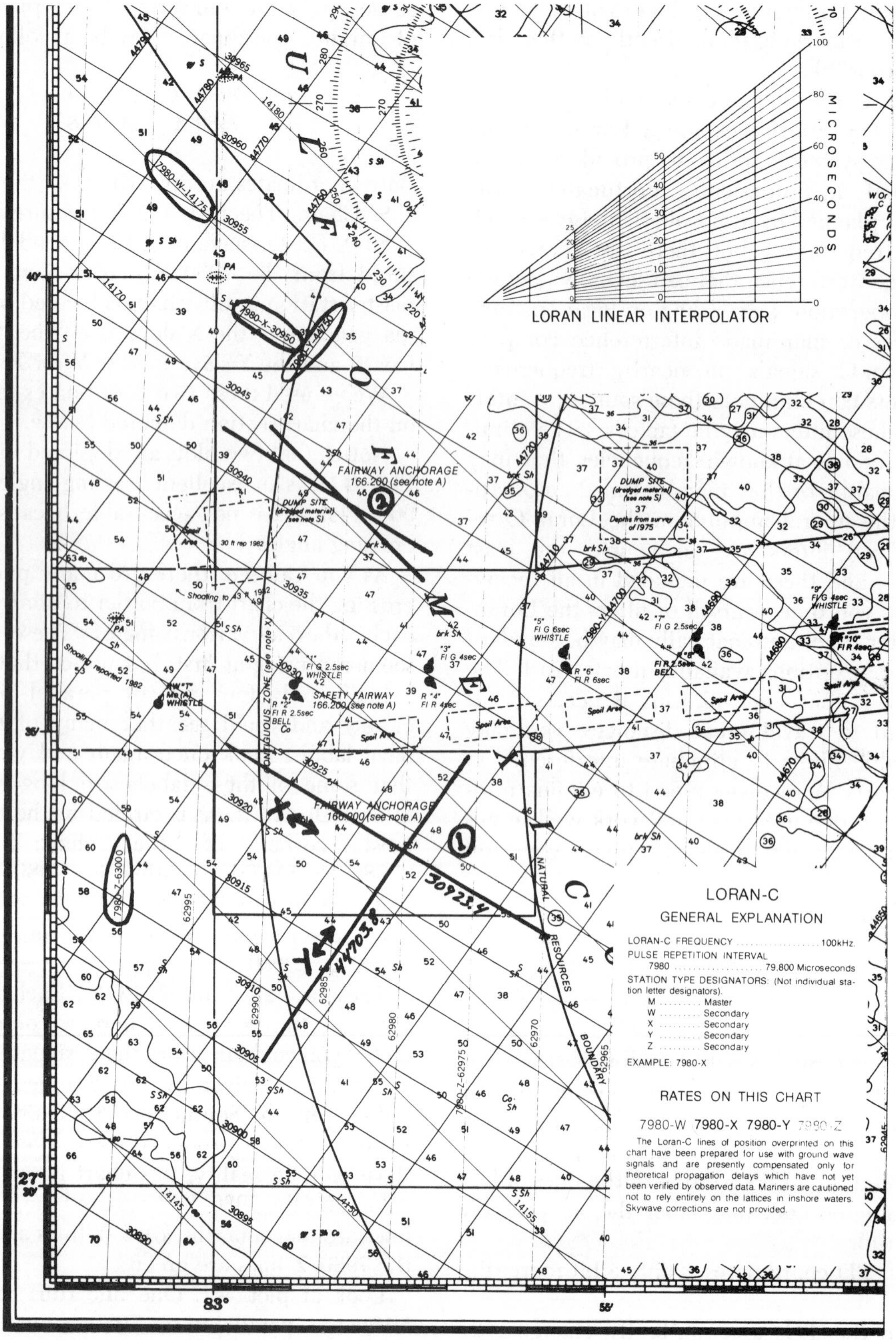

tween 7980–X–30920 and 7980–X–30925, being nearer 30925 than 30920. The other TD runs roughly NE-SW and is parallel to the 7980–Y set. Its exact value is 44703.8, and it is located between 7980–Y–44700 and 7980–Y–44710, being nearer 44700 than 44710.

To find the precise TD value for an LOP located between two printed TDs, we use the wedge-shaped Loran-C Interpolator that's printed on the chart. Notice that the three vertical lines on the interpolator are labeled in microseconds. The leftmost is labeled 0–25, the middle line is 0–50, and the rightmost is labeled 0–100 microseconds. Use the middle and rightmost scales to find intervals of 0–5 and 0–10 microseconds, respectively. Lines drawn upward and to the right from a common point at the extreme lower left are spaced evenly so that any vertical line drawn on the interpolator will be subdivided into equal spaces. Because the distances between adjacent printed TDs on a chart vary widely, use a pair of dividers to transfer a given TD spacing to the interpolator. Intermediate points are found by referring to the appropriate scale.

If you're plotting *from* the chart and want to find the value of a Loran-C TD that runs through a point located between printed TDs, use your dividers to measure the distance between the adjacent printed TDs. Note the numeric difference between the two adjacent TDs: 5, 10, 25, 50 or 100 microseconds. At some position along the interpolator, the distance from bottom line to top line is the space between the points of your dividers when the points are perpendicular to the bottom line. Use a straight edge to draw a light vertical pencil line across the interpolator at this position or simply make a light tick mark on the bottom line to locate the position. This transfered distance is divided by the interpolator into equal distances or intervals.

Now go back to the plotted point and pick off the distance from the point to the adjacent printed TD line having the lower value. Transfer the distance between the plotted point and the printed TD with the lower value to the interpolator at the position previously marked. Put one point on the bottom line and the other point directly above it. Using one of the three scales,

the value in microseconds of the distance transfered can be found. Add this value to that of the printed TD from which you measured to compute the TD value for the plotted point.

The job is half complete.

Repeat the process to find the TD value of the point in terms of the set of printed TDs most perpendicular to the first set. This establishes a pair of Loran-C TD chart coordinates. This value is subject to the limitations spoken of earlier, what the Coast Guard calls "absolute accuracy", and may be in error by as much as 1/4 mile or more. Until better charts are printed, that limitation on the accuracy of plotted TDs is inescapable.

On the other hand, if you maneuver your vessel to a location that is clearly marked on the chart, you can check the accuracy of the printed Loran-C TDs by comparing the TD values obtained by using the chart, dividers and interpolator with the TD values displayed by your Loran-C receiver. If the values agree closely, you may be in an area where absolute accuracy is better than average. If the values do not agree, you may want to change the ASF factor in the receiver so the figures do agree. Remember, however, that other navigators operating *without* ASF calibration will *not* obtain the same readings you do after the ASF adjustment. Decisions based on Loran-C information must always be made with ASF in mind.

Working *from* the Loran-C, i.e., plotting TDs displayed on the receiver, employs the interpolator in reverse. Look again at sample plot #1 on the chart above. This plot crosses the 7980–X TD (30923.4) with the 7980–Y TD (44703.8). At the moment this fix was made, the Loran-C receiver display read X–30923.4 / Y–44703.8 in microseconds.

Again, the value of having a receiver that displays two TDs at once can not be overemphasized. Another nice feature employed by some units is an "instant memory". A single touch of a button causes the TD displays to freeze . . . holding the TD coordinates of the boat's location at the time the button was pressed. This feature could mean life or death for an unfortunate crewmember lost overboard. At the cry, "Man overboard!", the helmsman needs only to press the freeze display button, write down the coordinates carefully (and double-check their accuracy against the display), then plug those same coordinates into the receiver's computer as a waypoint and return to the precise position of the accident. The freeze display button should be pressed as quickly as possible, preferably simultaneously with the man overboard cry. A boat making even 10 knots soon will be far beyond swimming distance. A Loran-C with a freeze mode can return quickly to within 100 feet of the recorded position in many areas. The freeze display function also is popular with commercial and sportfishermen who want to mark the location of a school of fish detected by the chart recorder so they can make a slow turn and back down right on top of their prospective catch.

The fix depicted by the chart shown above was taken when the Loran-C receiver display read X–30923.4 / Y–44703.8 microseconds. The navigator recorded these coordinates and noted the time.

The next step is to find the approximate position of the two LOPs. An inspection of the chart reveals that the TDs bordering 30923.4 are 30920 and 30925. The TDs bordering 44703.8 are 44700 and 44710.

Now the interpolator is used. In the approximate area of the fix, use dividers to measure the distance between adjacent printed TDs. Transfer this distance to the interpolator as before. Subtract the lower value from the measured value to find the interval. In the case of the X-TD, the interval is 3.4 microseconds. At the position where the dividers just span between top and bottom lines of the interpolator, measure up from the bottom a distance equal to the 3.4. (The distance between adjacent X-TDs is 5 microseconds, so use the 0–50 scale and divide by 10.)

Finally, use the dividers to pick off the 3.4 microseconds distance from the interpolator and mark this distance from the 30920 printed TD to find the location of a point that has a TD value of 30923.4 on the 7980–X master-slave pair. Draw a line through this point parallel to the 7980–X printed TDs. You are somewhere on this line, give or take ¼ mile.

Repeat the procedure for the other displayed TD to find the Y-coordinate.

Where the lines intersect is your location, +/− ¼ mile, more or less. Remember, the repeatable mode is far more accurate than the absolute (charted) mode. When ASF is applied correctly, however, charted positions can be quite accurate—in many cases more accurate than even the sharpest pencil point can depict.

Piloting

The lastest Loran-C receivers are more than mere devices for finding your position. They are powerful piloting tools. Not all units marketed today offer every feature described here, but most include at least a few.

Waypoints can be entered into the Loran-C's

Using a card-type Loran-C interpolator.

memory in either TDs or lat/lon coordinates. Some units are programmed with enough memory to store dozens of waypoints. Others remember only a few. A waypoint may be recalled from memory using a waypoint number or, in some gear, by entering an alphanumeric key such as "TRAP82". The latter may be easier for some of us to remember, but numbered waypoints can be recorded conveniently on 3x5 cards with complete descriptions.

The number of waypoints you will store will depend upon the type of boating you do. Towboat operators making routine trips up and down the Mississippi may want to program waypoints for every dangerous turn or obstruction. The coastal pilot making repeated runs along a shore where frequent course alterations are necessary may want to enter waypoints for each aid to navigation along the way, and also offshore rocks and shoals. Commercial fishermen may want a receiver that can remember the coordinates of every lobster pot or fish trap. Sport fishermen may need the waypoints of only a few good spots. Weekend sailors may be satisfied with programmable waypoints just sufficient to recall the channel marks along the course back into port.

There are two modes of waypoint entry: manual or automatic. In manual mode, the operator enters the lat/lon or TD coordinates of each waypoint through the front panel. In the automatic mode, the operator merely presses a single button to record the instant coordinates at any given location.

Waypoints entered in either mode can be returned to again and again (with corrections for ASF applied as necessary).

If lat/lon coordinates of a set of waypoints for a string of aids to navigation down the Chesapeake Bay are programmed into your Loran-C receiver, you can use the Loran-C to find your way through rain or fog from marker to marker. If you calibrate for ASF at the first marker, using the automatic mode by entering the lat/lon coordinates of that first marker when you're close abeam, the next marker ought to pop out of the fog just at the moment the Loran-C receiver says it should. Arrival at succeeding markers may not be so accurate, however, because the required ASF

compensation may differ greatly between Baltimore and Norfolk. For this reason, it is necessary to update the ASF calibration from time to time—the more often the better.

Most units can alert the helmsman when the boat reaches a selected distance from a waypoint. For large ships or towboats pushing long strings of barges, managing a simple change of course at a waypoint can be a complex maneuver, and preparations must be made early to alter course. On a small boat, the alarm may be helpful in alerting the crew that an obstruction has been safely passed. In no case, however, should these alarms be relied upon without reference to other navigational information and a keen eye on deck.

An anchor watch feature is similar to the waypoint alarm feature but works in reverse. Instead of beeping when the boat reaches a selected distance from a waypoint, the Loran-C is programmed to beep if the boat moves beyond a certain selected distance from the waypoint—in this case the spot where the anchor was set. If the anchor drags, the Loran-C beeps.

Of greater use than arrival alarms are the cross-track error and steering features. Cross-track error is the amount your boat is offset from your intended track. Cross-track error may be caused by current, leeway, or sloppy helmsmanship. Some Loran-C units can be set to beep when the cross-track error exceeds a preset limit—thus preventing you from being blown off course into shoal water, for example.

The great-circle course and distance to the next waypoint are displayed by most of the Loran-C receivers on today's market. Distances may be in nautical miles, statute miles, kilometers, or some other units. Many units even display your speed made good over the bottom and estimated arrival time based on that speed.

Most units provide complete information with a single glance at the receiver's display windows. Others require the operator to select different "screens" to read the various numbers needed for piloting by Loran-C. Keep this in mind when buying a new unit. The coordinates of your present position plus the course and distance to the next waypoint should be available at a glance without any additional button-pushing. In addition, the memory number of the active waypoint should be displayed. If speed made good over the bottom also is displayed, so much the better.

A few units offer automatic sequencing of waypoints. This is useful for those who expect to navigate by Loran-C from waypoint to waypoint to waypoint. A series of waypoints can be assigned to a sequencing queue for the computer to reference one at a time. As the boat reaches a waypoint, the computer automatically switches to the next waypoint and displays the new distance and course to steer accordingly. This feature is advantageous when inexperienced crewmembers are standing long tricks at the wheel without supervision.

As with all forms of electronic navigation, *do not rely on Loran-C alone*! Use every available source of navigational information including radar, soundings and visual bearings.

Interfacing

The Loran-C industry is not yet totally agreed on a standard for computer interfacing to autopilots, radar, satellite navigation equipment, course plotters, and other gear. But, some ideas are emerging, and the fog of confusion is beginning to clear. The National Marine Electronics Association has proposed a standard industry leaders are beginning to adopt. This standard likely will undergo modification in the months ahead.

The problem is akin to what the microcomputer industry is facing regarding an industry-wide standard for floppy disk data formats.

Data formats are used to define the speed of transmission and the sequence of data words in a stream of pulses between computers. A stream of data pulses may contain many words or just a few. A data stream may include identifiers at the start of each transmission that tell the receiving computer what information is to follow. A data stream may contain error-checking codes at the end of each transmission to confirm the content of the message sent. Each word in a data stream may be composed of different numbers of individual pulses or bits. The speed of transmission, or baud rate, may differ from format to format.

The receiving computer must know what format the transmitting computer is using or else the data stream it receives is meaningless.

Because the industry hasn't completely agreed on a standard format, and because the analysis of any individual format is quite meaningless except to an engineer designing interface equipment, it is difficult if not entirely useless to recommend one or another format. Be aware that there *are* several formats in use—and that a device programmed to respond to one format will not work at all when it's connected to a Loran-C using another format. The foreign format is just like a foreign language. Unless the two interconnected devices use the same data format, they will not talk to each other!

It may be wise to buy all your marine electronics equipment from one manufacturer—especially when the gear is expected to talk to each other via interfaces. If one manufacturer doesn't

Dual Loran-C receiver with built-in navigational computer.

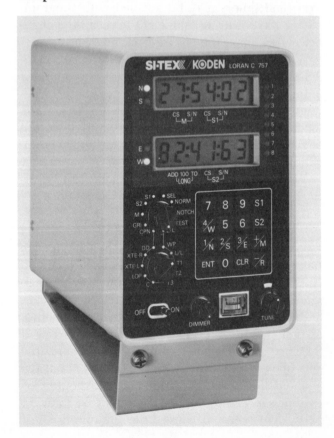

make both items of gear, e.g., a Loran-C and autopilot, then consult the manufacturers' literature to see what data formats are used by each item of gear.

Format names like 4800 baud NMEA 0180 modified, or 1200 baud NMEA 0182 can be confusing. After checking the literature carefully, ask the salesperson if the formats of the equipment you want to interface are compatible. Ask him to guarantee that the two will work together. Get him to put it in writing *and* agree to refund installation costs if the equipment won't work together.

Be cautious. This is still a developing phase of the marine electronics industry. There are surprises in store for the unwary buyer who assumes too much.

Conclusion

Even if you're not yet ready for a Loran-C, the foregoing information will give you a jump-start when you finally bite the economic bullet and put one aboard. Prices are expected to tumble soon. A few well-placed sources claim the units will someday sell for well under $100 and become a fad, like CB's. In time, they say, Loran-C computers will be built into digital watches so you can tell time and precise location with one glance at your wrist.

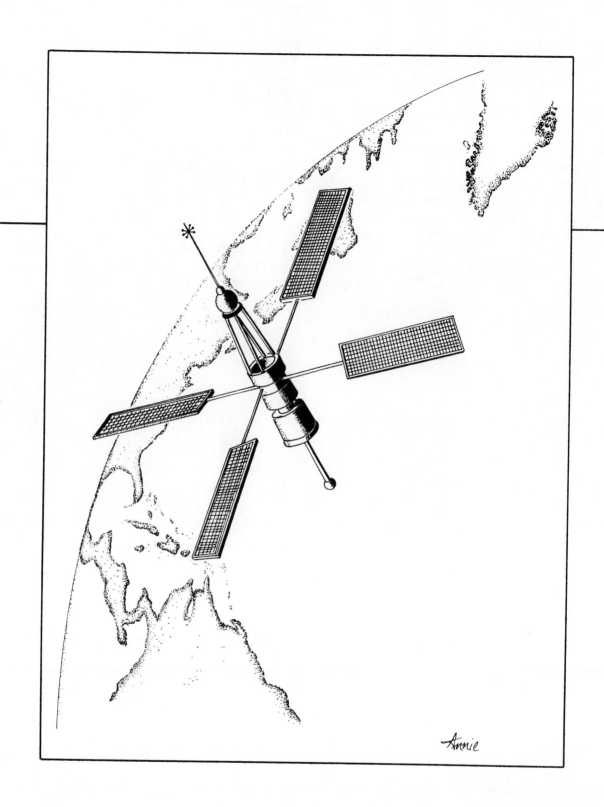

CHAPTER 2

Satellite Navigation

Introduction

When the Russians launched Sputnik I in 1957, scientists monitoring the satellite's radio transmissions back to the earth discovered something interesting. The frequency of the radio signals varied measurably as a function of the satellite's relative velocity overhead. When the satellite was "rising", its transmission frequency was higher than when the satellite was "setting".

This phenomenon is familiar to us all. When a race car speeds down a straightaway in our di-

Doppler effect.

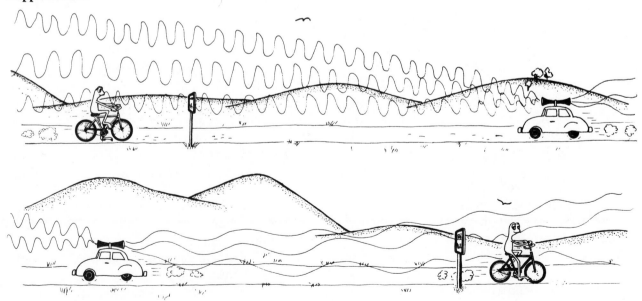

rection, the pitch of its powerful engine lowers dramatically when the car passes by us and begins moving away. The same frequency shift is observed in radio signals received from man-made satellites circling the earth. When a satellite passes overhead and is dropping away from us toward the horizon, its radio frequency is noticeably lower than when the satellite is rising.

This phenomenon is known as the Doppler effect, after Johann Christian Doppler (1803–1853) who first wrote about the change in the observed pitch (frequency) of sound waves and predicted that light waves should be similarly affected by relative velocities of the earth and distant stars. Radio, of course, had not yet been invented.

The amount of such a change in frequency resulting from the relative velocity of wave source and observer is called Doppler shift.

The Doppler effect is described in the following figure. In the first drawing, a sound source and observer are moving toward each other. (It doesn't matter if one or both are moving. It's the relative velocity that causes the effect.) In the second drawing, the two are moving apart. The pitch of the sound is a function of how many sound waves reach the observer's ear in a given length of time. When the observer and sound source are moving *toward* each other, the number of sound waves striking the observer's eardrum per unit of time is greater than when the two are moving apart.

Two scientists at the Applied Physics Laboratory of Johns Hopkins University took a special interest in the Doppler shift observed with Sputnik I. They theorized that careful frequency measurement of a satellite's transmissions could be used to determine the satellite's orbital parameters. These scientists were able to determine the satellite's position, velocity and altitude solely from Doppler shift measured by a single receiver on the earth.

As work progressed, other scientists began to wonder if there might be some other use of Doppler shift from satellites. They reasoned if one could find an unseen satellite's position by measuring its Doppler shift from a precisely known position on the earth then, conversely, one could find one's own position (such as a navigator

aboard a boat at sea) by measuring Doppler shift of radio broadcasts from a satellite that transmits its precise position back to the earth.

The amount of Doppler shift, i.e., the amount by which the received frequency varies from the actual transmitted frequency, is a function only of the relative velocities of the transmitter and receiver. It is *not* a function of the distance between them. In the calculation of lines of position in celestial navigation, the observation of the apparent altitude of a star is converted to a line of position on the earth. Similarly, a series of "observations" of the Doppler shift from a satellite of known position can be converted to navigational information.

Using minicomputers (microcomputers were not yet available), and inputting precise orbital data obtained by other means, these scientists were able to develop algorithms that yielded accurate results—and the concept of satellite navigation was born.

Within one year, the Transit program was funded. In 1964 the first Transit satellites were placed into polar orbits, circling the planet every 107 minutes. Today there are five satellites in operation with spare satellites and booster rockets in reserve to replace any that malfunction.

Tracking stations located in Maine, Minnesota and Hawaii follow the paths of the five satellites, measuring their precise positions as they pass overhead. Each tracking station transmits its measurements to a computer center in California where orbital data is compiled and re-transmitted to the satellites.

This data includes precise predictions of future orbits. The orbital data is stored in the satellite's computer memory to be re-broadcast to shipboard receivers (and other position-fixing equipment using the Transit system).

The shipboard receiver, in addition to measuring the Doppler shift, obtains precise orbital data from the satellite itself. It then transmits the Doppler shift measurements and orbital data to its built-in computer for conversion to navigational information.

In 1967, the first commercial use was approved. Today the Transit system is used throughout the world aboard military, commercial, and pleasure boats. Shipboard equipment is priced from $2000, depending on options and accuracy.

More expensive satellite navigation sets receive satellite transmissions on two frequencies (150 MHz and 400 MHz). This "dual channel" equipment is somewhat more accurate than the less expensive "single channel" (400 MHz) units. The reason for this is in the difference between the effects of ionospheric refraction on the two wavelengths. An error in the system is introduced when the ionosphere "bends" the angle of radio waves passing through the ionosphere. The amount of bending depends on wavelength. Long and short waves do not bend the same amount. By using two frequencies, the effect of ionospheric refraction can be computed, and a correction can be applied within the satellite navigation computer to cancel the effect entirely. Dual channel equipment is capable of fixing positions to better than +/− 40 meters (about 120 feet), while single channel units provide fixes no better than +/− 100 meters (about 300 feet).

Unfortunately, these accuracies are obtainable only at fixed locations. As soon as a vessel gets underway, certain unavoidable errors reduce accuracy considerably.

Unless these errors are compensated, satellite navigation is not accurate.

Fix Interval Errors

From the user's perspective, satellite navigation equipment, as it exists today, is extremely simple to use. Accuracy is good. Reliability is excellent. But there are limits.

At times, all five satellites are on the other side of the planet. Only when a satellite is high enough above the horizon is it possible for the onboard receiver to obtain navigational data and compute a fix. The navigator who relies on satellite navigation alone may be without a fix for 1–½ hours or longer, depending on latitude.

Moreover, unless the orbital paths of satellites,

Satellite navigation computer (left) on modern passenger liner.

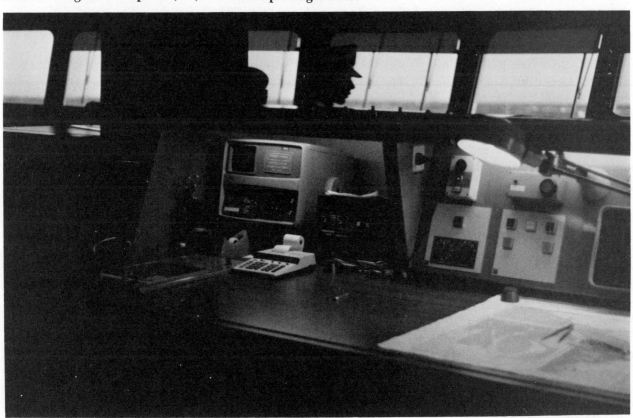

also called "birds", cause them to rise more than 10° above the observer's horizon, significant errors may result. On the other hand, if a bird flies much higher than 75° above the observer's horizon, other errors may result. Only birds reaching maximum altitudes between 10° and 75° can provide accurate fixes. Many satellite navigation receivers ignore data transmitted by birds failing to pass through the 10° to 75° altitude window.

So, even with five birds are flying at all times, there may be long periods between acceptable passes when no navigational data (or unacceptably imprecise data) is available. During these periods, other navigational data is needed to compute continuous dead reckoning (DR) positions which, as you will see, are necessary for accurate satellite navigation fixes.

The average time between fixes is a function of the observer's latitude. From the equator to the tropics, north or south, the interval between acceptably accurate fixes averages ninety minutes. At 50° latitude, the average time between fixes is about one hour. Inside the arctic or antarctic circles the average time between fixes is 30 minutes.

The time required for the satellite navigation receiver and microcomputer to obtain accurate fix data from a bird passing through the altitude window varies from 10 to 16 minutes. During this time, the satellite travels some 4,400 to 7,000 miles. Unless the satellite is above the horizon for a sufficiently extended period so complete Doppler measurements can be made with the satellite both approaching and receding, no fix is possible.

Speed and heading information can be manually programmed into the satellite navigation computer so that a running DR position is maintained. The operator merely inputs the true heading made good and speed made good over the bottom, and the computer maintains a continuous DR position readout until the next satellite pass.

Some equipment includes an interface to the speed log or the steering compass or both, so that speed and heading information is automatically updated in the satellite navigation computer. More on this shortly.

Ship Velocity Error

The accuracy of a position fix by satellite depends on the satellite knowing a ship's velocity—meaning both a ship's speed *and* direction. An error of one knot causes an error of $\frac{2}{10}$ nautical mile in the fix position. The error has a greater effect on longitude determination than on latitude, and so is most pronounced when the vessel's course is northerly or southerly. On easterly or westerly headings, latitude error is most pronounced, and longitude error is reduced. Feeding the navigation computer accurate velocity data all but eliminates this error.

In this sense velocity is the vector product of both speed and direction. Knowing speed over the bottom, for example, is insufficient. The actual course made good is also required. If speed over the bottom is known, but the course is in error, the position fix also will be in error. Conversely, an error can arise if course made good is accurately known but speed over the bottom is not known.

True heading and speed (over the bottom) must be known to obtain maximum accuracy from the Transit system,

Some units permit manual entry of vessel speed and heading. As long as the vessel remains on course and continues to make good a constant speed *over the bottom*, the satellite fix will be okay. The most accurate information will, of course, be that displayed immediately after computation of the satellite pass. At all times after the pass, DR position accuracy depends upon the accuracy of speed and heading data.

To improve accuracy (and eliminate human error), some higher priced units provide automatic speed log and/or compass interfaces. Other units offer an interface to the Loran-C (works only within range of Loran-C coverage).

Compass Interface

Either gyro or magnetic compasses may be interfaced to input true heading to the satellite navigation equipment.

A gyro interface is not particularly expensive, but the gyro compass is. If your vessel is already equipped with a gyro having a stepper or synchro output, this is the interface to choose.

A gyro compass is unaffected by magnetic variation, but ship speed does affect gyro compass readings. Errors, at worst, are on the order of one or two degrees however. If absolute precision is required, a speed log interface to the gyro may be added, thus eliminating even that source of error.

Magnetic compasses can be interfaced to satellite navigation equipment, and these installations are far more economical for small craft operators. A special compass is required, however. It is not practicable to interface to a standard steering compass.

The same rules for installation of steering compasses apply to the installation of a satellite navigation interface compass, except that many interface compasses are self-compensating. The computer in the satellite navigator can read an interface compass and create its own deviation table while you steer through a 360° circle. This internal compensation is automatic. Moreover, some equipment also knows what variation to apply, so that the compass interface data is corrected to true headings without operator intervention.

For long voyages, a compass interface may not be required. However, if many course changes are made within a short period of time, the next satellite fix will not be accurate unless each change is manually entered into the computer at the exact instant the course change is effected.

Finally, unless the satellite equipment is given the correct heading continuously, the DR position displayed between satellite updates will be in error.

Speed Log Interface

Interfaces to various types of speed logs also are available to automatically provide speed data for improving satellite fix accuracy.

Only Doppler speed logs, however, provide accurate speed over the bottom. Other logs read speed through the water (See Chapter 14 on speed logs.), and these are *not* accurate under all conditions. Besides the fact that they can not measure actual speed made good over the bottom, they have other problems that reduce accuracy. Most speed logs read speed through the water by measuring the rotation of a tiny paddle-wheel impeller mounted on the hull below the waterline. The faster the spin, the higher the boat's speed through the water. But impellers can become fouled with weed, barnacles and other marine growth. Hull shape, angle of heel, severity of wave action, and other hydrodynamic factors also reduce speed log accuracy. An accuracy of +/− ½ knot may be the best you can expect.

It's important to remember that speed through the water is not speed over the bottom. A current can alter speed over the bottom by as much as several knots.

Satellite navigation computers need to know speed over the bottom. Doppler logs provide true speed by measuring actual motion with respect to the bottom. Doppler logs are limited, however, by water depth. Doppler logs are also quite expensive. They are commonly used only on ships or large yachts.

If a standard log is installed, with a compass interface, an error of ½ knot through the water plus current over the bottom will be introduced.

However, the effect of current can be calculated by a few of the better satellite navigation computers. For example, suppose a speed of 6 knots at a heading of 060 is input to the computer. A satellite passes by, and a position fix is computed. From that fix, then, until the next satellite whizzes by to provide another fix, the computer updates the DR position from the speed and heading information being sent to it via the log and compass interfaces. DR accuracy is best just after a satellite fix and is least just before the next fix. At subsequent fixes, however, the computer can be programmed to note the difference between the DR position and the satellite fix position. This difference is a function of the errors in speed and heading data being sent to the computer from the log and compass. The computer can calculate the amount of set and drift experienced between satellite fixes, and it can then do two things more: (1) It can report the current set and drift to the operator via the display panel, and (2) it can be programmed to use the current set and drift data in all further calculations of the running DR between satellite passes.

If a Doppler log is not used to determine speed made good over the bottom, then a satellite navigation system should be selected that can compute and compensate for set and drift. Some limited improvement is possible with a paddle-wheel type speed log that can be interfaced to the satellite computer.

On the other hand, if you anticipate remaining within the skywave range of Loran-C coverage, and if you now have or plan to have a Loran-C unit on board, another option is available for maintaining accurate DR positions between satellite fixes.

Loran-C Interface

The satellite navigation system can be interfaced to Loran-C equipment, and no other interfaces are required—so long as you are operating within the skywave coverage area of Loran-C.

As discussed above, during the intervals between satellite passes (as much as 1½ hours at times) the satellite navigation equipment is "blind". Loran-C, on the other hand, always knows where it is. The problem with Loran-C is its limited range. Once you sail beyond the limits of groundwave coverage, the accuracy of Loran-C is questionable. Even within groundwave coverage areas errors are introduced (See Chapter 1.) by land-path propagation (secondary phase error).

An ideal electronic navigation device is achieved when Loran-C and satellite navigation work together.

The satellite navigation system doesn't know where it is between satellite passes. The Loran-C system doesn't know how much secondary phase error or skywave error is affecting its pulse arrival times. However, the satellite navigation computer can tell the Loran-C unit where they both are located (at least once every 1–½ hours), and the Loran-C unit can adjust its time delay readings to agree with the satellite fix position.

The result is a self-adjusting Loran-C that

Course plotter.

"knows" how much secondary phase error and skywave error to apply to its readings.

In turn, the Loran-C unit continues to receive constant data from its shore-based transmitters and calculates speed made good over the bottom. This is fed to the satellite navigation computer to improve the accuracy of its data.

After two or three passes, *both* instruments are displaying latitude and longitude, course made good, distance to the next way point, and other navigationally significant information with an extremely high degree of accuracy.

It is essential, therefore, that you select both the Loran-C and satellite navigation equipment with interfacing in mind, even if you aren't yet ready for satellite navigation equipment. At this time the industry has not agreed to data format and other interface standards, so buy cautiously. If there is any question about the ability of the units to talk to each other, make that function an element in your purchase contract. When you contract equipment selling for more than $500, most courts will ignore the so-called verbal agreement. Get it in writing. Many Loran-C units and satellite navigation computers will *not* communicate. Make the sale contingent upon their doing so.

Operation

Operating a satellite navigation system should be simple. Unfortunately, some manufacturers make it extremely difficult by requiring complex entry of specialized codes to access displays. Satellite navigation should be a hands-off process requiring no more than an occasional glance at the display to see where you are. There are no knobs to tune, no channels to select. The units should be self-functioning.

Unfortunately, some manufacturers insist on showing all data on positions, course and bearing to waypoints, and other goodies, on a two or three-line liquid crystal display. It won't fit! One display may show only position in latitude and longitude, or amount of set and drift, or great circle and rhumb line course to a selected waypoint. All information is not displayed at once.

In order to see more data, a separate display mode must be selected—and this is where the problem comes in. Some units are more logical than others, and all require a bit of thought to access the required display. Special mnemonics may be used. Color-coded buttons are another idea. Whatever the process, some button pushing is needed to access the desired information.

The alternative is a larger display—at greater cost. Many of the better units show all data on a single display, usually a CRT. The only button pushing is for starting the equipment and manually feeding speed and heading.

On the other hand, some of the less expensive units do use a logical process for accessing sub-displays—and liquid crystal displays do draw far less current from ship's supply batteries than standard CRT displays. If sub-display access seems easy to use, there's no reason to insist on having all data displayed at once on a larger CRT display. If the sequence of button pushing seems

Satellite receiver displaying latitude and longitude.

unnecessarily complex, perhaps a more logical unit is the answer.

Start-Up

Satellite navigation computers need several items of information to get started.

One of these is the approximate time. The satellite navigation computer must be told the correct time (GMT/UT) before it can decode the timed signals from the spacecraft. This time must be accurate to within 15 minutes. The computer will resolve any error less than 15 minutes by reference to the data transmitted by the spacecraft and correct itself to the nearest second. After start-up and the first pass of a satellite, the unit will provide an accurate time standard that can be relied upon for celestial navigation or other purposes.

The computer also must be told the height of the satellite navigation antenna above local sea level. This is simply the distance from the water's surface to the base of the antenna when your boat is on an even keel.

A related fact that must also be input is geoidal height of local sea level. The earth is not a sphere. It is, in fact, a rather lumpy ball whose surface may deviate from a perfect sphere by as much as 100 meters. Telling the computer how high its antenna is above sea level isn't enough. The satellite navigation system needs to know how high the sea is at your location, with reference to the geoid/spheroid differential. This can be done directly or indirectly. The direct method is to input geoidal height from the values printed on a geoidal map that shows the local differences between spheroidal sea level and geoidal sea level throughout the world. Such a map is shown in the following figure.

The indirect method of telling the satellite navigation system how high the geoid is at your initial location is to input your precise latitude and longitude and let the computer estimate its location based on a few passes of the spacecraft, compare its estimates with the value you input directly, and compute the geoidal height based on the difference. All units may not offer this function, however. Consult the manufacturer's literature.

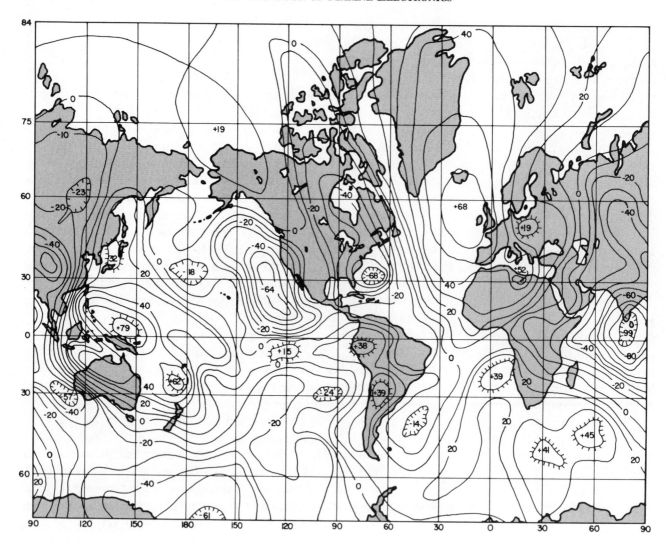

Conclusion

Clearly, navigation by satellite is on the ascent.

As new techniques develop, as more equipment is manufactured and sold to end users, as smarter use of microprocessors is made, as component and equipment costs drop, other navigation methods, such as Loran-C, may soon be obsolete.

The sky is the limit, but we aren't there yet.

In fact an even more accurate satellite system called Global Positioning System (GPS) is being built at this time and will replace today's Transit system by the middle of the next decade. Experts predict that all GPS satellites will be in constellation by 1992 and, by 1995, commercial gear will be available to private users at prices equivalent to what we now pay for Transit satellite navigation equipment. The GPS satellites will not fly around the planet like Transit satellites, and continuous fixes will be available at all times.

The Transit satellite navigation system should be around at least until the end of this century—but by the year 2000 both Transit and Loran-C will be relics.

Transit satellite navigation equipment can not tell you where you are during the intervals between satellite passes. It requires speed and heading input to maintain an accurate DR and to insure that the satellite fixes themselves are accurately determined.

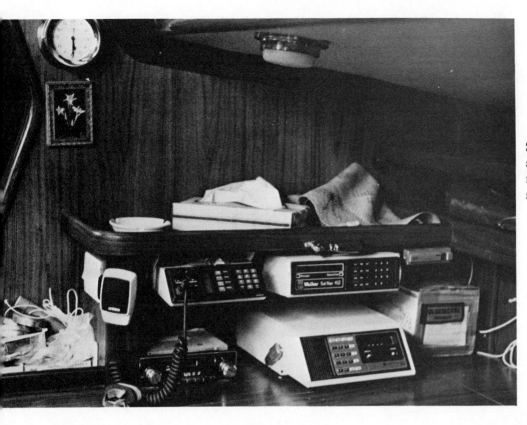

Satellite navigation unit and other gear in navstation of French sailboat.

Every 1 knot of error in the ship's velocity causes an error of 2/10 nautical mile in the satellite fix. Unless speed and heading (i.e., velocity) are precisely known, satellite fixes can not be accurately determined.

For offshore work, satellite navigation is ter-rific. It is a worldwide system, operating 24 hours a day. It works in rain or shine. It is reliable and relatively inexpensive.

It has limits but, within those limits, it is a useful aid to those who sail beyond the range of Loran-C.

CHAPTER 3

Radio Direction Finders

While daily advances in marine electronics science continue to dazzle us, radio direction finding, the simplest and oldest form of radio navigation, is still used regularly in every kind of craft from sea-going passenger liner to cod dory.

The beauty of RDF is its low cost, simplicity and reliability. For less than $300, you can equip your boat with electronic navigation. If you want to spend more, you can buy the bells and whistles, but a functional RDF unit need not cost more than a few hundred dollars—while more exotic electronic navigation equipment can cost well into the thousands of dollars.

Despite the existing popularity of Loran-C and Sat-Nav equipment, the older RDF system has much to defend it. Both loran and satellite systems rely on complex circuitry and depend upon a relatively few government-operated transmitters—transmitters that can and occasionally do go off the air. RDF bearings, on the other hand, can be taken on hundreds of marine beacons and on commercial broadcast stations.

Both Loran and Sat-Nav use external antennas usually mounted high in the rigging where they can be destroyed by dismasting or by lightning (an event that does happen from time to time). Both Loran and Sat-Nav receivers will be rendered totally useless by lightning unless the external antennas are disconnected or grounded when it strikes. Most RDFs use a ferrite rod antenna mounted inside the unit itself.

There's not much to go wrong inside an RDF unit. Most units consist of nothing more than a simple AM broadcast radio receiver with a separate tuning circuit so that low-band beacon stations (100–500 KHz) can be received. The antenna on top is nothing more than a longer version of the same ferrite rod antenna that's been used in transistor portables for decades. The ferrite rod antenna may be gussied up in a fancy rotating dome with an azimuthal ring and pointer to facilitate reading relative bearings to a distant transmitter—but inside the fancy dome is a simple ferrite rod antenna just like the one in the radio you take to the beach.

RDF works in the dark, in fog, on any kind of vessel. It is less expensive than other forms of electronic navigation and may, under certain conditions, be significantly more reliable.

At such reasonable prices, every boat that ventures far from shore should carry one. Many boat owners can afford a spare.

Principles

At close range, radio waves travel in straight lines. They don't curve to the right or left and, although they may bend a bit around the horizon or bounce back and forth between the earth and a high-altitude layer of ionized gas known as the ionosphere, they do so by following nearly perfect great circle courses from transmitter to receiver.

Because of the straight line propagation characteristic of radio waves, directional antennas can be used to take bearings on distant stations by detecting the direction from which incoming radio waves are travelling. This principle has been understood and used since the pioneer days of radio.

When a ferrite rod antenna is broadside to an incoming signal, the strength of the detected signal is greater than when the antenna is turned end on to the incoming waves. As the radio energy passes over the antenna, an electrical current is induced in the antenna. When the antenna is broadside to the approaching radio waves, the induced current is at its peak, and more radio energy is presented to the receiver.

Loop antennas, used on some RDFs, are most sensitive when aligned with the path of incoming radio waves and least sensitive when the loop is broadside.

When a ferrite rod antenna is rotated around a vertical axis, the signal strength from any distant station will vary from a maximum (when the rod antenna is broadside to incoming waves) to a minimum (when the antenna is end on). The positions of the antenna when incoming signal strength is at an absolute minimum are called null points. At the nulls, the incoming radio wave path is directly in line with the rod, giving the operator an accurate bearing to the transmitting station.

Finding these points is called null tuning. A meter or other electronic indicator can be used to determine the precise points at which the incoming signal strength is at a minimum, or you can use your ear to estimate when signal strength is at a null. Using radio volume instead of a meter or other is called "aural null" tuning.

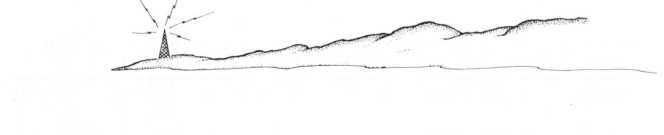

Directional antennas. When a ferrite rod antenna is turned broadside to a transmitting beacon, the meter indicates a high signal level. When the antenna is turned end-on to the beacon, the meter indicates a minimum reading, or "null."

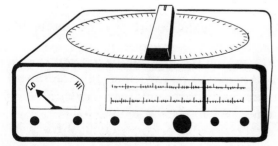
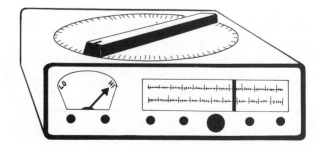

Automatic direction finder.

But, a radio beacon may be located in either of *two* opposite directions—both in line with the RDF antenna but 180 degrees apart. In other words, the incoming radio waves appear to come from opposite directions.

The problem of 180 degree ambiguity is eliminated by using a separate "sense antenna" to detect which of the two possible bearings is the actual bearing of the transmitting station.

Manual radio direction finders use a simple telescoping whip antenna similar to the telescoping whip antenna on a portable FM radio. The whip antenna is extended manually, and a sense switch is activated to determine which of the two ambiguous directions is correct. With the sense antenna extended and the sense switch activated, the ambiguity disappears.

Automatic direction finders (ADFs) pick the correct bearing with no operator intervention required. The true direction of the radio beacon transmitter is indicated without ambiguity.

Features and Innovations

The best recent RDF innovation is digital frequency readout. With the older dial-type frequency indicators, one was never certain just what frequency he was tuned to. Unless you heard the station you were looking for, you were never certain just where it was located on the dial. All you could do was tune back and forth in the general area and hope to hear it beeping at you.

With a digital readout all that is ancient history. All you need to do is set the dial to the beacon frequency and wait. If the station is transmitting (and if you're within range) you'll hear it! You can set the digital readout to the beacon frequency you are interested in, and relax. No more twiddling the dial back and forth while waiting.

Frequencies and schedules for RDF broadcasts are listed in publications 117A and 117B of the Defense Mapping Agency Hydrographic/Topographic Center. These publications are available where charts are sold.

RDF equipment that works at VHF frequencies is available. It typically costs more than conventional RDF gear and is designed primarily for air-sea rescue work, rather than navigation. This gear is just beginning to be seen in the pleasure boat market.

A recent RDF idea, uses a microprocessor-controlled receiver and directional antenna to measure radio bearings from several transmitters at once. The unit computes your position from known positions of the transmitters and reports latitude and longitude. At this time the idea is still in its infancy, but there's little doubt that we'll see other uses of microprocessors in RDF,

Manual direction finder with digital frequency readout.

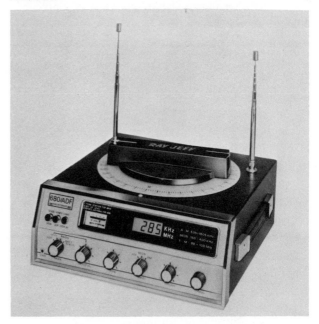

both for enhanced signal processing and complex interpretation of positioning data.

Piloting

But don't let technology lead you into shoal waters. RDF is not accurate!

RDF is limited by the vagaries of radio in general, the quality of equipment, the skill of the navigator, and a vessel's rigging that can interfere with the direction of incoming radio waves.

Generally speaking, RDF can't provide bearings more accurate than about +/− 3 degrees . . . at best. Quite often the potential accuracy of RDF is far less than +/− 3 degrees, and that is a total of 6 degrees possible error (+ 3 degrees added to −3 degrees).

The fact that an RDF azimuth ring is calibrated to the nearest degree or even tenth of one degree means nothing. Errors creep in. Many inexpensive RDFs have azimuth rings marked at intervals of 2 degrees. The unwary may assume that bearings taken by such units are accurate to 2 degrees. It just isn't so!

Bearings taken by RDF are *relative* bearings, i.e., bearing angles relative to the boat's heading.

Fix accuracy limits. An RDF bearing may be in error +/−5° or more. The area of most probable position is within the black triangle.

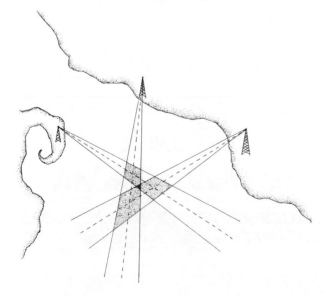

If the steering compass is accurate to +/− 1 degree (an excellent compass), and the helsman can steer no closer than +/− 2 degrees, and the RDF is readable only to the nearest 2 degrees, the possible error may be 5 degrees or more!

Do not assume that radio bearings can be plotted as rhumbline bearings on the common Mercator chart. Radio waves follow great circle courses, and radio bearings are great circle bearings. As such they can not be plotted as straight lines on Mercator charts except at latitudes very near the equator or where the distance between the transmitting station and radio direction finder is on the order of a few tens of miles or where the bearing is directly north or south. In high latitudes, the great circle bearing to a radio beacon may differ considerably from the rhumbline bearing, and the greater the distance between transmitter and radio direction finder the more this is true. Bearings nearly east or west are affected more than bearings nearly north or south.

If a Lambert projection chart is used, there need be no correction for great circle error. Straight lines drawn on Lambert charts describe great circles. Radio bearings on Mercator charts are corrected using a conversion table. Such a table may be found in the appendix of this book.

The greater the distance between a transmitting station and an RDF receiver, the more correction is needed before the bearing can be plotted on a Mercator chart. In temperate or tropical latitudes, little or no correction may be needed when plotting radio bearings from beacons nearer than 100 miles. In higher latitudes conversion may be needed even with closer beacons. At extreme latitudes, RDF use should be confined to conning only, i.e., steering beacons within a few miles of the vessel.

RDF Deviation Table

Although incoming radio waves travel in straight lines from the transmitting antenna to your boat, they do funny things as they approach a metallic hull or travel through wire rigging. Electromagnetic waves induce currents in conductors around which they travel. These induced currents in turn cause the conductors to re-radiate as antennas. The re-radiated radio waves may travel in new and unpredictable directions.

The result is that incoming radio waves do not travel in a perfectly straight direction once the waves begin to interact with the hull and rigging. Depending upon boat size, hull material, rigging arrangement, and other related factors, the *apparent* direction of incoming waves may be altered by several degrees—and the alteration is not constant but changes from location to location on the boat.

This anomaly is similar in principle to the problems encountered with magnetic compasses aboard any boat with ferro-magnetic fastenings or structures, or carrying high current equipment like welders or power winches. A magnetic compass will not indicate the same heading at all locations on the boat. Local magnetic anomalies interfere with the earth's magnetic field, causing the compass heading to deviate from the actual local magnetic heading. Some deviation can be corrected by installing compensating magnets near compass locations but, in most boats, some residual deviation always remains to introduce an error between compass bearings and actual local magnetic bearings. These residual errors are tabulated in a chart called a deviation chart, which determines what error, if any, exists between what the compass reads and what it should read.

Radio direction finders also have deviation errors caused by the hull and rigging. These errors also differ from location to location on most boats. If an RDF is used at several locations on board, an RDF deviation table should be prepared for each.

Even hand-held RDFs are susceptible to errors caused by rigging. If you hang on a stay to lean outboard and take your RDF readings away from the rigging's influence, bearing accuracy may be improved. However, some surprising errors may remain. Just for fun sometime, take radio bearings on an antenna you can see with your unaided eyes. Pick one that's at least 5 miles away. Shove the helm down and sail in circles. You may be surprised to discover that the RDF doesn't always point at the transmitting antenna!

An RDF deviation table is prepared in the same manner as a compass deviation table. Find a location where the water is smooth, a spot where

TABLE 3-1

RDF RADIO DEVIATION TABLE

RDF Rdg.	Radio Bng.	Dev.	RDF Rdg.	Radio Bng.	Dev.
000°	002°	2°E	180°	182°	2°E
010°	013°	3°E	190°	193°	3°E
020°	024°	4°E	200°	204°	4°E
030°	033°	3°E	210°	213°	3°E
040°	042°	2°E	220°	222°	2°E
050°	051°	1°E	230°	231°	1°E
060°	060°	0°	240°	240°	0°
070°	070°	0°	250°	250°	0°
080°	079°	1°W	260°	259°	1°W
090°	088°	2°W	270°	268°	2°W
100°	097°	3°W	280°	277°	3°W
110°	106°	4°W	290°	286°	4°W
120°	117°	3°W	300°	297°	3°W
130°	128°	2°W	310°	308°	2°W
140°	139°	1°W	320°	319°	1°W
150°	150°	0°	330°	330°	0°
160°	160°	0°	340°	340°	0°
170°	171°	1°E	350°	351°	1°E

you can steer in circles without being disturbed. A spot where a beacon antenna can be clearly seen with the unaided eye is best. Lacking that, pick a spot where the actual magnetic bearing to a transmitting antenna is known with accuracy. The station need not be overly powerful, but its signal must be clear. Don't use a station beyond a mountain or behind a city skyline. A station within 10 or 20 miles is best.

Steer in slow, tight circles, taking bearings on the station as you turn through 360 degrees. Note the relative RDF bearing at 10 or 15 degree intervals and record the difference between what the RDF says and what it *should* say. This is the RDF deviation. The following is an example of an RDF deviation table.

If the RDF indicates a greater relative bearing value than the actual magnetic bearing, the RDF deviation is westerly. If the RDF indicates a smaller relative bearing value than the actual magnetic bearing of the transmitting antenna, the RDF deviation is easterly.

RDF deviation is applied according to the same rules used to apply compass deviation.

Radio Bearing to RDF Reading: West is best and East is least.

Relation of RDF bearing to boat heading. To obtain radio bearing, add the compass heading of the boat to the RDF bearing.

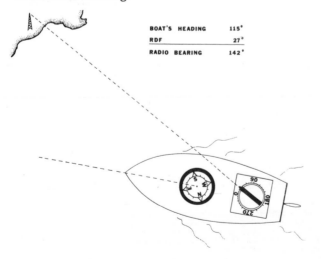

BOAT'S HEADING	115°
RDF	27°
RADIO BEARING	142°

From the actual radio bearing to the RDF reading add westerly and subtract easterly radio de-

viation. From RDF reading to actual radio bearing, add easterly and subtract westerly radio deviation.

Taking Radio Bearings

Another source of error in using RDF to find bearings to the antennas of distant transmitter locations is the need to convert the radio bearing to a magnetic bearing that can be plotted on a nautical chart.

Taking Bearings with a Console RDF

Console model RDFs do not contain their own compasses. Only by comparing the RDF bearing to the steering compass bearing is it possible to obtain a bearing that can be plotted on a nautical chart. This can be a tedious task for a navigator working alone.

The RDF is aligned with the vessel's lubbers line (the fore-and-aft line), and relative radio bearings are compared with the compass heading to determine the compass direction of the radio bearing. Because one can not be looking at the compass and at the RDF simultaneously, the process of determining relative radio bearings and converting to compass bearings is quite involved.

Moreover, the RDF should *not* be located near the steering compass. At least six feet should separate the two. Otherwise the magnetic RDF components can interfere with the steering compass, resulting in incorrect magnetic bearings. (This is true for *any* radio—especially those containing built-in loudspeakers. Keep them away from your steering compass.)

The best way to take radio bearings, therefore, is to work with a second crewmember. One person steers while watching the compass carefully. The other person attends to adjustments on the RDF.

At the precise instant the navigator finds a clear and convincing null, she shouts, "Mark!" The helmsperson reads the steering compass at that same instant and reports back. The navigator records the compass heading, applies compass deviation and adds the relative bearing indicated by the azimuthal pointer on the RDF to obtain the magnetic bearing of the radio beacon.

Note that compass deviation must be applied to the compass heading, not the radio bearing. Enter the compass deviation table with the compass heading reported by the helmsperson, extract the compass deviation and apply it to the compass heading to obtain the magnetic heading of the boat before adding the radio bearing.

For example, suppose the navigator adjusts the RDF receiver and slowly rotates the directional antenna until reaching a perfect null. She shouts, "Mark!", and the helmsperson shouts back "three-oh-eight". The navigator reads the azimuth pointer on the RDF at 204 degrees. If compass deviation at 308 degrees is 5 degrees easterly, the magnetic bearing to the transmitting beacon is found as follows.

308° compass + 5° easterly deviation = 313° magnetic
313° magnetic + 204° relative = 517° magnetic
517° magnetic − 360° redundancy = 157° magnetic

Because 517° is greater than 360°, we say it is redundant. The navigator subtracts 360° to get 157°, the actual magnetic bearing of the beacon.

Note: This is not a true bearing. To convert to true bearings, apply local variation. Consult the bibliography in the appendix for a list of piloting titles that explain variation.

Taking Bearings with a Hand-Held RDF

Hand-held RDFs contain their own compasses, eliminating the need for the complex procedure described above. However, compasses built into hand-held RDFs have small cards rendering RDF compass bearings less precise and therefore less reliable than those taken with larger compasses. Small card size limits accuracy. In fact, it can be said, the bigger the compass card, the better the compass (within reasonable limits).

A small compass card is not subjected to the same rotational torque forces from the earth's magnetic field as is a large card. Where insufficient magnetic interaction exists between the compass card and the earth's magnetic field, compass bearings are less accurate. The magnifying lens in a hand-held RDF merely makes the numbers more readable—it does not improve the card's response to the controlling magnetic forces.

Moreover, like a steering compass, the magnetic compasses in RDFs also need compensation for each point in the boat where they are used. This compensation is in addition to the radio compensation already mentioned. Magnetic de-

Handheld RDF being used at the taffrail outside the rigging where radio deviation is minimized.

The bridge of a modern passenger liner is alive with complex marine electronics. (*Capt. Michael Buffington*)

viation errors may amount to several degrees depending on the RDF's location on the boat.

In practice, however, only one table need be prepared for each location. Because the process of taking radio bearings with a hand-held RDF and comparing these with charted magnetic bearings is a single-step process, any deviation observed contains both radio deviation and compass deviation. When the deviation is applied, the result is a magnetic bearing that can be plotted on a chart.

Make no mistake about it. Unless your boat is a non-metallic dinghy with no rigging or metallic spars to interfere with radio and magnetic fields, an RDF deviation table is required for *all* locations on board where the unit is going to be used.

Radio Beacons

Virtually any radio station that can be tuned in on an RDF can be used for direction finding. The most reliable frequencies are between 100 KHz and 1600 KHz.

Aero beacons work well. So do AM broadcast stations. Again, however, stations located at great distances may require correction for the difference between great circle and rhumbline plotting—especially at high latitudes.

Special direction finding beacons are erected by government agencies at key points along the coasts of the world to help with navigation. A few offer simultaneous sound/radio transmission to permit calculating distance to the beacon by using a stop-watch. These stations are listed in Coast Pilots and other government publications and can be identified by special chart notations. During restricted visibility, these stations transmit radio pulses and sound a horn, bell, or claxton

Radio Direction Finder with dial-type readout.

at the same instant. The time interval between receiving the radio signal and hearing the horn can be converted to distance by a simple formula.

$$\text{miles} = \text{seconds} / 4.8$$

If accuracy is not critical, just divide by five. In other words, if five seconds after hearing the radio signal you hear the horn, the radio transmitter is one nautical mile away, more or less. If you time the interval precisely using a stopwatch, the distance can be found with better accuracy.

Some radio beacon stations offer RDF and compass calibration services by appointment. One example is Thomas Point Light just off Annapolis Harbor in the Chesapeake Bay. Contact a local Coast Guard station for instructions.

Conclusion

Many types of radio direction finding equipment are on the market today. Some are more suited to marine use. Others are employed by aircraft and ground vehicles. Specialized directional antennas and associated receiver circuitry have been developed to make possible the measurement of relatively precise bearings to any transmitting radio station.

It's a good idea to carry at least one hand-held RDF unit if you're going offshore. It's also a good idea to carry a spare set of batteries in a sealed plastic bag.

If you have Loran-C and/or satellite navigation equipment, so much the better. But when you need the backup, a simple RDF will see you through.

Caution: Radio bearings are taken on transmitting antennas, which are not always located at the same position as a station's studio or business offices. Nautical charts show the positions of beacon and commercial radio station transmitting antennas.

Radar

For coast and harbor navigation, nothing is as helpful as a radar unit. Radar can "see" through rain, fog and the gloomiest night, using its electronic eye to show landmasses, daybeacons, buoys and boats.

Range and distance to any radar target can be found directly from the radar display. Navigation by radar is precise and easy. Position fixes can be plotted quickly from information displayed, and changes in position are immediately updated on the screen to provide a constant picture of your position and the positions of all radar targets nearby.

Options include adjustable range rings with digital readout of distance to any displayed target, azimuth cursor with digital readout of bearing to any displayed target, range alarm to alert the operator when any target moves within a preset distance from the radar-equipped vessel, color displays for bright and readable images, north-up or course-up presentations, relative-motion or true-motion presentations, anti-collision functions to detect the existence of hazards, off-centering function to shift the display for better views of nearby targets, remote display to permit simultaneous monitoring from more than one

Color radar.

navigation station, target enlargement to enhance the size of target pips at distant ranges, plotter overlay so eraseable markers can be used to plot changing target positions right on the screen. And that's just a few. We'll examine the options in a subsequent section.

Principles of Operation

RADAR, is an acronym for RAdio Detection And Ranging.

Radar works by bouncing radio pulses off the targets and timing the interval between transmitting and receiving the pulses. The position of a rotating antenna at the moment an echo is detected provides the means of determining direction to the target.

The principle of radar is similar to that used by electronic depth sounders, except that radar uses ultrahigh frequency (UHF) radio waves instead of ultrasonic sound waves, and radar uses a rotating antenna while depth sounders use a fixed transducer.

Radar units transmit pulses of radio energy from a slowly rotating antenna (sometimes called a scanner). Whenever the pulses reflect from a distant object, some of the energy returns to the scanner. The direction in which the scanner is pointing when a reflection is detected is the direction of the target causing that reflection.

Thus, range *and* bearing are displayed on the radar screen.

In older radar units, an "electron gun" in the display tube is aimed in the same direction as the rotating scanner up in the rigging or out on top of the wheelhouse. When a radar echo is detected, the electron gun fires a burst of high-energy electrons at the phosphor coated screen, causing the phosphor coating to glow at that point, making a pip appear on the screen. The retentivity of the phosphor-luminescent coating inside the CRT causes the pip to continue glowing for several seconds—usually until the scanner rotates to that bearing again when the pip may be re-painted by another burst of electrons.

Newer radars use microcomputer circuitry and display pips on the screen using the same technology your personal computer uses to create graphics displays. In some units the computer decides which pips are false echoes and which are caused

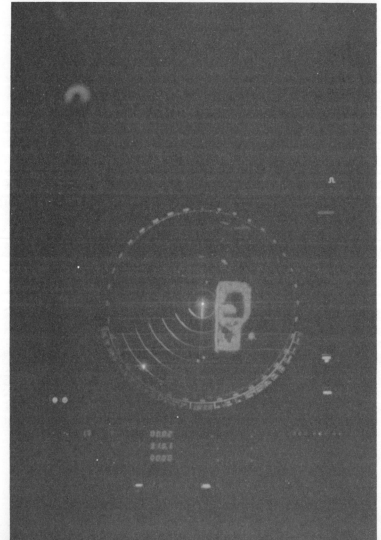

Radar view of ship channel in Tampa Bay.

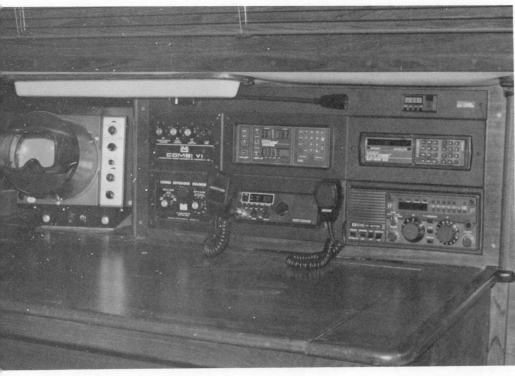

Radar at navstation. (*IMI Southwest*)

by real targets, thus eliminating interference and unnecessarily confusing pips on the display. This new technology is replacing the older and will be the standard before the end of this decade.

One unit that has just become available to small boat owners for less than $2000 (including scanner) features target tracking, range and bearing to selected target, and interfaces to a Loran-C and depth sounder to pack the most valuable piloting information into one display. The user can mark any target with a special cursor, and the radar computer will thereafter keep track of that target, displaying range and relative bearing. If the target gets closer than a selected alarm distance a buzzer sounds in the wheelhouse.

Radar pulses, like all other radio waves, travel through air at the speed of light, 328,000,000 yards per second. Thus a radar pulse will travel 164,000,000 yards to a reflecting target and return again to the radar antenna—a total distance equal to 328,000,000 yards—in one second.

In practice, however, far smaller distances are measured. Rather than millions of yards, a typical radar unit measures distances in hundreds or thousands of yards. The time required for a radar pulse to travel such short distances is, of course, much less than one second—indeed, millionths of seconds.

A special unit is used to measure such brief intervals: the microsecond (abbreviated μsec), equal to a millionth of a second.

In one microsecond, a radar pulse can travel one millionth of the distance it could travel in one second, or a total of 328 yards.

That converts to a target distance of 164 yards, since the total pulse travel distance is equal to the

Sixty-four mile color radar.

distance *out* plus the distance *back*. If the interval between transmission and reception of a radar pulse is exactly one microsecond, the distance to the reflecting target must be exactly 164 yards.

Of course, the math is done automatically by electronic circuits inside the radar transceiver. Radar targets simply appear as glowing pips located at their proper distance from the center of the radar screen—depending upon the range selected by the user.

The vessel's heading is represented by a line drawn from the center of the screen to the top center of the screen. This is called a "heading-up" display. A target bearing 090° relative to the vessel's heading appears to the right of center near the top of the screen. A target bearing 180° degrees relative appears below the center, toward the bottom of the screen. A target bearing 315° relative appears above and to the left of center.

A simple azimuth ring around the perimeter of the screen and a rotating cursor permit the navigator to measure precise bearings to targets by aligning the cursor with any target and reading the relative bearing to that target from the numbers printed on the outer azimuth ring. The rotating cursor may be a simple round frame with a wire hairline stretched across its diameter. In more costly units the azimuth ring and cursor are

interfaced to computer circuits that display bearings to targets on a separate digital readout.

The above figure shows a radar screen with the range set to 8 nautical miles. The maximum distance that can be seen with the radar set to this range is 8 miles. A target appears at the maximum range, near the edge of the screen, bearing 140°. Another target is marking at 4 miles, bearing 035°.

Note the concentric range rings at 1 mile intervals. These are added to the display electronically by the radar unit and, in most units, can be turned off when a clear and unobstructed view is required.

An adjustable range ring is an option with some models, standard equipment on others. A control on the unit causes the adjustable range ring to expand or shrink in diameter so that the ring can be made to intersect any selected target. When the ring intersects a selected target, the precise distance to that target is displayed by a digital readout. Without an adjustable range ring, distances must be estimated by interpolating between the fixed concentric range rings.

In the figure above, the range setting has been changed to 16 miles. Notice that a beach is now visible at 12 miles, bearing southwesterly and running NW-SE. The target formerly visible at

Radar screen on 8-mile range.

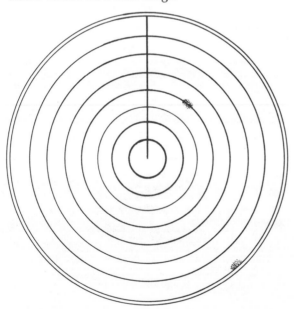

Radar screen on 16-mile range.

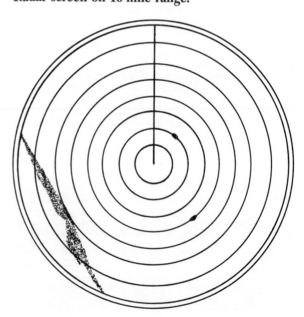

the edge of the screen when the unit was set to the 8 mile range is still visible but now appears halfway out on the screen.

Concentric range rings now appear at 2 mile intervals. Range ring placement is automatically selected for each range setting.

Radar Weather

Although radar can usually see through rain, a heavy shower may reduce sensitivity to targets within and beyond the area of rainfall. Extremely heavy rain can form a radar-opaque curtain, through which nothing can be "seen". Even a light shower may obscure especially small targets. A subsequent section explains how to tune the radar controls to maximize radar sensitivity on a rainy day.

Ironically, a real plus favoring the installation of radar even in small craft is its ability to detect rain. A radar screen provides a detailed weather map, showing clearly what's in the surrounding area within radar range. A 24–mile radar unit sees 1809 square miles. A 48–mile range radar unit sees 7238 square miles. And those are square nautical miles!

Squall lines and rain showers are clearly visible. A weather-wise navigator can easily pick the best course to follow, considering the positions of squalls showing on the radar screen.

Racing sailors plan courses to make best use of the winds associated with rain squalls depicted on the radar screen. With a little experience, a sailor can cut several minutes or even hours from a passage by tacking early to avoid an expected wind-shift or changing course to intercept a favorable air flow.

Radar will be the heart of this complex navstation. Note dropcloth protecting the chart table where tools are being used.

Limitations and Dangers

Radar provides a picture of what's out ahead, behind, and on either side. Radar can see through fog, through rain, or through the blackest night.

But radar can mislead and confuse.

For example, many radar units continually trace a bright heading marker line right up the center of the screen to show the course that's straight ahead. This bright trace on the screen also can obscure a target dead ahead—such as an approaching ship steaming straight toward you at 20 knots. If the heading marker can be switched off when not needed, targets dead ahead will be clearly visible without the heading trace to obscure them.

Another common error occurs when the selected range is changed without re-adjusting the receiver's sensitivity. If, for example, the radar had been used at short range for navigating through a harbor and was then switched to the 48 mile range upon passing the sea buoy on the way out into open water, the sensitivity control (also called the gain control) may need to be re-set so that distant targets will be picked up at the new range setting. The sensitivity required for close range work is less than that required for longer range settings. If the sensitivity is not re-adjusted after changing to the longer range, the radar receiver may not detect weak targets. This, of course, can cause some unpleasant surprises.

If the range setting is switched without advising the navigator of the change, another hazard will exist. Suppose a child is permitted to play with the controls while the navigator attends to some other duty. If the range had previously been set to 16 miles, and the child changes the range to 1 mile, the navigator may mistakenly believe a target 500 yards ahead is actually 4 miles away. The results, of course, could be catastrophic.

It is the navigator's duty to check the range control setting and all other adjustments *before* interpreting any radar display.

The advertised maximum range displayable on a radar screen may exceed the capability of individual units. Radar performance can not be increased by advertising or by printing larger

Radar on bridge of modern passenger liner.

Radar installation on bridge of motoryacht.

numbers on a control console. It is easy to modify a radar set by adding a switch with extra positions so the range can be set to 32 or 64 miles. However, the ability to actually "see" a radar target at such distances depends on more expensive factors, e.g., transmitter power, height and quality of antenna, receiver sensitivity, and a host of other things including installation. A range switch that can be set to 64 miles does not of itself guarantee that the radar can actually detect targets at 64 miles—especially small targets. When buying a new radar unit, write into your sales agreement exactly what performance you expect from the unit—then insist upon it. If your application requires a certain minimum range performance, make the dealer guarantee that performance—*in your boat*.

Radar has limitations. Be wary of them.

Pips aren't always what they seem.

Radar can only see objects that can reflect radar energy. An old wooden piling poking its dangerous head a few inches above the waves may not appear on the radar screen. A small fiberglass boat may be invisible to radar. The size and intensity of pips depends upon how much radar energy the target can reflect.

Round objects or objects that slope away from the radar may not reflect strongly. Square objects or objects that present large, flat surfaces to the radar usually will return strong echoes.

However, radar only sees the *near side* of target objects. It can not determine how "deep" a target is. For example, a steep shoreline may show up on the radar screen as a solid line with nothing apparent beyond the line (unless tall buildings or other structures behind the shore reflect the radar pulses farther inland). An island between the radar equipped vessel and the shore may appear

**Two views of Tampa Bay
from Japanese freighter.**
(*photos by Jim Byrne*)

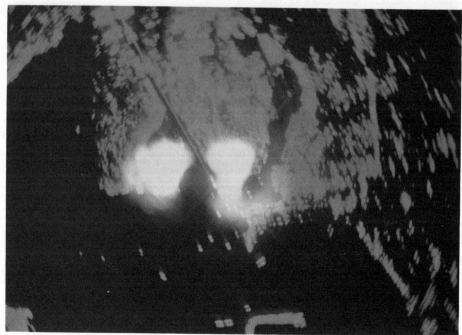

on the radar screen as a promontory, hiding the mainland shore behind it in a radar "shadow". A low, offlying beach may be entirely invisible to radar, while higher dunes inside the beach itself show clearly on the screen. The effect, of course, is the impression that the shoals along the shore are farther away than they actually are. A common danger.

The consequence of relying too strongly upon the information provided by the radar set may be disastrous.

In the following sections, some radar characteristics and their effect on the presentation of target pips is examined.

Pulse Length

The ability of a radar set to see nearby targets or to discriminate between two targets at the same relative bearing but separated by a short distance depends upon the length of the radar pulse transmitted by the scanner.

Pulse length depends upon the length of time the transmitter is turned on during each transmitted burst of radar energy. Pulse length is also called pulse duration.

At the start of each pulse transmission, a train of radar waves begins to move away from the scanner. The train continues to lengthen until the transmitter is turned off.

Effect of Pulse Length on Minimum Range

Let's examine how the length of that pulse affects the minimum radar range at which targets can be detected.

For the purpose of illustration, let's see what happens when pulse duration of 1 μsec is used. The physical length of a 1 *usec* pulses is 328 yards. At the instant of transmission, the pulse begins to move out from the scanner. Exactly 1/2 μsec later, the leading edge of the pulse is 164 yards from the antenna—but the antenna is still transmitting. If a radar target exists at 164 yards, the pulse will reflect from the target and move back toward the scanner antenna so that at the end of 1 μsec, the reflected pulse has returned to

the scanner. At the same instant, the transmitter turns off and the receiver turns on, the reflected pulse is detected, and a pip is displayed on the radar screen at 164 yards.

Note, however, that any target closer than 164 yards can not be detected with a pulse duration of 1 μsec, since the transmitter will not have turned off by the time the reflected pulse returns to the scanner. Any target inside 164 yards will be missed if pulse duration is 1 μsec or longer.

For short-range work, a shorter pulse duration is required. With pulse durations of 0.1 μsec, targets as close as 16.4 yards can be detected and displayed. So-called "river radars" used by towboats and other craft navigating congested waterways transmit very short pulses so that targets within a few yards of the radar can be detected and displayed on the screen.

To find the minimum target detection range from the shortest pulse length, multiply the pulse duration (in μsec) by 164. The product is the minimum detectable range in yards.

Study the specification sheets. Note pulse durations (pulse lengths) for various units. If your type of boating requires radar detection of short-range targets, install a unit that uses shorter pulses on

Sixteen-inch ship radar display. (*Furuno*)

close-range settings. Remember, the numbers printed on a switch do not determine range performance. The laws of physics *do*. Short-range detection requires short pulses.

Effect of Pulse Length on Discrimination

If the radar pulses are too long, two targets in line with the radar but separated by a short space may fuse together and appear as one pip on the radar screen. A shorter pulse permits the two targets to appear as separate pips on the screen. Shorter pulses also cause pips to paint more distinct images of target objects.

If pulse duration is 1 μsec, pulse length is 328 yards. If a pair of ships are anchored 164 yards apart, for example, and if the second ship is directly beyond the first, a 1 μsec pulse is not going to distinguish between them but will display them as a single pip. As the leading edge of each pulse reflects from the first ship, some of the energy continues on toward the second ship and reflects from it. Since the two boats are less than 1μsec apart, the two reflections join together, moving back to the radar as one pulse—instead of two—and a single pip is painted on the screen.

Reducing receiver gain (sensitivity) may aid in separating a pair of pips, but other targets may disappear as a result.

If pulse duration is 0.1 μsec, instead, a different situation exists. The shorter pulse reflected from the first ship is on its way back to the radar before the remainder of that pulse reaches the second ship. By the time the reflection from the second ship begins its return trip to the radar, the first reflection is complete. The two reflections are separated in time and space, so a separate pip is painted on the radar screen for each.

If discrimination between targets located in the same direction is needed—as is the case when running channels where range markers are separated by short distances—short pulse durations are required to separate the pips.

Effect of Pulse Length on Maximum Range

The primary disadvantage of short pulse lengths is that range is limited. Short pulses contain less energy. Weaker pulse energy results in weaker target reflections. The longer the range of a target, the more critical is the power of a reflected pulse.

The least expensive way to increase radar pulse power is to increase the duration of each pulse. Longer pulses contain more total power than short pulses and will provide detectable reflections at greater range. The trade-off, however, is loss of targets at close range and the inability to discriminate between any two targets situated near each other.

Many radar units automatically use longer waves on longer range settings. The fact that targets close in may be lost, and that discrete targets situated close together may disappear should be kept in mind when operating the radar where pulse length is automatically lengthened.

Effect of Scanner Height on Range

Like VHF radio, radar range is essentially line-of-sight. No matter how powerful the transmitter or how sensitive the receiver, a mooring buoy bobbing its round little head a few inches above the surface of the bay will not be seen on a radar screen at 48 miles! An offshore lighthouse or large ship, on the other hand, may appear clearly.

Radar *can* see a short distance beyond the visible horizon, however. To find distance to the radar horizon, take the square root of your scanner's height (in feet) and multiply by 1.22 to get distance in nautical miles.

There are unusual conditions, however, in which the maximum radar range may be in-

Seventy-two mile radar. (*Furuno*)

TABLE 4-1

DISTANCE TO RADAR HORIZON

SH	HD	SH	HD	SH	HD	SH	HD
6	2.9	36	7.2	90	11.4	200	17.1
10	3.9	40	7.6	100	12.0	240	18.6
14	4.5	50	8.5	120	13.1	280	20.1
18	5.1	60	9.3	140	14.2	360	22.8
24	5.9	70	10.0	160	15.2	440	25.2
30	6.6	80	10.7	180	16.1	600	29.4

SH = scanner distance from waterline.
HD = horizon distance in nautical miles.

creased by many miles. If a layer of warm, dry air forms over a layer of cool, moist air, targets may be detected far beyond the maximum ranges normally observed. The radar waves are confined between the surface of the earth and the discontinuity between the overlying air masses. But, the long range targets detected by this tunnel effect may confuse the display.

If cool, moist air moves over a surface layer of warm, dry air, radar performance may be shortened below the predicted maximum ranges.

Effect of Radar Frequency Band

Most commercial radars sold today transmit in the X-band, at 9400 MHz. Waves at this frequency are only 3 centimeters long, so antenna sizes are manageable for small craft. X-band units work well in most applications, providing crisp pip images.

One limitation of the X-band, however, is its limited range. All is well up to 32 miles or so in most weather conditions, but the short, 3 centimeter waves tend to be dispersed by particulate matter in the air—spray, dust, rain, etc.—so that signals returning from distant targets are weakened.

Shorter radar waves also are dispersed by fog—defeating a principle reason for installing radar in the first place!

Longer waves provide greater range by penetrating dust-laden or spray-filled air without dispersion. More energy reaches the target, and more energy is returned in the reflected pulse. The result is improved long-range performance.

Some small-craft radar manufacturers offer S-band units. The S-band frequency is 3050 MHZ, with wavelengths at 10 centimeters. These longer waves reach farther targets, but larger scanners are required, and less target discrimination is possible—i.e., the pips are not quite as crisply defined on the radar screen.

Most small-craft users will find X-band radar adequately meets their needs. Large ships may install both.

The problem with S-band radars on small craft is that longer range is not possible without greater antenna heights, anyway. If the highest location for mounting a scanner on your boat is only 24 feet above the water, long-distance radar ranging may be moot, since only the tallest targets would be visible at great range.

Horizontal Beam Angle

Horizontal beam angle (or horizontal beam width) is a measure of the ability of the radar to distinguish between two targets located next to each other at the same distance but separated by a small bearing angle. If the horizontal beam width is too great, the two targets will merge and appear as a single pip on the radar screen.

The problem arises with the scanner antenna. A small scanner can't provide narrow horizontal beam angles. The following table shows the effect of scanner size on horizontal beam angle.

If horizontal beam width is 2° (common in small craft radar units), bearing imprecision is +/− 1°. Point targets, such as RaRef buoys, do

SCANNER SIZE AND BEAM ANGLE

SCANNER SIZE	HORIZONTAL BEAM ANGLE
30″	3.8°
37″	2.8°
44″	2.4°
48″	1.9°
72″	1.2°
84″	1.0°

not appear as distinct points but as parts of an arc 2° wide! When plotting such point targets, measure bearings to the center of the pip.

Plotting errors can crop up when a large, unusually shaped target returns an unbalanced reflection. The target may not be located at the center of its pip. With especially large targets, bearings plotted from the center of the pip may be unreliable. If bearings are taken of one edge of the pip, however, and corrected for ½ the horizontal beam angle, the error can be minimized. Bearings taken to the edge of a pip, rather than to its center, are called radar tangent bearings. A

Effect of horizontal beam angle. The actual edge of a radar target will be displaced toward the target's center by one-half the horizontal beam angle.

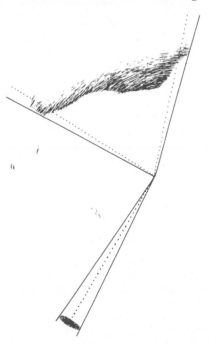

tangent bearing measured to the right edge of a pip should be reduced by ½ the horizontal beam angle, while a left tangent bearing of the same target will need to be increased by the same amount. If horizontal beam angle is 2°, subtract 1° from all right tangent bearings; add 1° to all left tangent bearings.

Two ships anchored near each other at the same range but separated by 2° (the horizontal beam width), will appear as a single pip on the radar screen—and, the pip will be 4 degrees wide! Unless the navigator is aware of the idiosyncrasies of the machine, he may interpret the pip as an island rather than a pair of ships.

Vertical Beam Angle

Vertical beam angle is the up-down size of the radar beam. A narrow vertical beam angle should only be used from stationary, land-based positions. A pitching motorvessel or heeling sailboat may miss targets if a narrow beam angle radar unit is installed.

Vertical beam angles of 20–25° are common. Narrower beam angles should be used with caution. The following figure shows why.

Radar Controls and their Functions

We are now ready to examine all those controls!

Many radar sets seem far more complicated than they really are. Those many knobs and switches actually are quite easy to understand when examined one at a time—taking each in turn to see just what function it performs. In the following sub-sections, each control and its function is examined.

Brightness

Also called brilliance or intensity, this control is similar to the brightness control on your TV set at home. Turning this control clockwise causes the pips to brighten or intensify. The control should be adjusted so that pips are clearly visible, but

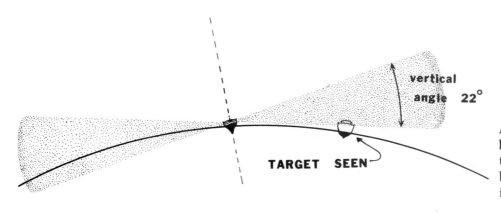

BOAT HEELED 10°

vertical angle 22°

TARGET SEEN

A pitching motorvessel or heeling sailboat may miss targets if a narrow vertical beam angle radar is installed.

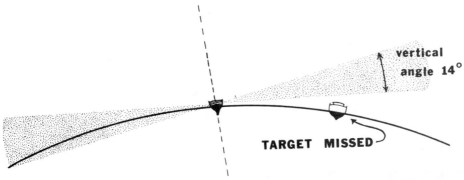

BOAT HEELED 10°

vertical angle 14°

TARGET MISSED

Radar scanner mounted on mainmast.

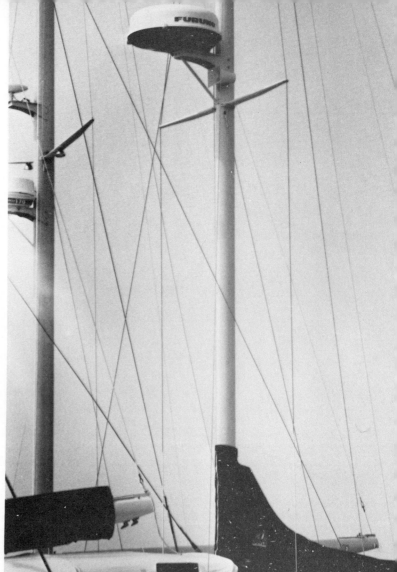

Radar scanner mounted on mizzenmast.

background areas remain black. Set the control so that any further increase causes the background to turn from black to grey. Once the unit has warmed up, this control should need no further attention.

The brightness control does not affect radar sensitivity.

Gain

Also called sensitivity, this control *does* affect radar performance by increasing the efficiency of the receiver section.

The gain control does not affect transmitted power.

This control should be adjusted after *every* change of radar range setting. The control should be set so that *only pips* are displayed on the screen.

When the gain control is set too high, an effect called "blooming" occurs. The screen lightens where no targets exist. The screen glows or "blooms" near pips. Whenever blooming is detected, reduce gain until the blooming effect just disappears and only pips are visible.

Do *not* reduce the gain beyond that needed to prevent blooming. Pips will be missed if the gain is not properly set.

Tuning

The tuning control may be the most misused, and yet it can be the most critical in terms of radar performance.

The tuning control adjusts the receiver circuits to the same frequency as the transmitter circuits. Because of changes in temperature, physical stresses, and other factors, the frequency of a radar transmitter may vary over a period of time. Unless the receiver is tuned to the same frequency, however, radar pulses reflected from a tiny distant target may be missed entirely.

The radar receiver must be tuned to the transmitter, just as your car FM must be tuned to the broadcast transmitter. And, just like the car FM, the weaker the signal becomes, the more critical is the tuning.

Watch the tuning indicator when adjusting the tuning control. Pay no attention to the radar screen. The "best" picture on the radar screen may not be the "correct" picture. Use the tuning indicator.

Sea Clutter

Also called swept gain or sensitivity time control (STC), this control reduces the effect of unwanted echoes near the radar by reducing receiver gain during the first few microseconds after each pulse is transmitted.

Return from waves, sleet, rain, snow and other interfering targets is often called clutter—thus, the name. Clutter makes it difficult to detect actual targets at close range. Since solid targets usually reflect radar pulses more efficiently than rain or snow or wavetops, reducing sensitivity at close range does not necessarily prevent detection of navigationally significant targets.

A danger exists, however. If the sea clutter control is set too high, *all* targets at close range may be eliminated, and those pips marking targets at greater range may be weakened.

Use the sea clutter control sparingly.

Rain Clutter

This control may also be called differentiation or fast time constant (FTC) control.

The rain clutter control makes it possible to reduce display of rain targets on the screen. Like the sea clutter control, this control should be used with caution as it has the effect of reducing sensitivity to small targets.

Always return the rain clutter control to its disabled setting when rain or other precipitation is not actually present.

Horizontal

Also called X Shift, this control moves the entire display left or right. For normal use, this control should be adjusted so the center of the sweep is in the center of the screen.

Vertical

Also called Y Shift, this control moves the entire display up or down. For normal use, this control should be adjusted so the center of the sweep is in the center of the screen.

Range Ring Brightness

Also called marker brightness, this control adjusts the brilliance of the range rings. In order to prevent the possibility of obscuring pips on or near the range rings, the range ring brightness control should be adjusted so that the rings are comfortably visible, not overly bright.

When piloting in congested waters, reduce range ring brightness so the rings don't interfere with your radar view.

Range

This control determines the radar range in effect.

With some sets, changing the range also changes the number of range rings, With other equipment, the number and position of rings does not change. Problems may result if the range is inadvertently changed without the navigator's knowledge. Always check the range setting when returning to the radar screen.

After changing the range control, the gain con-

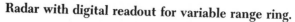

Radar with digital readout for variable range ring.

trol should be re-adjusted for maximum target response.

Range Marker

This control positions the adjustable range ring which, when placed over a target, provides the user with accurate ranging data, usually in the form of a digital reaout either in nautical miles, yards or meters.

Radar ranges are more accurate than radar bearings.

Focus

This control adjusts the relationship between the electron gun and the beam control coils. Adjust for sharpest pips.

Piloting

Radar is a piloting tool.

Its range is limited, and its ability to detect targets at a distance depends upon the target. Every target does not appear. Some are conspicuous, others are completely invisible.

Only the near edge of a target appears on the screen. The rest of the target is usually obscured.

Target height is also indistinguishable by radar. Intensity of a pip may give some indication—strong echoes being returned by tall objects—but short, metallic objects can cause stronger pips than tall, wooden objects. In general, only range, bearing, and apparent width of objects are discernable by radar.

Because of radar's limitations, safe piloting re-

Hand-held radar. User aims radar manually. When target echo is detected, a tone is heard. Pitch of tone indicates distance to target. (*Controlonics Corp.*)

quires a due regard for the many possibilities of mistakenly interpreting the real world represented by a particular radar display.

Visual Identification of Pips

Whenever possible, radar users should take visual bearings of targets before plotting their position on the chart. One of the most common errors in radar piloting is made when a navigator assumes the pip he sees is whistle buoy #27, when in fact the pip is caused by a steel-hulled workboat anchored for the night.

If visual identification of targets is impossible, due to an unusually heavy fog, darkness or precipitation, look for pips that can be unquestionably identified on the chart. If an unusual line of markers appears on the chart, look for that same line of pips on the radar screen.

Always compare radar screen displays with an actual eyeball view when possible—especially in congested harbors, in rivers, in channels, and along featureless shores where shoals make out from the beach. Compare radar pips with visual images of low-lying islands, different types of buoys and other aids to navigation, boats and weather patterns. Compare the radar images of various types of shorelines—with and without dunes, vegetation, hills, mountains or hotels. Study the appearance of pips returning from RaRef buoys and markers (those on which special radar reflectors are installed) and compare pips returning from other aids to navigation without RaRef devices.

Take notes.

Advance planning is always a good idea. Don't wait until visibility is zero before plotting possible radar targets. Use an indelible marker to locate on your chart the positions of beacons and buoys equipped with radar reflectors. Note where low beaches may be invisible to radar and where high dunes and hills can be expected to confuse the radar display images. Note targets that might be useful for ranging, especially radar-conspicuous landmarks at bends in rivers and channels.

A permanent scrapbook of radar images can be made by using a camera with fast film (ASA 400 or higher). If the wheelhouse is darkened and the radar brilliance control turned up a bit, photos of the radar screen are easy. During daylight hours, a hood can be used on the radar screen. With a large enough aperture, it may be possible to shoot at ⅙₀th second so the camera can be hand-held. If a longer exposure is required, use a tripod or other steady mount. Photographs of radar displays at harbor entrances, for example, may prove invaluable when the soup closes in to shut off the outside world. You are blind except for the view through your radar screen. If you mark the photograph to show which pips are buoys and which were other vessels present when the photo was taken, you can use the photograph as a supplement to your chart.

Never rely on just the radar. Continuously consult the depth sounder, compass, RDF, Loran-C, or any other navigational device at your disposal. If any two gadgets disagree, STOP! Throw out an anchor, if necessary. Do not proceed until you have found some logical reason for the discrepancy.

Do *not* rely on radar alone!

Radar Fix by Plotting Target Distances

If target pips can be positively identified, the following methods may be used to obtain charted fixes. A few rules set the stage: (1) if two lines of position are used, the lines should be as nearly perpendicular as possible; (2) if three lines of position are used, the ideal intersecting angle is 120° (six interior angles of 60° each); (3) reference objects should be positively identified; (4) possible margins of error should be plotted or at least noted in the logbook; (5) all lines of position should be labeled with the time and the method used to take the bearing (e.g., visual, radar, etc.).

The most accurate radar fix is obtained by two or more radar ranges. The chartwork is the same as that used to plot a fix by vertical sextant angles. Circles of position (COPs) are used. At the position of each identified pip, place the point of a pair of compasses, and draw a circle corresponding to the target range as displayed on the radar screen. Do the same at another pip. If the circles

Radar reflectors in the rigging
cause stronger echoes to appear
on the radar screens of other
craft. Without the radar
reflectors, these boats would be
nearly invisible to radar.

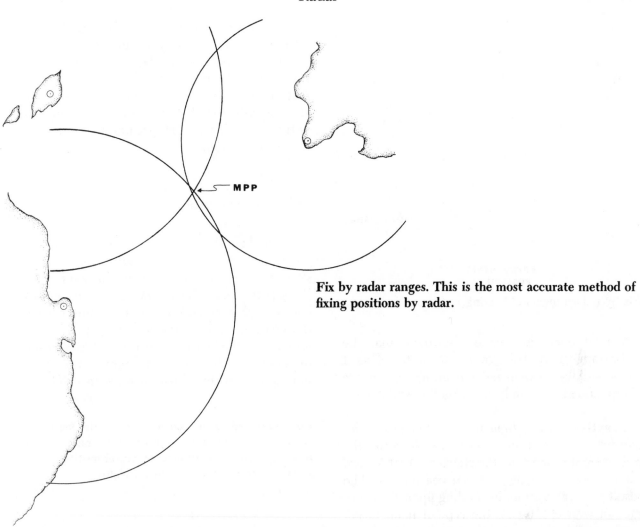

Fix by radar ranges. This is the most accurate method of fixing positions by radar.

intersect, the most probable position (MPP) is at or near the intersection.

Remember, however, the angle at which the circles intersect is critical, *and two circles always intersect at two points*. Only one point can be your position. Any ambiguity can be resolved by plotting another COP on the range to a third object—preferably situated opposite the first two targets.

Radar ranges are more accurate than radar bearings, so fixes obtained by plotting radar range COPs can be more accurate than fixes obtained by plotting radar bearing lines. This is especially true where a variable range marker is used to obtain a digital readout of distance.

However, apparent radar distance to some types of targets may be misleading. Islands with long, low, sloping beachfronts, for example, may appear on the radar to be farther away than they really are. The radar pips may indicate the position of inshore bluffs, missing the beach entirely. The chart, on the other hand, may show only the perimeter of a small island—i.e., where the beach actually meets the water. A mistake of this kind can cause unwanted surprises.

Radar Fix by Plotting Range and Bearing

If only one target is available, and only if that target is positively identified and on the chart, a fix can be plotted by the familiar range and bearing method. Both values are taken from the radar

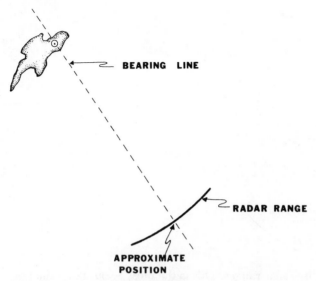

Fix by radar range and bearing.

The most common error in plotting fixes is the assumption that if two lines intersect in a single point, that must be the boat's position. In fact, this will only rarely be the case. The better method is to indicate the limits of accuracy and assume only that the fix position is somewhere within those limits. Any greater assumption may result in problems.

Collision Avoidance

If you and another vessel are on a collision course, the bearing of the other vessel will remain constant while the range between you will decrease. If a pip appears to be another vessel on a collision course with you, turn the radar azimuth ring so the bearing cursor intersects the pip. If the pip remains on the bearing cursor and draws closer to the center of the screen, the target *is* on a collision course. Alter course at once to avoid colli-

screen at once. Remember, however, that the radar range is probably more accurate (in most cases, see above) than radar bearings. Errors are compounded when only one target is available for a fix.

Plot the bearing *from* the charted target, *toward* the DR position of your boat. Measure the radar target range *from* the charted target *toward* the DR position along the radar bearing line. The result is your position, depending upon the accuracy of your chartwork, the type of radar target used, and whether or not the target selected is in fact the target shown on the chart.

Radar Fix by Crossed Bearings

This is the least accurate type of fix, since radar bearings are limited by the vessel's motion, steering errors, and the radar's horizontal beam width. Bearings taken when at anchor in a calm harbor will, of course, be more accurate than bearings taken while the boat is pitching about in heavy weather. Another error can result from the fact that the strongest radar return from a distant object may not be from its exact center.

Radar fixes by crossed bearings are plotted in the same manner as fixes by crossed bearings obtained by any other method.

Fix by crossed radar bearings. This is the least accurate method of fixing positions by radar. Radar bearing accuracy is limited by vessel motion, steering errors, and radar beam width.

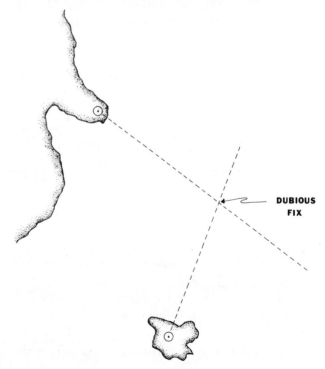

sion. Make your turn sharply. Alter course by at least 20° so the other vessel will not mistake your intentions.

Radar Hazards

Radar is dangerous!

Radar energy from a rotating scanner can cause blindness, severe burns or even death. The energy transmitted by scanners on U.S. Navy vessels, for example, is so intense that birds perched in the rigging when the radar is activated are literally cooked on the first rotation. Not a pretty thought, but serious injuries can result from careless use of even small boat radar units.

Radar is the same energy used in microwave ovens, and pulses from a typical small boat radar are many times more intense than the 600 or so watts of radiation used in household "radar" ovens.

NEVER look into the beam of a transmitting radar scanner. Permanent retinal damage or total blindness can result.

Do not permit any part of your body to pass through the beam. Even though you may feel nothing, internal tissue will be damaged with possibly serious long-term consequences.

Scanners should be mounted high enough to prevent their scanning the deck, wheelhouse, or any area of the boat where personnel may be working. Even small doses of radar energy can be harmful if the victim is exposed continuously for long periods.

Radar scanner mounted atop its own mast at taffrail of SORC competitor. Note that scanner is above the heads of the crew.

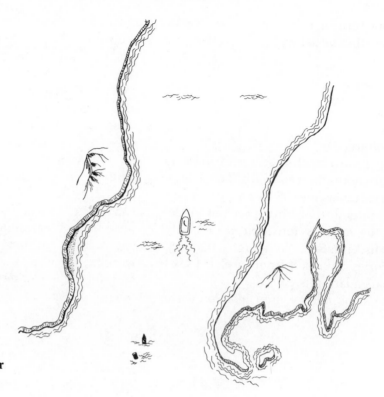

The "real world" and its radar
image.

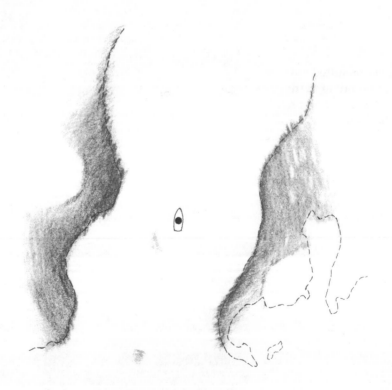

When approaching other vessels close aboard, when entering a congested harbor in clear visibility, and always when tied to the dock where radar is never needed—shut it off!

And, never open the transmitter or scanner chassis of a live radar set. Lethal voltages are present inside all radar units. If you require repairs, hire a licensed technician. The FCC issues a special commercial radar endorsement required of all who adjust or make repairs to radar transmitters. We're talking *thousands* of volts here, so KEEP OUT!

Conclusion

Radar paints a picture.

With it you can see the shoreline, other watercraft, or an unlighted offshore buoy bobbing invisibly on oily midnight waves ahead—waiting to make shipwreck of any small boat that strikes it in the night.

Radar can see.

But, radar can not talk. It will not tell you what to do. If you bump bottom, when you thought you were in 60 feet of water, the radar will just keep on flashing as though nothing whatever had happened. It can not tell you why you bumped. It can not tell you where you are. It can only paint a picture of radar targets nearby. All else is meaningless to the radar. It does its job, and you must do yours.

Practice is important. Pips do not reveal much about what targets look like out in the real world. They don't look like buoys and ships and shorelines. But patterns do exist, and pips offer clues to their targets' identity—clues you can learn to interpret through practice.

Radar can be wonderful—especially in heavy fog with rocks on either side, at night in roaring rain with shoals ahead, on an unfamiliar coastline where the navigation aids seem to disappear in the background city lights on shore—but radar can't see everything! And what it sees may not be what it seems to be.

Communications

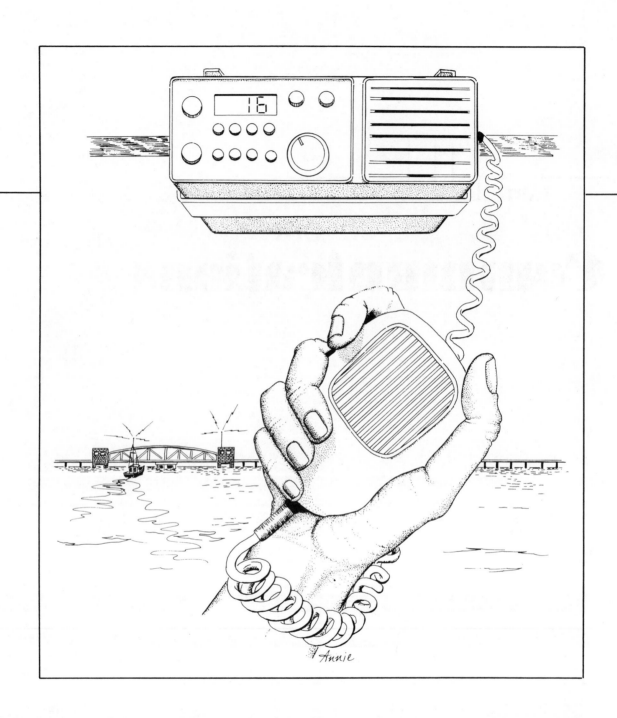

CHAPTER 5

VHF Radiotelephone

Introduction

Marine VHF radio is useful for communications out to about 50 miles. VHF stands for Very High Frequency, using frequencies above 150 MHz where waves are shorter than 2 meters. These high frequencies and short waves have the advantage of being immune to atmospheric static and unaffected by the time of day. Of all the forms of marine radio communications, VHF is the most used.

VHF is the primary mode of communications for pleasure craft and commercial vessels—CB and "ham" radio installations notwithstanding. If you are near shore and need to make a call, for any reason, someone is certain to hear you. Almost every boat afloat has at least one VHF on board, and some have two or three! The FCC requires that a VHF radio be installed *before* a license is issued for any other marine radio. The reasons are sound ones.

Within its range limits VHF radio communication is reliable. The equipment is relatively inexpensive, simple to operate, and requires no complex antenna or ground systems to perform satisfactorily.

Range *is* limited, however. But, then, limited range is one of VHF's advantages—channels aren't plagued with interference from distant stations (as the older AM frequencies were). Typical

Radio room on modern passenger liner.

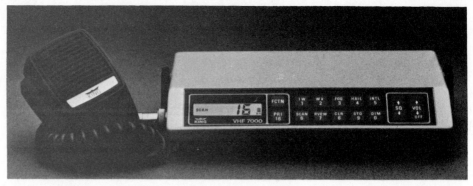

VHF transceiver, foghorn, loudhailer. (*King*)

maximum boat to boat range with deck-mounted antennas is 15–20 miles. Mounting the antenna at the masthead increases the maximum range to 25–40 miles under ideal conditions. Maximum range from boat to shore, where the shore station antenna is mounted atop a high tower or on a coastal mountain, is 45–70 miles. These ranges are estimated maximums based on the use of 3 db antennas (explained shortly) and maximum legal transmitting power (usually 25 watts).

Although range is limited, communications within the limited range is excellent—crisp, intelligible, and free from static.

But performance may vary widely, depending upon the quality of the radio and the quality of its installation. Although you can install your own VHF without the aid of a licensed radio technician, the radio's performance may suffer if the job isn't properly done. If you elect to install the radio yourself, follow the suggestions in the installation chapter later in this book. If you decide to pay a licensed technician to do the job for you, look over his shoulder, so to speak, and make certain the job is done according to these recommendations.

If you're in the process of buying a new radio,

pay particular attention to the important differences between units manufactured by different companies. Parts of this chapter are geared toward helping you choose the best VHF radio (from the dozens now on the market) by explaining the esoteric terminology used by VHF radio manufacturers in their specifications sheets. All those numbers really do mean something—and some are more important than others. By examining the specifications sheets, you can avoid bad bargains.

Also in this chapter we'll examine VHF antennas—the most important component of any radio installation. Which kind is best for your boat? How high should it be? Do you need a spare?

VHF Channels

Your VHF should feature a minimum of 12 channels. Unless you plan to tour Europe or investigate all the lakes and waterways of Canada, you probably don't need every available channel.

On the other hand, frequency synthesizers in the newest sets may be less expensive than added channel crystals. In fact, it is rare to find a VHF rig anymore that doesn't sport at least two dozen channels, and most boast 55 or more, including at least three receive-only weather channels. The price difference isn't worth the inconvenience of being limited, and there is the re-sale value to consider. A unit limited to only a dozen crystal-controlled channels is going to be a lot harder to sell when you finally decide to upgrade.

The law requires only three VHF channels: Channel 16 international distress, safety and calling channel, Channel 6 intership safety channel, and at least one working frequency.

Useful working frequencies include Coast Guard channel 22A for communicating with CG

VHF marine radiotelephone. (*Si-Tex*)

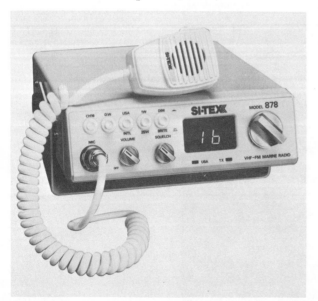

TABLE 5-1

VHF CHANNELS FOR U.S. RADIO USERS

DISTRESS, SAFETY & CALLING   16
 (No "rag chewing"!)
INTERSHIP SAFETY   6
 (Intership Safety ONLY!)
COAST GUARD COMMUNICATIONS   22A
 (Ship to CG Ship or Aircraft and Ship to CG Coast)
PORT OPERATIONS   1, 5, 65A, 66A, 12, 73, 14, 74, 63, 20, 77
 (Intership and Ship to Coast)
NAVIGATIONAL   13, 67
 (Intership and Ship to Coast)
NON-COMMERCIAL   68, 9, 69, 71, 78A, 72
 (Intership and Ship to Coast)
NON-COMMERCIAL   70, 72
 (Intership)
COMMERCIAL   1, 7A, 9, 10, 18A, 19A, 79A, 80A, 63
 (Commercial Intership and Ship to Coast ONLY!)
COMMERCIAL   67, 8, 77, 88A
 (Commercial Intership ONLY!)
PUBLIC CORRESPONDENCE   24, 84, 25, 85, 26, 86, 27, 87, 28
 (Ship to Coast Marine Operator)

coast stations, vessels or aircraft. The navigational intership and ship to coast channels (13 & 67) are working frequencies used by tugs and harbor craft, a ready source of valuable information. The public correspondence ship to public coast channels are used to make radiotelephone calls through the marine operator—several of these may be needed to take advantage of local telephone company services, but check with the telephone company to see which are used in your area.

Ask an old-timer which channels he uses most.

Channel Scanners

One advantage of using microcomputer chips in VHF radios is the ability to automatically scan selected channels. This can be a decided benefit at times.

The law requires you to monitor channel 16 for distress calls *whenever your radio is turned on.* Everyone should comply for the welfare and safety of all boat operators, but what if you want

to talk on another channel? You can't switch back and forth to listen for calls on channel 16.

But a scanner will do the job for you—automatically. For a small extra charge, you can own a VHF that constantly scans selected channels, including channel 16. The receiver electronically switches channels in sequence and, if an incoming signal is detected on one of the selected channels, the scanner stops to let you hear the call.

If you want to monitor more than one channel at a time, this feature may be worth the slight additional cost.

Channel-scanning VHF. (*Ray Jefferson*)

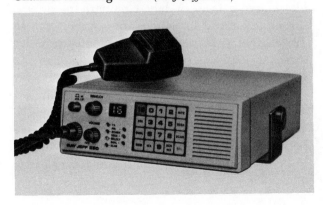

Even this ancient lateen rigged Italian vessel was equipped with modern electronics for its trans-Atlantic passage to America. Note rack of antennas at for'ard end of cabin trunk.

Remote Controls

Some manufacturers offer remote control stations to permit radio operation from the cockpit or in the chartroom or galley or wherever a remote control unit is located.

These can be very convenient, but consider an alternative before you buy. Compare the price of a remote control to the cost of a basic, no-frills, 12–channel VHF radio. You may be surprised to discover you can own a second radio (and an emergency backup in the bargain) for just a few dollars more than the cost of a remote unit. The added safety is worth considering. An inexpensive coaxial switch can be used to switch one antenna between the two radios, thus saving the cost and installation hassle of another antenna for the second radio.

Specifications Sheets

There are dozens of marine VHF radios on the market. No two are the same. Quality, added options, and price vary widely. How can a prospective buyer tell which radio is the best choice?

Local knowledge is a good source of information. How do your friends rate their VHF radios? What do local commercial operators say about various brands? Which works best for them? Actual hands-on experience is a good measure of quality.

But what can you do if a new VHF has just hit the market? What if none of your friends have any experience with the new model. How can you evaluate its quality?

The answer is the specifications sheet.

Reputable manufacturers proudly publish their

Study the specification sheet before you buy.

equipment's specifications. Other manufacturers may hide the truth with misleading specs, or provide specs that don't tell the entire story. A well-equipped marine electronics shop should be able to double-check the specs to make certain the radio you are buying is as good as the specifications sheet claims. If you're buying a new VHF, insist on seeing the specifications sheet. The following sub-sections should help you interpret the numbers so you'll know what you're buying.

Sensitivity by SNR

No matter how powerful your transmitter is or how high and efficient the antenna may be, you can't communicate with another station unless you can *hear* it. A fancy radio with lots of options, bells and whistles may be a poor bargain when compared to a less expensive radio with better sensitivity. In VHF equipment, receiver sensitivity is probably the single most important specification.

But be careful. The numbers may be confusing.

Sensitivity is often measured by the strength of an incoming radio signal (measured in microvolts at the antenna terminals) that is required to overcome the ever-present radio noise caused by static and electrical activity within the radio itself. This method of measuring is called the signal-to-noise or SNR method. It is a measure of how well a radio will receive weak signals.

Actual spec sheets may express sensitivity in two ways. Both tell us what signal strength is required to overcome noise inside the radio, but both do not measure the noise in the same way. The method discussed in this section is the SNR method. In the next section, we'll examine the SINAD method.

VHF and SSB transceivers mounted at navstation.

A typical spec sheet might give the following SNR spec for a receiver's sensitivity.

Sensitivity = 0.30 microvolts @ 20 db SNR

The initials, "db", stand for decibel, a unit used to compare the strengths of any two signals. The db is merely a mathematical invention that makes it easier for us to compare power levels. The following equation shows how the db is derived:

$$db = 10 \log (P^r / P^n)$$

In other words, take the logarithm (base 10) of the ratio found by dividing P^r (the strength of an incoming radio signal) by P^n (the strength of the noise trying to drown out the radio signal), and then multiply that logarithm by 10.

Some common values for dbs are given in the following table along with the ratio they represent.

TABLE 5-2

DECIBEL RATIOS

DB	RATIO
3	2:1
6	4:1
8	6:1
10	10:1
12	16:1
20	100:1
24	250:1
30	1000:1
40	10,000:1
50	100,000:1
60	1,000,000:1
70	10,000,000:1

In other words, 3 is 10 times the logarithm of 2:1, so a 2:1 ratio is expressed as 3 db; 6 is 10 times the logarithm of 4:1, so a 4:1 ratio is expressed as 6 db; 12 is 10 times the logarithm of 16:1, so a 16:1 ratio is expressed as 12 db; and 60 is 10 times the logarithm of 1,000,000:1, so a 1,000,000:1 ratio is expressed as 60 db.

That's all there is to it!

If a signal is twice as strong as the noise, we may say it is "3 db over" (the noise) or that the noise is "–3 db down" (below the signal). A 6 db signal-to-noise ratio (SNR) means the signal is four times as strong as the noise. A 60 db SNR means the signal is one million times as strong as the noise.

Now let's take another look at the first specification listed above:

Sensitivity = 0.30 microvolts @ 20 db SNR.

This spec tells us that an incoming radio signal with a strength of 0.30 microvolts will produce a signal-to-noise ratio equal to 20 db, i.e., the signal will be 100 times as strong as the noise. This 20 db SNR level is also known as "full quieting" in the industry, since a signal 100 times as strong as the noise will overcome *all* the noise and produce a quiet output at the speaker.

This navstation is complete with a handheld VHF on the chart table.

If a spec said,

Sensitivity = 0.50 microvolts @ 20 db SNR

we'd know the receiver wasn't as sensitive since *a much stronger signal is required* to quiet the receiver by the same 20 db, 100:1 SNR. Since more signal is required to quiet the receiver, the receiver is not as sensitive.

If a spec said,

Sensitivity = 0.30 microvolts @ 12 db SNR

we'd know it also is not as good, since a 0.30 microvolt signal produces only a 16:1 SNR (12 db) which is not full quieting.

SNR sensitivity specifications should tell you how strong an incoming radio signal must be to overcome internal radio noise by a certain db ratio (SNR). If a manufacturer says its receiver's sensitivity is 0.30 microvolts, but fails to specify the SNR that 0.30 microvolt signal causes, we haven't learned anything, since we don't know how effectively the incoming radio signal will overcome noise. Microvolt sensitivity must be given with a SNR value (usually in dbs), or the specification is meaningless.

The spec sheet should tell us how strong an in-

coming signal must be to overcome competing noise at a given SNR. If SNR isn't given, the specification is incomplete and misleading.

Sensitivity by SINAD

In practical VHF work, however, we aren't interested in full quieting. We want to hear speech coming through our VHF radio speaker. What we truly need to know about a prospective VHF radio is how strong an incoming signal must be to produce a certain "speech-to-noise ratio". So the radio industry invented another standard for specifying receiver sensitivity. This new standard is more meaningful since it gives an indication of how well the radio will perform when another station is *talking* to us. Most manufacturers include this specification *and* the SNR or full quieting spec. It is called the SINAD ratio.

SINAD sensitivity is a measure of how much *modulated* radio signal is required to produce a readable signal at the speaker. Modulation is a fancy term for speech or tones superimposed on a radio signal. Actual SINAD measurements at the manufacturer's lab are made with tones, but the numbers tell us how well speech will be received by the radio when operated in your boat.

Miniaturized VHF transceiver.

A typical SINAD specification might look like this:

Sensitivity = 0.30 microvolts @ 12 db SINAD

A 0.30 microvolt modulated signal at the antenna terminals will produce an output at the speaker in which the speech power is 16 times stronger than the noise level (12 db over noise). This is an acceptable figure.

Since VHF communications consists of speech, a 12 db SINAD specification is more meaningful than a 20 db full quieting spec. The full quieting spec tells how strong an incoming signal must be to completely overcome the radio's internal hiss. The SINAD spec tells how strong a signal must be before you can understand what the other person is saying amid the hiss.

When selecting a new VHF radio, examine all receiver specs carefully. If 12 db SINAD sensitivity is over 0.35 microvolts, the receiver is probably of poor quality. If 20 db full quieting is higher than 0.45 microvolts, don't buy.

Examine the following table. This table shows how receiver sensitivity affects range. In the first row are several possible values for receiver sensitivity based on the 12 db SINAD ratio. These values are in microvolts. In the second row are the corresponding ranges (in nautical miles) at

which each receiver can hear a 25 watt transmitter. The table assumes both boats have sailboat antennas mounted at the deck.

When you're studying specs on VHF receiver sensitivity, look for low microvolt numbers and high db numbers. Pay particular attention to the SINAD ratio. Remember: full quieting sensitivity is not as important to VHF communications as the SINAD ratio since SINAD sensitivity is a measure of the intelligibility of an incoming signal, while full quieting sensitivity is a measure of the amount of signal needed to overcome the hiss.

Squelch Threshold

Rotate the squelch knob on a VHF. Notice where the hissing noise stops. This is the squelch threshold. The control should be set just barely on the quiet side of this point for general use.

If an incoming signal is present at the antenna, the squelch circuit "opens" the receiver to the call. If an incoming signal is not present, the squelch keeps the receiver quiet, so you don't have to listen to the hiss.

If the squelch is set too high, weak signals won't get through, and you may miss a distant station's call. If the squelch is set too low, you can hear weaker stations, but the speaker emits a constant rushing hiss noise, *and* the receiver draws more current from the batteries.

Squelch threshold or squelch sensitivity is one of the specifications occasionally reported by manufacturers of VHF equipment. This figure, expressed in microvolts, is the amount of signal needed to overcome the squelch circuit and "open" the receiver to an incoming signal.

If this number is too big, only strong signals can overcome the squelch circuit. That's not good. On the other hand, if the number is too small, the squelch may admit unwanted interference, resulting in a noisy set that won't stay squelched. That's not good either.

TABLE 5-3

VHF RANGE VS. RECEIVER SENSITIVITY

SINAD	0.25	0.30	0.35	0.40	0.45	0.55	0.65	0.75	0.85	1.0
Range	22	21	20	19	18	17	16	15	14	13

Squelch threshold sensitivity varies. Values should not be much higher than the SINAD sensitivity of the receiver or lower than about 0.15 microvolts.

Receiver Selectivity

Adjacent channels in the marine VHF spectrum are separated at 25 kHz intervals. When you're listening to channel 16, you don't want to hear conversations on the adjacent channel. This is where selectivity pays off.

Selectivity, like sensitivity, is expressed in db values.

Here we use db to compare the strength of incoming signals on the selected channel with the strength of unwanted signals on adjacent channels. The best receivers will reject unwanted signals. Signals on the selected channel will come through many times as strong as signals on the adjacent channels. In fact, if signals on the selected channel aren't at least 1,000,000 times as strong (60 db) as signals on the adjacent channels, the radio is inferior. That may seem like a large number, but anything less is simply not good enough—especially if you're trying to hear a distant station at the outer limit of VHF coverage while the adjacent channel is being stomped on by a powerful ship or shore station nearby. The cross talk can wipe you out unless the receiver's selectivity is at least 60 db.

Selectivity is sometimes called adjacent channel rejection.

Taffrail antenna mount. Note supporting bracket on stern pulpit.

Intermodulation Rejection

Intermodulation is caused by the mixing of off-frequency signals to produce interference on the selected channel. Intermod problems may be unpredictable. Both the mixing stations causing intermod may be outside the marine bands. The off-frequency signals may originate from a local fire department, the highway patrol, or the radio transmissions from a fleet of cement mixer trucks. Intermodulation problems are greater near cities or busy harbors where other users of the VHF spectrum are active.

A good quality receiver will reject intermodulation by a factor of at least 60 db.

Image Rejection

Also called spurious response, image interference results from unwanted signals generated within the radio itself. Both the receiver and transmitter contain oscillator circuits as well as mixers, multipliers and amplifiers, all capable of generating whistles and whines that can interfere with incoming signals before they get to the speaker. Rejection of these images is an important specification that is reported by many reputable manufacturers. A good receiver should provide images rejection by a factor of at least 60 db.

Audio Power

This figure is a measure of how much sound you can get out of the speaker with the volume turned all the way up.

Less than 4 watts of audio power is probably unacceptable unless you intend to sit next to the radio whenever you want to listen to it. Handheld units provide less audio power (less than 0.5 watts is okay with a handheld rig), but they're designed to be carried with the user, not mounted on a bulkhead 20 feet away in the courtroom.

Also check the size of the speaker and where it's located on the unit. Many speakers are in the front where they belong, but a few are on the top

or bottom of the radio and end up muffled by the bulkhead or overhead once they're mounted.

Some radios offer an external connection to permit a second speaker to be mounted out on deck or in the wheelhouse nearer the helmsman. A remote control unit may also solve this problem by putting the speaker closer to the user.

Transmitter Power

All VHF marine radios manufactured for sale in the United States offer both low-power (1 watt) and high-power (25 watts). More power is illegal. Ability to switch to low power is required by FCC regulations. In other words, most VHFs offer no power options.

The handheld unit is an exception. Transmitter power in a handheld may vary from 1 to 5 watts or more, and selection of which to buy should be done carefully. These convenient radios are made to be carried with you. They have built-in batteries, usually NiCad rechargeables. But, rechar-

Handheld VHF. (*Apelco*)

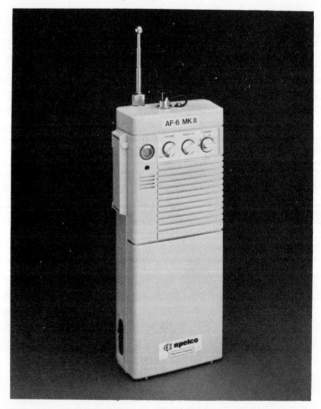

geable or not, the NiCad batteries are small and can't be relied upon to give unending hours of uninterrupted service. If the radio remains squelched (no noise from the speaker), these radios can be left on for as long as 12 hours or more before the battery goes dead. If signals are being received so the loudspeaker is blaring away most of the time, however, the battery can't last as long. And, if you happen to be long-winded and transmit at high-power, don't be surprised if the battery goes dead *much* sooner—possibly within an hour. Transmitting at low power, obviously, increases battery life.

A 5 watt transmitter in a handheld may be overkill for two reasons. In the first place, handhelds aren't intended to replace the main ship's radio; they're intended for dockside or short-range use where power is not essential. Remember, VHF is line-of-sight, and does not depend on power for its range, generally. Secondly, unless you plan to lug a pocketful of spare batteries around, you can't expect to talk long on the small built-in batteries if your transmitter power is 5 watts.

Good output power for a handheld is 1.5 watts high power, 0.15 watts low power. Use low power, and your batteries can last 10 times longer!

A note on so-called "linears" is needed here. It's possible to boost your transmitter's output beyond legal limits by adding a linear amplifier like those used by hams and outlaw CBers. These devices can multiply output to 100 or even 200 watts, but their use is punishable by fine *and* imprisonment.

In fact, the use of a linear may actually degrade the VHFs performance or even cause premature failure. The practice is not recommended.

Power Consumption

As discussed above, power consumption can be an important factor for sailors who need to conserve their DC batteries while the engine, generator, or other charging device is not operating. A 50 ampere-hour battery can deliver 50 amperes for one hour or one ampere for 50 hours—but that's all

you can get out of it. Once the battery's dead, the radio won't work and the engine may be exceedingly difficult to start.

Power consumption in VHF radios is rated in three modes: standby, receive, transmit.

In standby mode, the receiver is quiet—squelched. Current drain can be as low as 50 milliamperes (0.05 amps). Use of LCDs (the gray liquid crystal displays) instead of LEDs (the red or green light-emitting diodes) cuts down considerably on standby current drain. If your DC voltage supply is limited, weigh this figure carefully in your final selection.

In receive mode with the speaker active, current drain may be as high as 1.5 amperes, depending on the volume setting.

In transmit mode, current drain depends on transmitter power output and efficiency. At 25 watts, current drain will be near 5 amperes while transmitting. At low power (1 watt), current drain will be only 1 ampere or less. Figures higher than these may be acceptable in boats with excess DC power, but higher figures may indicate inefficient circuitry. Steer clear.

VHF Antennas

VHF performance depends more upon the antenna than any other single factor. Attention to the antenna and its installation will pay off with improved performance. There are several types of VHF antennas, different materials, and assorted mounting configurations. A poor antenna installation can actually *ruin* your radio.

Emergency Antenna

VHF antennas are not expensive. If you anticipate that foul weather or accident could result in the loss of your VHF antenna, you may want to carry a spare. If your boat is a sailboat, with a VHF antenna at the masthead, the best spare might be one you can mount on deck or clamp to a stanchion in the event of dismasting. If your boat is a motor vessel, the best spare might be a direct replacement.

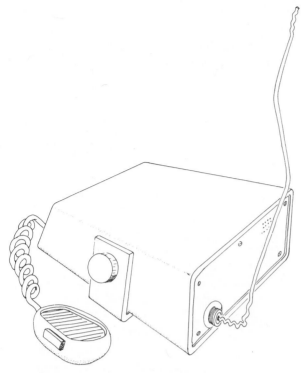

An emergency antenna can be made from any wire 18″ in length inserted in coax connector of VHF transceiver.

An emergency antenna can be made from an old coat-hanger (or any stiff conductive wire: copper, aluminum, steel). The optimum length for a unity gain vertical antenna is 1/4 wavelength. Since radio waves at VHF frequencies are just short of 2 meters long, a 1/4 wavelength vertical antenna should be about 18 inches (plus about 3/8 inch to push into the antenna connector on the radio). Take care the wire doesn't short the antenna terminal by touching both the center and outside of the socket.

Emergency antennas also are available commercially.

If you can dismount the radio unit and get it out on deck or higher, do so. The emergency antenna should be as nearly vertical as possible and away from other wires, rigging, metal spars, etc. When first installing the radio, some thought should be given to the possibility that you may want to operate it at some distance from the mounting bracket. Even if you never need to use

the radio in an emergency configuration, a servicing technician will appreciate your having left a few extra inches of cable behind the bulkhead so he can move the radio without disconnecting the cables.

Gain Antennas

VHF antennas differ in the amount of gain they provide. An ideal antenna for operation between two fixed, land base stations would be sensitive in only one direction, concentrating all radio energy in the direction of the other radio station. A boat, however, must listen for stations located in all directions. A directional antenna could cause serious problems.

VHF antennas, therefore, are not sensitive in only one direction. They are omni-directional.

But, sensitivity can be concentrated in a narrow wedge out to the horizon where other stations are located. It is rare that you'll be talking to an airplane flying several miles *above* your boat. Rather, you'll be talking to other boats or other shore stations on the horizon or just beyond it—in the horizontal. Antenna sensitivity, therefore, can be concentrated in the horizontal to improve performance without losing anything.

The amount of horizontal concentration is called gain. The gain of an antenna is measured by comparing the antenna's performance with a

This commercial emergency VHF antenna stores easily, unrolls for operation. (*Nautical Engineering*)

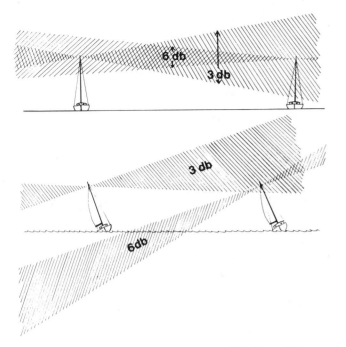

Why 6db VHF antennas are unsuitable for sailboats.

the water when what's needed is sensitivity *in the horizontal.*

On a sailboat, because they heel under the press of canvas, only one antenna is suitable—the 3 db gain antenna. If the antenna gain is too high, stations at the horizon will be missed. The antenna will either look over them or under them, and in either case there is loss of communications. Higher gain antennas are made for vessels that don't go from place to place with the lee rail awash.

If yours is a motor vessel, you can probably get by with a 6 db gain antenna. But if your vessel rolls wildly, as some motor-driven craft will do in moderate weather, you, too, should use a sailboat antenna, i.e., a 3 db gain antenna.

Antenna Location

The VHF antenna should be mounted as high as possible. If the highest point in your boat is a mast, mount it there. If the highest point is a stack, put it on the stack. If the highest point is the top of the wheelhouse, put it there.

Sailboats, of course, have the advantage of greater height. A few old salts may be heard to insist, however, that sailboat owners should mount their VHF antenna on the deck at the transom, so the radio will still be operable in the event of a dismasting. Their reasoning is only partially sound.

VHF communications is essentially line-of-sight. The higher the antenna, the farther you can talk. If you're worried about dismasting (an event

standard antenna with no gain at all (unity gain). Thus, using our comparison unit, the db, again, we say that an antenna that is twice as sensitive in the horizontal as the standard unity gain antenna has a gain of 3 db (2:1). An antenna that is four times as sensitive in the horizontal as a standard unity gain antenna has a gain of 6 db.

Higher gain antennas are available, but they are not widely used in small craft. Obviously, if the boat pitches and rolls about wildly in heavy weather, a high-gain antenna will focus its sensitivity up toward the clouds or down at the fish in

TABLE 5-4

VHF RANGE VS. ANTENNA HEIGHT

RECEIVER ANTENNA HEIGHT	TRANSMITTER ANTENNA HEIGHT							
	8	12	24	40	60	120	200	400
8	15	17	22	27	30	38	42	49
12	17	20	26	30	34	41	47	53
24	22	26	32	37	39	48	53	60
40	27	30	37	42	47	53	58	63
60	30	34	41	47	51	57	62	69

VHF antenna atop mainmast, SSB antenna on mizzen.

VHF, SSB and other antennas mounted at taffrail. Better to put VHF antenna at masthead.

Effect of VHF antenna height.

that occurs far less often than dockside yarn spinners admit), carry a spare that can be set up on deck.

The following table shows why antennas should be as high as possible. VHF radio waves travel in nearly straight lines from point to point. Propagation is said to be line of sight. A deck-mounted antenna may have an effective height of only 12 feet. A masthead antenna, even in a small cruiser, may have an effective height above 40 feet. Enter the table with antenna heights (receive and transmit) in feet to find the theoretical maximum range in nautical miles.

The table above estimates maximum VHF range using a 3 db sailboat antenna, a receiver with 0.35 SINAD sensitivity, and 25 watts of transmitter power. Typically, shore stations have far more power and antenna heights at 120 feet or above.

For example, compare the maximum range of communications between two boats with deck mounted (12 foot) antennas and the maximum range of communications between two boats with masthead (40 foot) antennas. The first pair can communicate up to 20 miles. The second pair can talk 42 miles—more than twice as far as the boats with deck mounted antennas. If two boats have their antennas mounted atop 60 foot masts, the range is 51 miles.

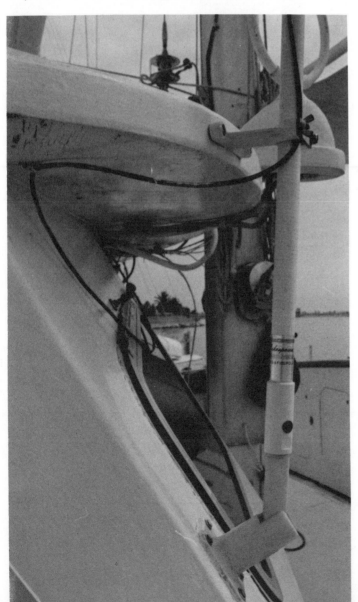

VHF antenna mounted on the front of a wheelhouse. A higher location is preferred.

Since shore stations have more power and far higher antennas than boats, ship-to-shore ranges are greater than ship-to-ship ranges. The theoretical maximum range between a boat with a masthead antenna at 60 feet and a shore station with its antenna mounted atop a 400 foot tower is about 69 miles.

Conclusion

As a final word of advice, once you've carefully perused the technical specifications, pay careful heed to the manufacturer's reputation. What do others say about their quality, reliability, and reputation for prompt and efficient dealer service?

Some VHF manufacturers produce gear for use by the military. In most cases, you'll find this is a good measure of the company and its product. Military specs demand the highest quality.

Also note that manufacturers who don't list certain specs on their equipment may have nefarious reasons. They may not want you to know just how poorly their equipment performs. Don't hesitate to insist on seeing the specifications before you buy.

Don't be swayed by silly options. If you need a loud hailer, buy one. Don't buy a VHF radio because it has a loud hailer built in. And, don't buy because the radio matches the stateroom decor!

Radios are technical devices. Their purchase requires you to make technical decisions. Apply the technical principles examined here. Unless the radio measures up, don't buy it.

There are certainly plenty to choose from.

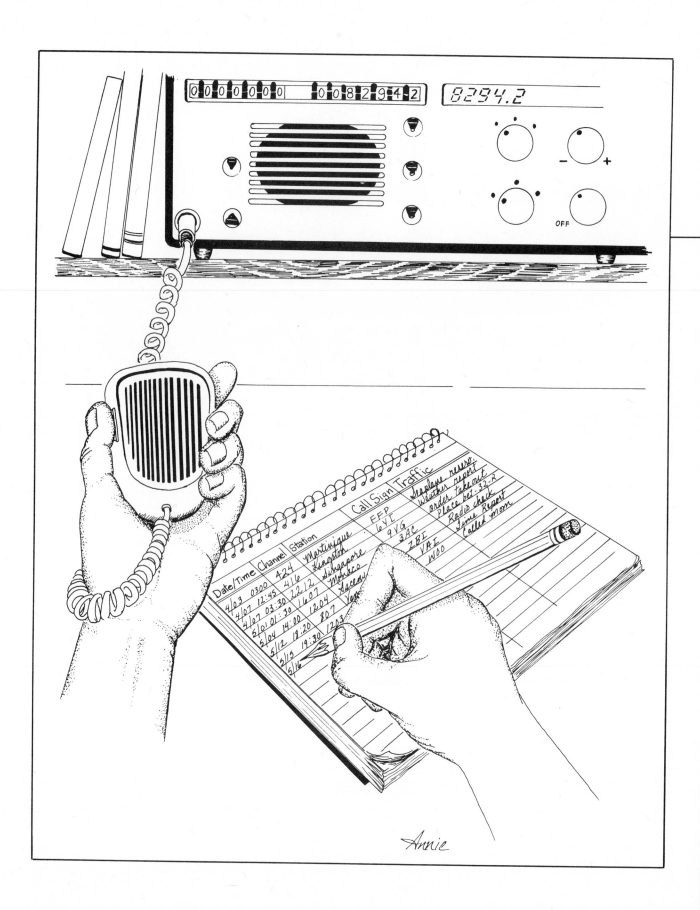

CHAPTER 6

Single Sideband

Marine SSB communications uses radio waves of varied lengths in the medium frequency (MF) and high frequency (HF) spectrum to transmit to virtually any part of the world at any time of day. With a marine SSB radio, you can talk with almost anyone—if you know how to use SSB effectively. You can place telephone calls from your

With SSB on board, you can call or receive calls from anyone—no matter how far you are from land.

dock or from thousands of miles at sea. You can call the Coast Guard for weather bulletins, navigational information, or for assistance in an emergency. And, of course, you can communicate with any other boat equipped with SSB—whether the other boat is 100 miles down the coast or 3000 miles away.

Telephone companies and private operators located throughout the world maintain radio watches on assigned frequencies to relay your call to the landline system. One of these stations is always within range. The following table lists stations that offer relay telephone service.

The Coast Guard monitors several channels on a 24–hour basis to render assistance to vessels in distress. These channels are listed in the following table.

In addition to monitoring distress calls, the Coast Guard broadcasts Notices to Mariners to warn of approaching bad weather or changes in aids to navigation. These messages are also broadcast on VHF, but vessels outside VHF range can receive the messages (and reply if necessary) on SSB. For a list of scheduled broadcast times and frequency channels, contact the nearest Coast Guard station.

TABLE 6-1
SSB TELEPHONE RELAY STATIONS IN U.S.
AT&T HIGH SEAS STATIONS

Coast Station KMI—California
Address:
American Telephone and Telegraph Company
Station KMI
P.O. Box 8
Inverness, California 94937
For technical information call:
(415) 669-1055

Coast Station	Channel Designation	Ship Receive (kHz)	Ship Transmit (kHz)
KMI	401	4357.4	4063.0
Point Reyes,	416	4403.9	4109.5
California	417	4407.0	4112.6
	804	8728.2	8204.3
	809	8743.7	8219.8
	822	8784.0	8260.1
	1201	13100.8	12330.0
	1202	13103.9	12333.1
	1203	13107.0	12336.2
	1229	13187.6	12416.8
	1602	17236.0	16463.1
	1603	17239.1	16466.2
	1624	17304.2	16531.3
	2214	22636.3	22040.3
	2223	22664.2	22068.2
	2228	22679.7	22083.7
	2236	22704.5	22108.5

Channels: 401, 804, 822, 1201, 1229
and 1602

GMT	TRFC	WEATHER
0000	X	X
0300	X	
0600	X	X
0900	X	
1200	X	
1500	X	X
1800	X	
2100	X	

Channels: 416, 809, 1202, 1203, 1603
and 2214

GMT	TRFC	WEATHER
0100	X	
0400	X	
0700	X	
1000	X	
1300	X	X
1600	X	
1900	X	X
2200	X	

Coast Station WOO—New Jersey
Address:
American Telephone and Telegraph Company
Station WOO
P.O. Box 558, Beach Avenue
Manahawkin, New Jersey 08050
For technical information call:
(609) 597-2201

Coast Station	Channel Designation	Ship Receive (kHz)	Ship Transmit (kHz)
WOO	410	4385.3	4090.9
Manahawkin,	411	4388.4	4094.0
New Jersey	416	4403.9	4109.5
	422	4422.5	4128.1
	808	8740.6	8216.7
	811	8749.9	8226.0
	815	8762.3	8238.4
	826	8796.4	8272.5
	1203	13107.0	12336.2
	1210	13128.7	12357.9
	1211	13131.8	12361.0
	1228	13184.5	12413.7
	1605	17245.3	16472.4
	1620	17291.8	16518.9
	1626	17310.4	16537.5
	1631	17325.9	16553.0
	2201	22596.0	22000.0
	2205	22608.4	22012.4
	2210	22623.9	22027.9
	2236	22704.5	22108.5

Channels: 410, 826, 1201,
1631 and 2205

GMT	TRFC	WEATHER
0000	X	
0400	X	
0800	X	
1200	X	X
1600	X	
2000	X	X

Channels: 411, 815, 1211,
1605 and 2210

GMT	TRFC	WEATHER
0100	X	
0500	X	
0900	X	
1300	X	X
1700	X	
2100	X	X

Channels: 416, 808, 1228,
1620 and 2201

GMT	TRFC	WEATHER
0200	X	
0600	X	
1000	X	
1400	X	X
1800	X	
2200	X	X

Channels: 422, 811, 1203,
1626 and 2236

GMT	TRFC	WEATHER
0300	X	
0700	X	
1100	X	
1500	X	X
1900	X	
2300	X	X

TABLE 6-2

EMERGENCY SSB CHANNELS

(2182 KHz) INTERNATIONAL CALL & DISTRESS

ITU CHANNEL	SHIP RECEIVE	SHIP TRANSMIT
424	4428.7 KHz	4134.3 KHz
601	6506.4 KHz	6200.0 KHz
816	8765.4 KHz	8241.5 KHz
1205	13113.2 KHz	12342.4 KHz
1625	17307.3 KHz	16534.4 KHz

Of course to take advantage of the SSB system, you need a high quality radio, properly installed with an efficient antenna and ground, so the transceiver can radiate its transmitted energy effectively and detect faint incoming signals. You also need a working knowledge of radio protocol and communication procedures, so the person on the other end knows how to respond to your call effectively. Finally, and perhaps most importantly, your set must be equipped with the necessary frequency bands to take full advantage of SSB's long-range potential. Some inexpensive radios operate only in the 2 and 4 MHz bands.

Coast Station WOM—Florida

Address:
American Telephone and Telegraph Company
Station WOM
1350 N.W. 40th Avenue
Fort Lauderdale, Florida 33313
For technical information call: (305) 587-0910

Coast Station	Channel Designation	Ship Receive (kHz)	Ship Transmit (kHz)
WOM	403	4363.6	4069.2
Ft. Lauderdale,	412	4391.5	4097.1
Florida	417	4407.0	4112.6
	423	4425.6	4131.2
	802	8722.0	8198.1
	805	8731.3	8207.4
	810	8746.8	8222.9
	814	8759.2	8235.3
	825	8793.3	8269.4
	831	8811.9	8288.0
	1206	13116.3	12345.5
	1208	13122.5	12351.7
	1209	13125.6	12354.8
	1215	13144.2	12373.4
	1223	13169.0	12398.2
	1230	13190.7	12419.9
	1601	17232.9	16460.0
	1609	17257.7	16484.8
	1610	17260.8	16487.9
	1611	17263.9	16491.0
	1616	17279.4	16506.5
	2215	22639.4	22043.4
	2216	22642.5	22046.5
	2222	22661.1	22065.1

Channels: 403, 802, 1206, 1601 and 2215

GMT	TRFC	WEATHER
0030	X	
0430	X	
0830	X	
1230	X	X
1630	X	
2030	X	

Channels: 412, 805, 1208, 1609 and 2216

GMT	TRFC	WEATHER
0130	X	
0530	X	
0930	X	
1330	X	X
1730	X	
2130	X	

Channels: 417, 810, 1209 and 1610

GMT	TRFC	WEATHER
0230	X	
0630	X	
1030	X	
1430	X	
1830	X	
2230	X	X

Channels: 423, 825, 1215 and 1611

GMT	TRFC	WEATHER
0330	X	
0730	X	
1130	X	
1530	X	
1930	X	
2330	X	X

MOBILE MARINE RADIO, INC.

Mobile Marine Radio, Inc. operates station WLO in Mobile, Alabama. The services provided by WLO and the procedures for utilizing these services are similar to those of the Bell System's stations previously described.

Mobile Marine Station	ITU Channel	Ship Receive (kHz)	Ship Transmit (kHz)
WLO	824	8790.2	8266.3
Mobile,	829	8805.7	8281.8
Alabama	830	8808.8	8284.9
	1212	13134.9	12364.1
	1225	13175.2	12404.4
	1226	13178.3	12407.5
	1607	17251.5	16478.6
	1632	17329.0	16556.1
	1641	17356.9	16584.0
	2227	22676.6	22080.6
	2231	22689.0	22093.0
	2237	22707.6	22111.6

All channels use USB mode.

To reach WLO from long distance to place a marine radiotelephone call, dial "O" and ask the operator for the "Mobile Alabama Marine Operator." Or, you may dial direct: (205) 666-2998

For further information write:
Mobile Marine Radio, Inc.
Station WLO
7700 Rinla Avenue
Mobile, Alabama 36619

or call the business office: (205) 666-5110

State-of-the-art SSB transceiver. (*Stevens Engineering*)

Others provide them all: 2, 4, 8, 12, 16, and 22 MHz.

Marine SSB communications is unique in that users can choose from six frequency bands, each with different wavelengths, and thus each with different transmission characteristics, shorter waves being produced by the higher frequency bands, and longer waves by the lower frequency bands. This difference in wavelengths gives SSB its flexibility. The following table shows the wavelength for each frequency band.

At any particular time of day, over any particular radio path, one wavelength will work far bet-

TABLE 6-3

SSB FREQUENCY BANDS AND WAVELENGTHS

BAND	WAVELENGTH
2 MHz	150 meters
4 MHz	75 meters
8 MHz	38 meters
12 MHz	25 meters
16 MHz	19 meters
22 MHz	14 meters

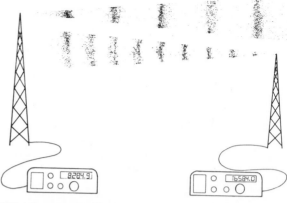

Effect of frequency on wavelength.

ter than another. A certain wavelength may work well between Nassau and Boston at noon, for example, while the same wavelength may not be able to get through just a few hours later in the day. Wavelengths that work perfectly at midnight may be useless after daybreak, and wavelengths that do the job in the early afternoon may be totally dead after dark.

Choosing the best frequency (and having equipment that permits the right choice to be made) is essential. Being able to select the optimum frequency to talk to New York, Miami or a ship anchored off the coast of Mozambique is the key to SSB success. If your radio can't transmit on all the necessary channels, you simply can't make

contact with stations far away—no matter how powerful your transmitter or how efficient your antenna system. Similarly, the most sensitive receiver is completely useless unless it can be tuned to a frequency that's getting through.

Buying an SSB Radio

Here are a few pointers to help you pick the best radio for your boat. Frills may not be necessary. They are often expensive, and a simple radio may be more reliable than one with many gadgets. The key question is: Does it meet your immediate and future radio communications needs? If it doesn't, don't buy—no matter how slick the gadgetry. Radio is radio.

If you communicate with agents or port officials in far-away countries, you may require high-power and high frequency bands in addition to

Time of day and SSB propagation.

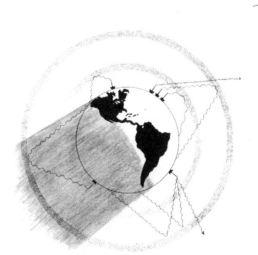

Synthesized SSB transceiver. (*Motorola*)

special antenna installations. Others, who need only local coastal coverage, can get by with medium-power and the lower bands with simple antennas. In general, 100 watts of transmitter power is ample. More than 1000 watts is overkill.

If you plan to use the SSB only through the marine operator for business traffic with clients ashore, you may get by with a limited number of channels. Otherwise you'll need extra channels to talk with ships, tugs, harbor masters or other shore stations at distances beyond VHF range. Frequency-synthesized radios offer maximum channel coverage.

If you're buying a radio to be used near your home harbor, a few channels in a low-power, crystal-controlled unit should work fine. You can probably pick up an inexpensive used set. If you later move to another area, however, or decide to operate farther offshore, this radio may be useless. You saved money in the beginning, but you now need more power and more frequencies. It might have been less costly to buy a radio with higher power and synthesized channels in the first place.

A versatile radio is easier to sell than one that has been channelized for a single location. If possible, buy a radio that can be used in many applications and locations. If the radio can meet the radio needs of a wide spectrum of mariners, it will be easier to sell when you're ready to move up.

This book would be incomplete without at least a few words about the bells and whistles being offered on todays SSB radios.

Marine radio is serious business. Commercial users depend on it. Disasters are prevented by it. One simply can't afford to own an unreliable radio.

Nevertheless, some manufacturers today add flashing lights, warning buzzers, and computer-type keyboards to their radios in hopes of catching buyers' eyes with innovative technology. Some of these features are useful, but others can contribute to premature failures. Common sense decrees that simple gear is less likely to fail than that which is preposterously complex.

Find a trusted marine radio dealer. Ask around. Find out who has been in the business longest and who has the best reputation. Let him help you with these decisions. If you need a buzzer to sound in the engine room when you receive an SSB call, then by all means buy a radio with buzzer. But, if you can get by without complexities—avoid them.

SSB and VHF Compared

Marine SSB is a long-range communications system designed to reach beyond the range limits of VHF. SSB is propagated by means of skywaves, radio waves that travel from place to place by bouncing off the ionosphere, a layer of electrically charged gases 25 to 250 miles above Earth's surface, so that radio contact can be made between stations separated by thousands of miles.

VHF communication is primarily line-of-sight. Radio waves travel from transmitting antenna

SSB and VHF in compact navstation installation. (*IMI Southwest*)

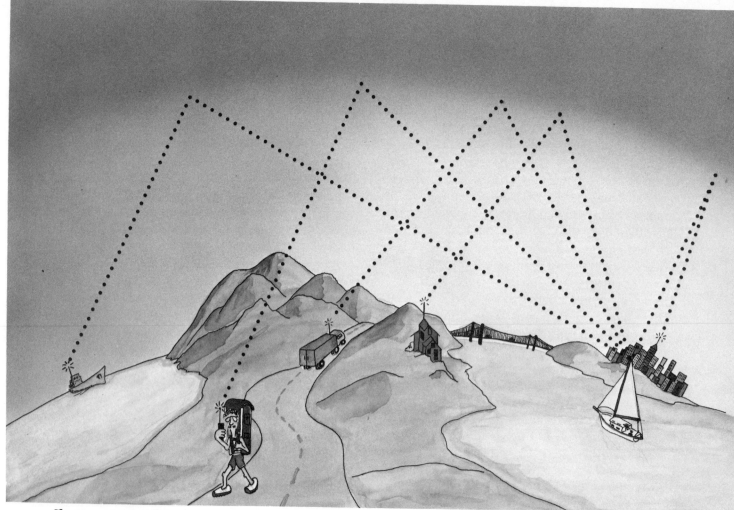

Skywave propagation.

directly to receiving antenna. There is no ionospheric bouncing to extend radio range. Being shorter than SSB waves, VHF waves simply penetrate the ionosphere and are lost in space. They won't bounce back to Earth. VHF waves may "bend" a small amount to reach around Earth's curvature and permit contact with stations a short distance (10–20 miles) beyond the horizon, but contacts beyond 50 or 60 miles are uncommon. VHF is strictly short range.

SSB should *never* be used for short-range contacts. That's what VHF is for. If you can work another station using VHF—use VHF—not SSB. This will reduce interference to distant stations. SSB waves travel thousands of miles before they dissipate. Careless use of SSB channels can interfere with communications between stations operating at tremendous distances. Operators who use SSB to talk to a boat just across the harbor or hull down on the horizon, instead of using limited-range VHF, are sometimes guilty of dis-

rupting important conversations oceans away! A local call on 22 MHz can impede a rescue operation on the other side of the planet!

The potential for unwanted interference from local SSB use is so great, the FCC forbids the installation of SSB equipment until VHF is on board. Before you can be licensed to use SSB, you must have VHF. That's the law.

Operating Principles

There are two modes of SSB communications: simplex and half-duplex. In simplex mode, the transceiver sends and receives on the same frequency. Stations listening in hear both sides of the conversation. This mode is used for inter-ship contacts. So-called "working channels" are commonly simplex. Simplex has an advantage in that an operator can listen before transmitting and, if he doesn't hear anyone talking, he can be relatively certain the channel is not in use.

In half-duplex mode (also called semi-duplex), the transceiver sends on one frequency but receives on another. This is the most common mode used for communications with Coast Guard and telephone relay stations ashore. Operation on the half-duplex channels requires careful listening *before* transmitting to make certain the channel isn't already in use. Important bulletins and announcements from a shore station must not be interrupted by calls from ships.

SSB channel assigments are listed in the following tables. Individual frequencies may change from time to time. Consult Notice to Mariners.

Different channels exist for each type of communications. Once you are familiar with which channels to use, you are ready to communicate. You can call another ship or boat. You can call the Coast Guard or pilot station ashore. You can even call your family at home or a business associate in his office via radio-telephone link. You can talk ship-to-ship in any ocean, ship-to-shore on any coast, and ship-to-telephone with any person anywhere a phone company has strung its wires.

If you maintain a radio watch and listen for your ship's name or station call sign on the scheduled traffic lists broadcast by the high-seas operators, you can receive calls from other ships, from shore stations, or from a pay phone in Des Moines, Iowa.

Frequency Options

All SSB radios won't operate on all SSB frequencies.

Lower priced units may operate on only the 4 MHz and 8 MHz bands, providing short to medium-range communications. For longer-range contacts, the higher frequency bands are needed.

If you need only local to medium-range communications, out to 300 miles or so, then an SSB transceiver capable of operating in the 4 MHz and 8 MHz bands with 100 watts or so should serve your purposes well. If you need greater range, a more expensive transceiver may be needed, with the 12 MHz band in addition to 4 MHz and 8 MHz. On the 12 MHz band, daytime contacts beyond 1000 miles are possible. If still

greater range is needed, you may require all six bands. With the higher frequencies, worldwide communications is possible.

Crystals

Some SSB radios still use crystals to control transmitting and receiving frequencies. Others use modern digital circuitry to synthesize operating frequencies.

Before the recent advances in integrated circuit technology, virtually all marine radios were crystal-controlled. Frequencies of both the transmitter and receiver were determined by carefully ground pieces of quartz mineral, slices of stone that have the peculiar property of vibrating at constant frequency when stimulated by an electrical signal. When kept at constant temperature and not exposed to moisture or external physical stress, a crystal will continue to vibrate at a fixed rate and can be used as a reference element in circuits that control the wavelengths transmitted by transmitters and the wavelengths to which receivers can be made sensitive. Old-timers would say their rigs were "rock-bound" because they were dependent on chunks of quartz mineral to fix their operating frequencies.

Crystal-controlled radios may cost less initially than those that are fully synthesized (depending on brand name and other features), but in the long run a synthesized rig may prove to be more economical. Initial savings in buying crystal-controlled equipment is not enough to offset the advantages of increased flexibility and reliability provided by channel synthesization.

Full-function HF radio. (*Marconi Canada*)

Crystals aren't expensive—$5 to $10 at most. But, if you decide to add channels to a rock-bound rig, you must tack on labor charges for an FCC licensed technician to do the work. When crystals are added, the transmitter should be re-tuned. Only the holder of a commercial General Radiotelephone or Second Class Radiotelegraph license is permitted by law to adjust a marine radio transmitter. The labor costs of adding channels to an initially inexpensive rock-bound rig may exceed what you saved by not buying a synthesized radio in the first place.

Frequency Synthesis

Crystals continue to be used in even the newest synthesized radios—but only *one* crystal is required. This single crystal serves as a frequency reference which is converted into all the other frequencies. Advantages include more frequencies, increased reliability, plus the ability to add features like dual frequency watch or frequency scanning.

Synthesized SSB transceiver. (*Intech*)

Scanners

Several manufacturers offer channel scanning capabilities as standard equipment with their frequency synthesized radios. This can be a decidedly helpful feature for those who don't want to miss any calls. Scanners permit operators to listen for traffic on several channels at once. The re-ceiver switches sequentially from channel to channel until an incoming signal is heard. The receiver then stops scanning so the operator can hear that call. When the channel is clear again, the receiver resumes its scan. Scanners permit the operator to monitor call and distress frequencies (e.g., 2182 kHz) while handling communications on other bands. It is well worth the slight additional cost.

Other Frequency Options

A few SSB radios on the market today can be tuned to *any* frequency in the MF and HF spectrum—even to frequencies that aren't marine SSB frequencies. This can have many advantages, but it may also lead to trouble—and caution is required.

If you're a licensed radio amateur, you may be able to use a general coverage rig to work stations in the ham bands.

However, the radio spectrum from 2 MHz to 22 MHz, includes many users other than hams and boat people. There are frequencies for radio-facsimile, radioteletype, and radiotelegraph in addition to radiotelephone. Users include foreign embassies, airlines, railroads, commercial broad-casters, and standard time and frequency services.

Finally, there are thousands of frequencies reserved for the use of military operations—ours *and* theirs.

You are absolutely forbidden to transmit on any frequency outside the marine SSB band (excepting licensed amateurs working other amateurs within amateur bands). Care must be exercised, therefore, to insure that your radio is not inadvertently switched to a channel outside the marine SSB spectrum. If such a radio is installed where personnel other than trained crew members may have access to the controls, the radio should be closely supervised or kept under lock and key to prevent improper use. Any competent technician can add a key-lock switch (like the ignition switch in your car) to your radio transmitter to prevent unauthorized use.

As licensee, you are responsible for the consequences of *all* improper uses of the radio. You can

Antennas on the *Nieuw Amsterdam*. The tall whip antenna with radials at its top is one of the SSB antennas on this modern passenger liner.

be held legally liable to any person who suffers injury as a result of interference caused by a radio licensed to you.

You can be fined. You can be imprisoned. You could even start an international incident. No kidding!

If your radio can be operated on frequencies outside the SSB marine bands, make certain it doesn't.

Speech Processors

Some units are sold with an option called a speech processor or speech compressor. Advertisements may claim the unit transmits the slightest whisper, imparting power and perception to each word, making communications possible under the most unfavorable conditions.

SSB radios without speech processors depend on the strength of the operator's voice to activate the modulation circuits that inject "talk power" into the transmitted signal. If the operator speaks softly into the microphone, there is little modulation. If the operator speaks too loudly, the signal may be over-modulated, causing distortion that can render the transmitted speech totally unintelligible.

Soft, high-pitched voices may fail to produce sufficient talk power to properly modulate the transmitted signal. Booming, deep-pitched voices may over-modulate, causing distortion.

What's needed is a circuit that will amplify weak voices and attenuate powerful voices, optimizing the modulation power to put just the right amount of speech in the transmitted signal. That's just what a speech processor does.

Communications scientists long ago discovered that speech is primarily composed of the frequencies between 300 and 3000 Hz. It is possible to attenuate all other frequencies and still retain the intelligibility of spoken language.

Frequencies above 3000 Hz or below 300 Hz add only personality, inflections, and emphasis. A spoken word can still be understood if all other frequencies are eliminated. Being able to convey

Not a good place to mount the SSB. It can get kicked here and will be the first thing to go out should the water rise above the cabin sole.

nuances of personality by speech inflection or emphasis may be desirable in an attorney's closing argument before a jury, but—in the world of SSB radio—the objective is simply getting the message through. When important information must be conveyed to a station far away, a station plagued with static or interference from other stations, we are satisfied if the words of our message are understood by the other operator. We aren't disappointed if every quality of our personality or attitude is indistinct.

Even average speakers, persons that speak at constant volume and an even pitch, can add miles to their SSB coverage by using a speech processor. Everyone varies the pitch and volume of her/his speech as she/he speaks. Connect a microphone to an oscilloscope, and you can see the changing frequencies and amplitudes you use as you talk.

Since the ability to convey intelligence, i.e., to be understood, depends primarily on vocal vibrations in the range of audio frequencies from 300 to 3000 Hz, intelligibility can be improved in a transmitted SSB signal by emphasizing the necessary speech frequencies and eliminating the others. A speech processor circuit between the microphone and the modulation circuit amplifies speech signals from timid talkers and limits signals from booming shouters. Frequencies above 3000 Hz and below 300 Hz are filtered out. All speech signals reaching the modulation circuits are emphasized for maximum talk power. A consistently efficient modulation results.

When shopping for a new SSB radio, if the

speech processing option isn't excessively costly, insist on it. It will improve the radio's performance, making it possible for you to get through when a radio without speech processing might not work at all.

The SSB Spectrum

The six frequency bands used for marine SSB communications each carry their own peculiar properties and potential to communicate a given distance at a given time of day. In general, higher frequencies (shorter waves) provide communications at greater distances. Lower frequencies (longer waves) provide shorter distance communications.

2 MHz Band

The lowest frequency SSB band is the 2 MHz band. This band has the longest waves (150 meters) and the shortest range. It is used for local radio contacts beyond the range of VHF. During daylight hours, maximum range is limited to about 60 miles. At dusk the band permits reliable communications to approximately 200 miles. During the night the 2 MHz band increases its reach. Just before dawn SSB stations several thousand miles away can be worked when there are no electrical storms (the lower bands are more susceptible to natural static). Ordinarily, however, the 2 MHz band is used for local communications from the VHF margin out to about 150 miles, depending on time of day. Although greater range is possible after dark, the higher frequency bands are less troubled with static and tend to provide more reliable communications.

The 2 MHz band includes the International Call and Distress Frequency for radiotelephone—2.182 MHz. This band should be included in every radio.

The 2 MHz band is called the LF band since it's in the Low Frequency portion of the radio spectrum. The remaining marine SSB bands are called HF bands since they are in the High Frequency portion of the radio spectrum.

4 MHz Band

The lowest of the HF bands in SSB is the 4 MHz band. This band begins to fade when the sun

Technician installing antenna coupler under bunk in aft cabin of motorsailer.

comes over the horizon at dawn, but communication out to 200 miles is possible until mid-morning. By noon, however, the band is stone dead and useless for communications beyond VHF ranges. Later in the afternoon, however, as the sun drops toward the horizon again, the band begins to revive. Just before sundown, the band may be active from 50 to 300 miles. After dark, close-range communications begins to deteriorate as the band reaches beyond nearby stations to make communications possible out to 1000 miles or more.

Daytime contacts are by groundwave propagation, radiation that travels along the surface of the planet. Between dusk and dawn, however, 4 MHz waves begin to bounce off the ionosphere. After dark, a skip zone is created. The waves jump over near stations, but stations farther away can be heard and "worked". An hour or so before dawn, communication is possible on 4 MHz with stations up to 2000 miles away, but stations nearer than 200 miles are within the skipped region and cannot be heard.

8 MHz Band

The 8 MHz band also is subject to daytime deterioration but, unlike 4 MHz, is still useful out to 300 miles at noon with virtually no skip. Afternoon distances increase to 700 miles or more but, as evening falls, the skip zone widens so that nearer stations are lost. By sundown, SSB contacts out to 1000 miles are possible, but stations closer than 300 miles are skipped. After dark, 8 MHz reaches still farther so that stations 3000 miles away can be worked with relative ease, while stations nearer than 500 miles are skipped.

12 MHz Band

The 12 MHz band is quiet most of the morning. Near noon both skip and maximum range extend. By mid-afternoon, the band is hot, and solid contacts to 2000 miles are commonplace, while stations nearer than 600 miles may be missed because of skip. After dark, 12 MHz range reaches out to 4000 miles or more, but the skip zone widens to 1000 miles so that contacts within that distance are unlikely.

16 MHz Band

The 16 MHz band behaves much like the 12 MHz band but provides somewhat greater ranges with

SSB antenna coupler mounted near SSB antenna on wheelhouse of *Aegis*. Note Loran antenna above loud hail speaker.

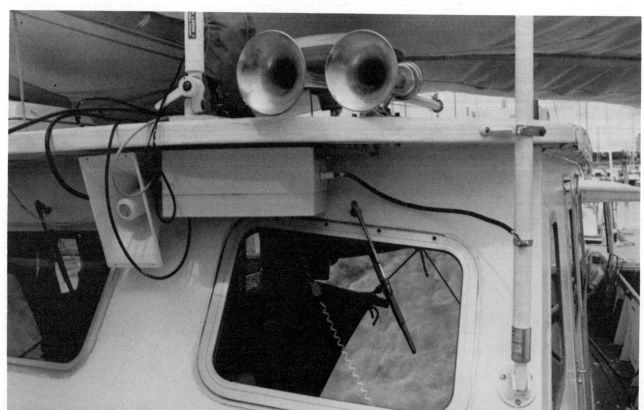

Studying the spectrum pays off.

increased skip distances. Contacts within 800 miles are rare. Evening contacts are possible with stations up to 6000 miles away.

22 MHz Band

The highest frequency band, 22 MHz, may be practically useless during periods of low sunspot activity (an 11–year cycle that peaked in late 1979 and should peak again sometime around 1990). When this band is open, maximum ranges may exceed 8000 miles! The band works best along a north-south radio path and dies shortly after dark.

Antennas

The antenna is the single most important part of your SSB installation. Unless the antenna efficiently radiates transmitted energy and, at the same time, effectively senses even the weakest incoming signals, the system simply can't perform acceptably.

SSB antennas can develop radio "hot spots", so take care not to touch the antenna while the unit is transmitting.

Choosing the proper antenna is partially dependent on the type of boat, its size, the layout of its rigging, etc. Sailboats have some advantages

over shrimp trawlers, for example. Each of the most commonly used antenna types is discussed in the sections that follow.

Whip Antenna

The easiest but not necessarily the most efficient antenna to install is the vertical whip. Usually 23 to 35 feet in length, these self-supporting antennas can be made to resonate at all SSB frequencies (with a tuner). Most are made of fiberglass, although a few are stainless steel rods. The fiberglass whips are lighter. The steel whips may need strong mountings to withstand the "whipping" that occurs during heavy weather.

In general, the SSB whip should be mounted high and in the clear, but height is not so critical with an SSB antenna as it is with a VHF antenna, since VHF range is a function of antenna height and SSB range is a function of frequency. Give height priority to the VHF antenna, but mount the SSB antenna in the clear as much as possible, away from wire rigging, booms and other antennas. Also take care not to mount the whip where it may be used as a handhold or as a belaying pin for a sheet or halyard!

Sailboats often mount SSB whip antennas at the taffrail. The presumption is that they will not be carried away in the event of a dismasting. Ocean racing rules require a taffrail whip, instead of a mast or rigging-mounted antenna. These rules make good sense from a safety perspective, but they do not make good sense from a radio perspective. A whip antenna will not radiate as well as an insulated section of wire (discussed in the next section). The best advice is to stow a whip below decks—ready for a dismasting—but insulate a length of wire in the rigging (usually the backstay) and use it for an antenna until (may you never be so unlucky!) you lose your stick.

Long Wire Antenna

An insulated long wire antenna is inexpensive and efficient.

It is, admittedly, difficult to replace in a sail-

Old-fashioned ceramic powerline insulator. These are ungainly, but they work well—and the stay will not fail should the insulator break since the wires loop through each other.

boat if the mast should be carried away in a storm. In larger vessels with raised deck structures fore and aft, a long wire can easily be strung between insulators. In sailboats, a section of the backstay is often insulated, using high-strength insulators designed for the purpose. Standard powerline insulators are *not* recommended.

One end of the long wire antenna is connected to the antenna tuner (coupler).

A long wire antenna will radiate far better at most SSB frequencies and provide greater range and reliability than any whip. Broken insulators and lost masts are rare. Today's stay insulators are stronger than the steel wire they're installed in. Use them and enjoy better SSB contacts.

Caution: If possible, avoid using a wire topping

lift with an insulated backstay antenna. The long wire antenna needs to be in the clear as much as possible. A wire topping lift (or any other wire rigging) can de-tune a long-wire antenna just by swinging nearby. If the topping lift should wrap itself around the backstay, as may occur in heavy weather when the boom is not vanged or the topping lift is not tensioned properly, the antenna may be shorted to ground—and the transmitter may be damaged. Keep the long wire antenna away from other wires. A length of pre-strained 3/8" Dacron braid rigged (as all good topping lifts should be) so the tension can be varied at the deck, will work at least as well as a wire topping lift, and it won't interfere with the radiating backstay.

Antenna Tuner

SSB antennas need a tuner (coupler). This is true whether you use a long wire or a vertical whip antenna. The tuner adjusts the apparent electrical length of the antenna, matching it to the transmitter's output frequency. Each frequency works well only if the antenna is tuned to the radio, and vice versa. If the channel is changed, especially between bands, the electronic relationship between transmitter and antenna needs to be re-adjusted. This is the purpose of the tuner.

The tuner is mounted between the radio and the antenna. The tuner should be independently connected to the vessel's radio ground and mounted as near the base of the antenna as possi-

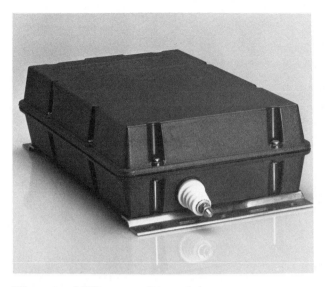

Waterproof SSB tuner. (*Motorola*)

Modern ceramic backstay insulator.

Antenna coupler mounted in hanging locker of aft cabin. Notice high voltage GTO cable connected to insulated terminal on top and wide copper strap connected to ground terminal on bottom.

ble. A single wire connects the tuner to the antenna. A coaxial cable connects the tuner to the radio. The wire from tuner to antenna is part of the radiating system. It should be routed away from all conductors and insulated to reduce shock hazard. All connections should be clean, tight and protected from salt air.

Many tuners today are self-adjusting. Microprocessors are used to create tuners "smart" enough to tune themselves. Others are set once by the installing technician and need no further intervention. Others require the operator to move a switch.

The automatic tuners can adjust to the boat's angle of heel, the position of the boom and other rigging, or even moisture in the air. They therefore provide optimum radiated power under all conditions.

Of course, complexity has its price—reflected in purchase and maintenance costs, as well as failure probability. The more complex an item of electronics (generally speaking) the more prone it is to failure. Weigh the alternatives. An automatic tuner with manual override may be best all around.

No matter which type you select, make certain the tuner is protected from salt air. Corrosion can destroy an antenna tuner in a matter of days. Many are designed to be mounted in the open. Others are not.

The Ground System

Getting an SSB signal off to a good start requires not only an excellent antenna but also a carefully

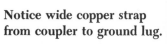

Notice wide copper strap
from coupler to ground lug.

planned ground system. The radio ground has been called the springboard from which waves of radio energy push themselves off on their electromagnetic trip across the vast ether of the universe. Another term for the radio ground system is "ground counterpoise".

As a rule of thumb, a ground counterpoise should provide at least 9 square feet of wide copper strap or similar radio conductor spread through the bilges, behind bunks, in the engine room, above the headliner—in short, wherever room and ingenuity can get it.

Ideally, the ground system should be planned before the boat is built. Then it can be molded into the decks or in the hull itself. Of course, if the hull is steel or aluminum, the ground installation is a simple matter of connecting the radio to the hull using wide copper strap. If the boat is fiberglass or wood, however, the problem is compounded. This is where the experienced marine radio specialist's skill pays off.

Wide copper strap must be used to connect grounding system for SSB installations.

Conclusion

Current technology provides unprecedented reliability and convenience—assuming the installing marine radio technician knows his business.

The most valuable feature of an SSB rig is flexibility of channel selection. Everything else—exotic bells and whistles notwithstanding—is merely secondary. The ability to select the frequency you need is even more important than power.

Assuming your equipment is top notch and installed properly, however, the rest is up to you.

Listen. Keep a log of who you hear, where they were located, where you were located, and what time it was. In a short time, you'll know the best bands for each range and time of day.

Remember: If you can hear the other fellow, the odds are in your favor that he'll be able to hear you, too.

SSB transceiver and remote control unit. (*King*)

CHAPTER 7

Amateur Radio

I remember one wet and chilly morning in the Chesapeake. Fog and drizzle obscured the bay. Dark clouds menaced overhead. It was a good day to stay on the hook.

We were anchored at Solomon's Island. Annie brewed coffee. I fired off the ham radio.

"CQ," I called. "This is W4MTS, marine mobile, anchored in the harbor at Solomon's Island."

"W4MTS!" the speaker blasted back. "You're just a mile away. Do you like steamed crabs?" I replied that we did, and the ham on the other end gave directions, "Up the east branch. You'll see our white dock. I'll meet you to handle the lines."

Though we thought it a bit early for crabs, I donned my foul weather gear, retrieved the hook, set main and mizzen, and worked cautiously up the creek. We found the dock, shared another cup of coffee, and swapped stories about radio, cruising, and the proper way to catch crabs. For lunch, we shared a bushel of those tasty arthropods, fresh from their traps, steamed in secret seasonings. Our new friends then drove us for supplies and told us how life was back in the 20's when they'd take the ferry to Tangier Island to go to school.

By the time we got back to our boat it was well after dark. A memorable day. And all from a simple "CQ!"

Why mention this non-technical encounter? To emphasize the enjoyment ham radio can bring to boating. It's happened dozens of times: in Marblehead, Baltimore, Key West, the Carolina sounds. Everywhere you go there are friendly hams—in their own boats or ashore—anxious to share a tall tale or swap ideas about antennas, bilge pumps or the best bait for mutton snapper.

With the proper gear and antennas, you can communicate with other boats across the harbor or over 3000 miles of open ocean. You can "read the mail" with the radio officer on a tanker in the South Atlantic or play chess with a handicapped person in Des Moines.

Amateur radio is rapidly gaining popularity with boating people everywhere. Ham radio is fun. It's a great way to make friends. It provides access to mail, communications with home, and information on technical boating topics. Finally, it offers a backup emergency communications option.

Amateur radio operators are licensed by the FCC. The novice license is for beginners, requir-

Bulletin board in radio room of ship. Note "QSL" cards from amateur radio operators.

ing a simple radio theory test, a passing knowledge of radio regulations, and a Morse code test at 5 words per minute (5 wpm). Almost anyone can pass the novice test with a little effort. The tests for general, advanced, or extra class licenses are a little more difficult, but anyone who makes an honest effort can pass the examinations. More information is provided in the chapter on licensing.

It's illegal to operate an amateur radio transmitter without a license. Particularly malicious radio outlaws are jailed *and* can be fined as much as $10,000. Since ham bands are as capable of world-wide communications as marine SSB, there must be regulations to prevent misuse. A ham operator can interfere with communications worldwide. Being a ham operator implies certain responsibilities. Operation outside the U.S. is permitted, but you may violate international laws if you don't get a local license. Prison terms can result from transmitting on ham bands in foreign waters, so check with local authorities before operating overseas.

If you're familiar with the propagation characteristics of marine SSB bands, you'll recognize the potential of ham bands for international communications. As with SSB, picking the best band for a particular time of day and distance is essential to success in the ham bands.

History of Amateur Radio

Not surprisingly, many of the early radio experimenters were also avid boatpeople. Marchese Guglielmo Marconi himself owned a marvelous yacht, a truly regal craft he named *Electra*. The earliest research work in radio was dedicated to the development of systems to facilitate navigation and communications for ships at sea. Radio beacons and directional antennas for coastal and harbor navigation were among the first applications of the new science. Safety on the sea was a prime consideration of the radio pioneers—and it still is.

They all were amateurs in those days. There was no FCC and a license was not yet required. Boys and girls of all ages listened to crudely fashioned radios with eager ears, hoping for an intelligent beep or toot to sound through the din of static crashes. It was exciting. They built receivers from old coils of wire, discarded razor blades, and whiskers from the neighbor's cat. The most ambitious built primitive transmitters and powered them by banks of homemade batteries. They experimented with antennas: top-fed, bottom-fed, end-fed, center-fed, long wires, short wires, no wires at all. They invented new circuits and revised old theories. They worked in basements, in backyards, on transoceanic steamers, on Cape Cod's beaches and on the barren outer banks of the Carolinas. The science of radio advanced—but the interest in the sea remained.

Today's radio pioneers are bouncing signals off the moon and sending messages around the world through the use of transmitters orbiting the planet in space satellites. But still, when a call is heard from a maritime mobile station, that call receives top priority. Special frequencies are set aside to facilitate radio communications with amateurs on boats throughout the world. These channels are not as reliable as those assigned for

WB4GQK at the printer and W4MTS at the computer on the motorsailer *Aegis*. This set-up is used to automatically receive weather maps and navigation bulletins for rebroadcast to amateur radio friends on the "Waterway Net."

marine HF-SSB or VHF-FM contacts, but they have certain advantages as you will discover in the following pages.

The Frequencies

Hams are licensed to operate in every part of the radio spectrum. In fact, the ham bands include

TABLE 7-1

THE AMATEUR RADIO BANDS

1.800–2.000 MHz	—	160 meters
3.500–4.000 MHz	—	80 meters
7.000–7.300 MHz	—	40 meters
10.100–10.109 MHz	—	30 meters
10.115–10.150 MHz	—	30 meters
14.000–14.350 MHz	—	20 meters
21.000–21.450 MHz	—	15 meters
28.000–29.700 MHz	—	10 meters
50.000–54.000 MHz	—	6 meters
144.000–148.000 MHz	—	2 meters
220.000–225.000 MHz	—	1 meter
440.000–450.000 MHz	—	½ meter

more frequencies than either commercial marine HF-SSB or VHF-FM. The list of ham bands given in the following table is only partially complete. Frequencies above those listed (up into the microwave and radar range where wavelength is measured in centimeters) are available to licensed hams for communications and experimentation.

Once you're familiar with the propagation characteristics of each of these bands, you can communicate with people all over the world. Learning the bands is one of the keys to success.

160 Meter Band

One-Sixty is just below the International Call and Distress frequency, 2.182 MHz. With transmitter power limited by the FCC on this band, daytime range is about 50 miles. Nighttime communications is reliable out to 200 miles.

80 Meter Band

Eighty meters is active from early evening through dawn, but daytime range is severely limited. After dark, contacts are common out to 300 miles. Just before dawn, 80 meters may be open to 2000 miles or more. Early evening finds many ham "nets" operating in the 80 meter band, using either Morse code (CW) or single-sideband (SSB) voice transmission. These nets handle traffic for stations throughout the United States and meet on a regular basis at pre-arranged frequencies.

40 Meter Band

Forty meters is popular with cruising hams, providing communications throughout the day with ranges at noon good to 500 miles or more. Contacts earlier in the morning may be possible out to 1500 miles. After dark the band is almost *too* good; foreign broadcast stations clobber ham communications with strange oriental music and news broadcasts from Siberia.

30 Meter Band

Thirty meters is new to radio amateurs. This small band of frequencies was once restricted to military and commercial use. It yields excellent contacts day and night. Daytime ranges reach 1200 miles. Nightime range may be 3000 miles. Operation on 30 meters is limited to Morse code.

20 Meter Band

Twenty meters is the busiest amateur band, except in the wee wee hours when propagation deteriorates. Daytime contacts out to 2000 miles are common. After dark, it may be possible to reach stations 4000 miles away. This band is home of the famous Maritime Mobile Net that meets from time to time throughout the day on 14.313 MHz to handle traffic for hams on boats throughout the world. Tune to this frequency sometime and listen in. At times you may hear stations calling in from every ocean.

15 Meter Band

Fifteen is erratic and undependable. When active, this band yields daytime contacts out to 8000. The band dies after sundown.

10 Meter Band

Ten meters is sporadic and very undependable. When it's hot, however, it's very hot. When it's dead, it's stone cold. Some days you can't talk across town. Other days you can talk with weak stations on the other side of the planet.

6 Meter Band

Six meters, once popular for local work, is not much used anymore. It is a midrange band providing contacts out to about 150–200 miles under ideal conditions.

2 Meter Band

The 2 meter band is, for some, the most useful. This band is used by local repeaters—automated stations run by local clubs. Repeaters receive and then re-broadcast transmissions from mobile stations using high-powered equipment and exotic antennas mounted atop tall buildings or towers. A low-powered, hand-held 2 meter transceiver can communicate with stations 100 miles away through the use of a repeater. The 2 meter band behaves much like the VHF marine band, except that hams aren't limited to 25 watts transmit power! With a 2–meter rig installed in your boat, you can make phone patches through local 2 meter repeaters just as you do with VHF—only you don't go through the marine operator. Many clubs operate open repeaters and let anyone use their autopatch to make telephone calls via 2 meter radio. Other clubs operate closed patches, requiring the user to access the repeater with a secret code. But club dues are seldom steep, and club membership can aid anyone who wants to learn more about radio and electronics.

Above 2 Meters

Higher frequency bands are available for amateur use. Range is limited to line-of-sight (with the exception of experimental work being done with repeaters in amateur-owned satellites or the occasional contact achieved by bouncing microwave signals off the moon's surface). Boating hams primarily use communications bands from 160 to 2 meters.

Net Operation

Special frequencies are used by hams on boats. Networks or "nets" are scheduled on these frequencies throughout the day to provide convenient meeting places for those who travel about upon the oceans. Traffic includes weather and navigational bulletins, phone patches to home, and contacts with other boats. Some of the net frequencies have been used to organize rescues, but ham radio is not a reliable emergency radio system. More on this later.

Hundreds of other nets meet daily as well, at all hours and on every band, to satisfy the interests of everyone. There are nets for computer enthusiasts, nets for campers, nets for pilots, nets for stamp collectors, and nets to handle traffic. A few of the nets most useful to hams on boats are listed in a table in the appendix. This list is by no means exhaustive, and the times and/or frequencies may vary.

A more complete net listing is available from: Seven Seas Cruising Association, P.O.Box 38, Don Pedro Island, Placida, Florida 33946. Send $5 and a S.A.S.E.

The Waterway Radio & Cruising Club is a friendly group of boating folk meeting daily at 0800 Eastern Time on 7.268 MHz (lower sideband). Every morning old friends and new get together to exchange notes on boats and harbors, charts and equipment, good fishing and diving lo-

Ham rig tuned to 7.268 MHz used by the Waterway Net.

cations from the Caribbean to the Coast of Maine. Shore stations make phone patches for families on vacation from the Bahamas to Boston, enabling sailors to make certain all is well at home. Arrangements are made for mail to be forwarded so the skipper can pick up his correspondence at the next port. Float plans are filed for those intending long offshore passages, and all stations listen closely for the check-in call from boats underway. This net frequency is busy throughout the day, informally convening on the even hours. Everyone is welcome to check in.

They even have their own burgee!

For membership and current roster, send $4 and S.A.S.E. to: Waterway Radio & Cruising Club, c/o Fred Dennerline, KA4STX, 2364 Northeast 28 Court, Lighthouse Point, Florida 33064.

The real workhorse frequency in the ham bands is 14.313 MHz. Throughout the day this 20 meter frequency is home for nets busy handling message traffic and arranging phone patches for maritime mobile stations. Ships and yachts exchange messages with each other and with stations ashore all over the world. This is probably

Before transmitting on any frequency, listen to make certain the frequency is not already in use.

the busiest of all ham frequencies. Check-in procedures are strictly formal. They have to be. Traffic is so heavy that stations calling in must be sent off frequency to meet elsewhere and exchange their messages. The 14.313 frequency is too busy for anything but making contact. All day and on into the evening, the litany continues. Stations from every ocean call in to get their messages ashore. "CQ Boston! CQ Quito! CQ San Francisco!"

Listen to some of these frequencies. That's the best way to get an idea of the services available.

Getting Started

You don't have to be a licensed ham to begin enjoying the fun and excitement of amateur radio. Indeed, many of us began as shortwave listeners. Listening can be the best way to get started. Tune around. If your receiver has a beat frequency oscillator (BFO) control, turn it "on" and tune carefully. Single-sideband reception requires careful tuning to pull intelligible speech from the garble of Donald Duck sounds. If your receiver is designed to pick up SSB, of course, tuning is far easier. Give it a try.

The American Radio Relay League (ARRL) operates a high-power station from Newington, CT. The station's call sign is W1AW. Scheduled bulletins and code practice sessions are broadcast throughout the day. Any good quality shortwave set can pick up these transmissions. For a schedule and frequency list, write: ARRL Headquarters, Newington, CT 06111.

While you're at it, ask for a list of ARRL publications. The ARRL represents the amateur radio fraternity, lobbying for radio amateurs at the FCC and at international conferences. ARRL efforts have contributed greatly toward making amateur radio what it is today.

In addition to lobbying for amateur rights, coordinating its National Traffic System, organizing contests and operating awards to stimulate experimentation and station improvement, the ARRL is busy publishing up-to-date educational materials: license study guides, operating manuals, electronics handbooks, logbooks, books with ideas for those who build their own equipment, antenna books, and many other publications of interest to hams. The ARRL kit, "Tune In The World With Ham Radio", includes a cassette tape containing Morse Code practice sessions and a book to help you learn about the code, radio theory, and setting up your own station. The kit sells for $8.50.

Equipment

Part of the fun of amateur radio is building your own gear. Complete plans for high-powered SSB transmitters, VHF handheld transceivers, radio-teletype demodulators, even circuits that automatically translate Morse Code into plain English are published from time to time in radio magazines. Your library has dozens of books such as "The Radio Amateur's Handbook" with all the details, schematic diagrams, lists of parts and tools, even how to put up an antenna and get your rig on the air. Several companies offer kits for amateur radio equipment, with step-by-step instructions.

Building is fun, but it's not everyone's chowder. Some of us are too busy. We haven't the time or the interest to build our own gear. We want to get on the air as quickly and as painlessly as possible.

So, if you're going to buy, what should you look for?

First on your radio shopping list should be a high-quality, general coverage receiver. Digital frequency readouts are common today. Insist on one. The best will display frequency to the nearest 100 Hz or better, letting you pre-set the receiver precisely so you don't miss calls. General coverage lets you tune in Navy weather and navigation bulletins as well as the ham bands. With the proper interface, you can receive facsimile or radioteletype transmissions, too. High frequency broadcast programming is another benefit of having a general coverage receiver on board. It's always a pleasure to listen to a Sherlock Holmes mystery on the British BBC Network, or listen to the Orioles win another baseball game on our Armed Forces network, AFRTS. These broadcasts

can be picked up anywhere in the world on a good general coverage receiver with a tuned antenna.

Standard time broadcasts are essential for precise celestial navigation. A comprehensive list of stations broadcasting time and frequency standards worldwide is provided in the appendix. All listed frequencies can be received within the spread of a good general coverage receiver.

A QRP (low-power) transceiver is an excellent second choice. You can work European or South American stations easily with less than 5 watts of transmitted power, using nothing for an antenna but a length of copper wire hoisted into the clear on a spare halyard. When you're ready to buy a more powerful rig, stow the QRP in a watertight container with a fresh 12V lantern battery and a length of antenna wire to be used in an emergency. The QRP rig is lightweight and portable. Set up your station at the foot of a palm tree on some deserted beach or transmit from the craggy top of an island mountain for some exciting worldwide contacts.

Next on your shopping list is an all-mode transceiver for HF (high frequency) work on all bands (160–10 meters) and at medium power (100 to 200 watts). With 100 watts of power, most maritime mobile stations have little or no difficulty making contacts, provided the antenna and ground systems are properly planned and connected. A few still use tubes in the transmitter, but the best for seagoing use are completely solid-state—using power transistors in the transmitter instead of battery-draining vacuum tubes. Unless your boat has a 110 volt AC generator, insist on a transceiver that works from the boat's 12 volt battery supply.

Several of the latest medium-power HF rigs have built-in general coverage receivers. You can transmit on the ham bands but listen on any HF band and parts of the MF and LF bands. The best of these can pick up stations from 100 KHz to 30 MHz. In fact, an HF transceiver with a built-in general coverage receiver may cost only a small amount more than a general coverage receiver by itself. This is certainly worth keeping in mind when you go out to shop for a shipboard station.

Many HF sets provide an RF (radio frequency)

power control to permit reduction of output power to QRP levels. This energy-saving feature is important to the battery-conscious cruising sailor who must conserve his reserve current. If the transmitter is pumping 120 watts up to the antenna, it is probably consuming at least 240 watts because of efficiency losses. And 240 watts at 12 volts is a whopping battery drain of 20 amperes. Only the stoutest battery can last for long with a 20 ampere drain. After a few brief "QSO's" (contacts) at high power, the battery is certain to go kaput. When buying an HF transceiver, look for the RF power control. It may have other names, e.g., "carrier level" or "output", but its function is the same. Study the specifications sheet carefully and quiz the salesperson.

If you expect to do much Morse Code work, pay a little extra for a set of code filters. Occasionally, when you're working another code station, a second, third, fourth, or fifth code station will move near your frequency, causing interference ("QRM") to your QSO. The interfering code will be slightly higher or lower in pitch. With a set of filters, you can tune out the QRM so only the station you want to hear comes through. Filters are especially helpful when you're trying to work a weak station while all around you are stronger stations.

Some mid-priced HF transceivers have dual variable frequency oscillators (VFO's) so you can listen to a station that is sending on one frequency then answer that station by transmitting back on another frequency. This is essential for certain modes of communications. The process, called "duplex",is distinguished from "simplex", in which both transmit and receive frequencies are the same. The ability to operate duplex can be a valuable feature and should be considered.

Many of the digital rigs can memorize sets of frequency and mode settings. These memorized channels can then be reselected as they are needed, or they can be reprogrammed to new frequencies and modes. A few transceivers can scan through their memories, stepping from channel to channel in sequence, stopping when a signal is heard. The models with built-in general coverage receivers can be programmed to step through the marine SSB frequencies, for example,

listening for weather or navigational bulletins. The more important marine SSB frequencies are listed in the chapter on marine single-sideband.

It bears mentioning that a few synthesized ham transceivers can be modified to transmit and receive on marine SSB channels or other non-amateur frequencies. A word of caution, however: Operation of such modified rigs outside the ham bands is a serious crime within the continental U.S. or its territorial waters. Ham rigs are not FCC approved for operation on the commercial HF-SSB frequencies (or any non-ham frequency).

Another handy feature available on some of the newer rigs is the ability to scan *between* any two pre-programmed frequencies. This is an ideal option for those times when you're listening for a scheduled call from a friend who agreed to meet you on 14.260 MHz, for example. Since her radio may be an older dial-type model that's not as accurate as your digital dandy, her call may be transmitted anywhere from 14.255 MHz to 14.265 MHz, depending on the accuracy of her dial. If you have the scanner option and can automatically scan between pre-selected frequencies, you can let your radio tune itself up and down the band between 14.255 MHz and 14.265 MHz. You won't have to sit in front of the radio waiting and cranking the tuning knob back and forth while listening—the radio will do that for you.

Of course, if she has one of the newer rigs like yours, you should be able to meet at any time, precisely on frequency to the nearest 100 Hz (0.1 KHz). Make certain the rig you buy has a band setting to let you tune in one of the time standard broadcasts listed earlier in this chapter. These stations also provide exact frequency references. For example, the WWV broadcast at 10.000 MHz is *precisely* 10.000 MHz—to better than the nearest cycle! A good mid-priced transceiver (or general coverage receiver) should provide a control to calibrate the digital readout to one of the time standard broadcast signals. You should be able to put the receiver in upper sideband mode, for example, tune until the digital readout is precisely 10.000 MHz (or any of the other time standard frequencies), then adjust a calibration control until the pitch of the received tone goes down to nothing. This is called "zero beat". Note

WB4GQK aboard *Aegis* on Tampa Bay chats with friends on boats in the Abacos and Chesapeake via ham radio.

that WWV sends an audible 1000 cycle tone along with the time ticks. The audible tone is absent during the last 15 seconds of each minute and during the 46th through the 51st minutes of each hour. It is during the "tone off" period that the transceiver should be adjusted to zero beat. With a well-designed radio, calibrating to WWV will be sufficient for the accuracy needed to operate at all frequencies.

Many transceivers include a "marker crystal" (or offer it as an option. This marker crystal can be zero beat to WWV and used to check your frequency on the other bands at 25 KHz or 100 KHz intervals. These should be calibrated carefully to WWV for best results. Note that the zero beat tone becomes sub-audible at around 50 cycles per second. By careful tuning, however, you will find a point where the transceiver's "S-meter" wiggles back and forth at the zero beat frequency. As you continue to adjust the calibration control, you will find a point where the meter moves back and forth still more slowly and, by "tweaking" the control just so, you can make the meter needle stop altogether. At this point the marker crystal is

adjusted to precisely match the incoming signal from WWV and can be used to set your transceiver with precision.

Antennas for Amateur Work

Everything imaginable has been tried as an antenna. A few that have been known to work (at least on certain frequencies) include an aluminum window frame in a city hotel room, barbed-wire fencing, rain gutters, even an old bed spring. Honest!

Antennas are frequency-conscious, however. What works well at one frequency may not work at all on another. If you have room for a tower and can mount a rotating three-element beam for each operating frequency, you're in good shape. Few of us have room in the backyard for such elaborate antennas, let alone on our boat.

Almost any insulated conductor that can be supported in the air above your deck will function as an antenna. An extreme example is a steel or aluminum mast totally insulated from the sea and connected directly to the radio transmitter. Such an arrangment may work well at certain frequencies—but it presents a serious lightning hazard and is not recommended. Masts should be grounded to the sea to prevent lightning damage to the boat and crew.

A frequent antenna choice of sailboat owners is the insulated backstay. Those who argue that insulators weaken the stay can use a simple long wire hoisted to the masthead on its own halyard, a fiberglass whip antenna, or even a horizontal dipole or inverted vee. These antennas are explained in the following pages. Boats have been sighted with ungainly three-element beam antennas mounted at the masthead, but this is not the norm and, unless you're planning to stay in sheltered waters, a beam antenna at the masthead is highly discouraged. The choice is yours, however. Experiment. That's part of the fun of amateur radio, after all.

An ideal boat antenna may simply not be possible for HF amateur use. The shortest optimum radiator for a vertical antenna is 1/4 wavelength long at the operating frequency. At the bottom of the 80 meter band, at 3.500 MHz for example, a 1/4 wavelength vertical radiator is 67 feet long. (To find 1/4 wavelength in feet, divide 234 by the frequency in megahertz.) If you carry a tall mast and can hoist a 67 foot insulated wire from the deck to the masthead, you may be able to radiate effectively on the 80 meter band. Insulate the top end of the wire and connect the bottom end to your transceiver. The vertical is one type of "end-fed" antenna, meaning the radio is connected to one end and nothing is attached to the other end. (The transceiver should also be connected electrically to the earth by a secure ground or seawater contact.)

Unfortunately, you have other wires up there hanging from the mast, shrouds and stays, wire halyards, topping lifts—electrical conductors that can interfere with the antenna. If your mast is aluminum, it too will interfere with the antenna's radiation. The following figure shows a vertical antenna mounted in the clear (away from other wires and interference) over an ideal ground. Note that the radiation pattern is omnidirectional. Except for short vertical antennas

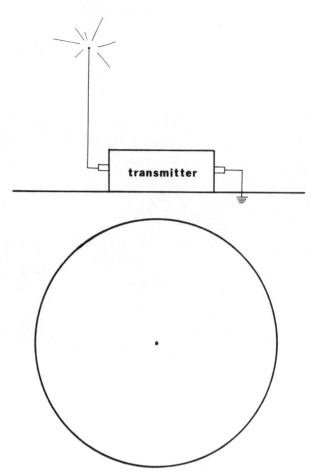

Vertical antenna and its radiation pattern.

mounted atop the mast for use on marine or amateur VHF, this omnidirectional pattern is a theoretical ideal. In practice, a vertical antenna hoisted in the rigging will have directional characteristics—and may not resonate at the cut length.

On large ships with two masts widely separated, a horizontal dipole or ½ wavelength antenna may be strung between the masts, but here the ideal length is twice that required for a vertical. To find ½ wavelength in feet, divide the constant 468 by the frequency in megahertz. For example, if you want to know how long a ½ wavelength dipole should be at 21.1 MHz, divide 468 by 21.1 to get 22.18 feet, which converts to roughly 22′ 2⅛″).

Unless your boat is very large indeed, a horizontal dipole antenna may be a difficult alterna-

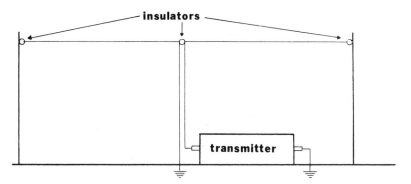

Horizontal dipole and its radiation pattern.

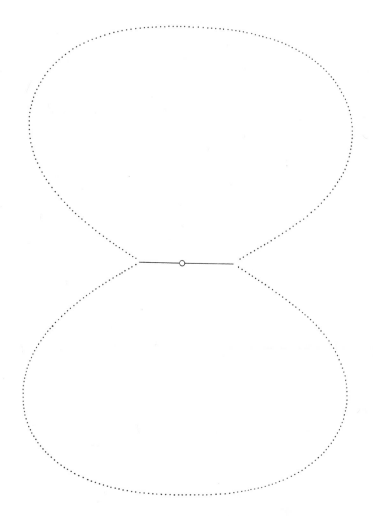

tive. The horizontal dipole and its directional radiation pattern are shown in the following figure. Note that the antenna is most effective when working stations that are broadside to the span of the antenna wire. Also note that the antenna is center-fed.

A third type of antenna, and one commonly used for on-board amateur radio work, is the inverted-V antenna. The inverted-V is essentially

nothing more than a horizontal dipole with its center supported from a mast or halyard and its outboard ends brought down to the deck. It is center-fed. The inverted-V requires but one mast and needs less space than the horizontal dipole. The angle between the legs of the inverted-V should be 90 to 120 degrees but, where space is limited, an angle smaller than 90 degrees can be used. The "468" formula used to cut a dipole may

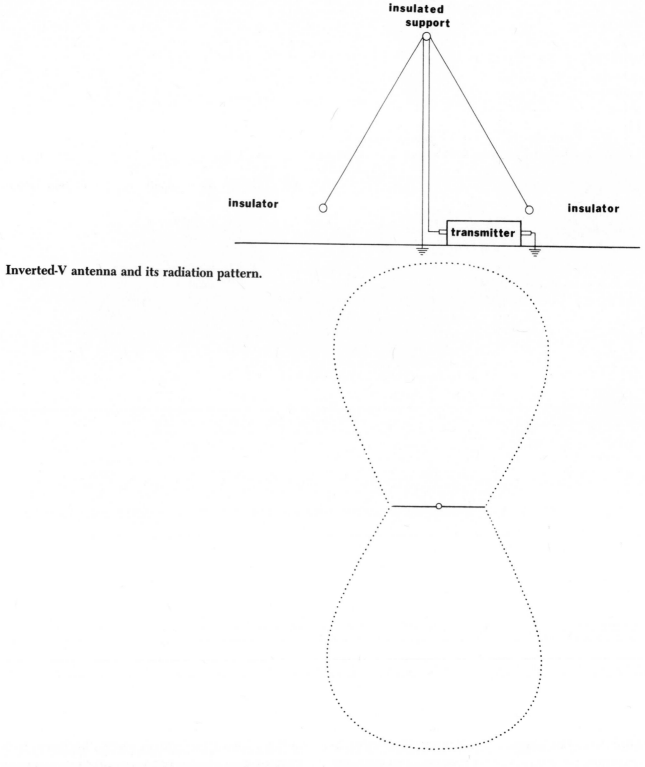

insulated
support

insulator

insulator

transmitter

Inverted-V antenna and its radiation pattern.

yield an inverted-V antenna that is just a shade too long for the operating frequency; slight pruning of the ends may be required to obtain a perfect match. Matching antennas to the operating frequency is explained in the following section.

Tuning the Antenna

Each of the above types of antenna can be fed with RG–8 or RG–58 coaxial cable (standard radio antenna cable available at all radio supply houses). Using coaxial feed these antennas will work well at the frequencies for which they are cut—but they won't perform well at other frequencies. Certainly in the limited space available aboard a boat one can't install a different antenna for every frequency. That's why we rely on an antenna tuner (also called a coupler or matching network).

All antennas react differently when connected to a radio transmitter. At one particular frequency, we say the antenna is resonant at its fundamental. At any other frequency, the antenna is not fundamentally resonant. Antennas work best at resonance, The following discussion, explaining (qualitatively at least) why this is so, has been included only because you'll need to know something about it in order to pass your FCC exam for an amateur license. (Don't be alarmed if it isn't immediately clear. It wasn't immediately clear for any of us who now hold licenses.)

A radio transmitter is nothing more than an AC (alternating current) generator that reverses the direction of electron current flowing in an antenna at a rate known as radio frequency, back and forth, back and forth, so many cycles per second. (One cycle per second is now known as a Hertz.) The rate of reversal is what we call radio frequency. Stations working the maritime mobile net in the 20 meter band at 14.313 MHz, operate by reversing the electron current flow in their antennas at the rate of one complete cycle 14,313,-000 times each second.

During half of each cycle the transmitter pumps electrons in one direction and, during the other half of each cycle, the transmitter pumps them in the opposite direction. The electrons aren't pumped into the space surrounding the antenna but are kept moving back and forth within the antenna. The rapidly reversing current flow sets up an alternating magnetic field that radiates outward from the antenna. At the same time, polarity changes in the antenna create an alternating electrostatic field that also radiates outward from the antenna. If either one of these fields were created by itself without the other, the effective range of radio would be very short.

In reality, however, the two fields interact to produce what is known as a reversing electromagnetic field, a composite of the reversing magnetic and the reversing electrostatic fields. The magnetic and electrostatic fields form an alternating oscillation between the two kinds of forces to complement and keep each other going, radiating into space—in short, *radio*.

A transmitter reverses the voltage at its antenna terminals twice during each cycle. The current direction also reverses twice during each cycle, but the current reversals occur ¼ cycle after the voltage reversals. The voltage is said to lead the current by ¼ cycle (90 degrees), and the current is said to lag behind the voltage by ¼ cycle (90 degrees).

Now remember that it is current in a conductor that causes a magnetic field to be created around the conductor—just like an electromagnet can only pick up scrap metal while current flows in its coil. The above diagram shows the two moments in each cycle when current in the antenna (and consequently the magnetic field around the antenna) is at its greatest—at one point a maximum in the positive direction, and ½ cycle later maximum in the negative direction.

But an electrostatic field requires no current. In fact, the name electro*static* means "stationary electrons".

In the space of ¼ cycle, the electrostatic field and the magnetic field reverse alternatel). At the beginning of every cycle, the voltage applied to the antenna terminals is at its maximum positive value, but the antenna current is zero; the electrostatic field is at its maximum positive value, and the magnetic field is zero. Just ¼ cycle later, the applied voltage is zero, and the current is at its maximum positive value; the electrostatic field is zero, and the magnetic field is at its maximum positive value. After another ¼ cycle, half-way through one complete cycle, the applied voltage is now at its maximum negative value, and the current is again zero; the electrostatic field is at its maximum negative potential, and the magnetic field is zero.

This ¼ cycle relationship affects the resonance of lengths of wire used for antennas. Voltage and current vary inversely at the top and bottom of the ¼ wavelength vertical antenna. When current is zero at the bottom of the antenna, voltage at the top is at a peak—either positive or negative. When current is at a maximum at the bottom of the antenna, voltage at the top is zero.

This balanced condition occurs *only* at a resonant frequency, i.e., when the length of the vertical antenna is equal to ½ the distance one wave travels in one cycle, i.e., ¼ wavelength.

The distance one wave travels in one cycle depends only upon the number of waves being generated per second. The speed of each wave is a constant—approximately equal to the speed of light and essentially the same in air, vacuum, or copper wire. This speed is 300,000,000 meters per second. Thus, if a transmitter reverses its antenna terminal voltage 100,000,000 times each second (100 MHz) it will send 100,000,000 waves of radio energy up the antenna every second. Each wave travels at the constant speed of 300,000,000 meters per second. A single wave at 100 MHz, then, will travel only 3 meters up its antenna before the transmitter creates another wave to follow it. The length of a radio wave at 100 MHz is 3 meters.

Remember: If 100,000,000 waves travel along an antenna at 300,000,000 meters per second, each wave can only be 3 meters in length. If the radio frequency is 10 MHz, then 10,000,000 waves are generated every second, each wave traveling along the antenna at the constant speed of 300,000,000 meters per second, and the wavelength is 30 meters. An ideal vertical antenna for 10MHz is ¼ wavelength long (7.5 meters or about 23.4 feet).

Notice that the transmitter is between the vertical antenna and the earth ground, alternately pumping electrons up into the antenna or down out of the antenna and into the earth. With a horizontal dipole or inverted-V antenna (or other center-fed antenna) the transmitter pumps electrons alternately between the two sides of the antenna, each side being ¼ wave in length.

When the length of a radiating element of an antenna is just right, e.g., ¼ wavelength, a phenomenon known as standing waves occurs. The rate of voltage reversals imparted by the transmitter just matches the rate of wave movement up and down the antenna. A perfect ¼ wavelength antenna element has perfect standing waves along its length, and the standing wave ratio (SWR) is said to be 1:1—a perfect match.

If a higher frequency is transmitted into the same antenna, the waves are too short for the element and there are no perfect standing waves—the antenna doesn't match the frequency. If a lower frequency is transmitted into the antenna, the waves are too long for the element and again there are no perfect standing waves—another bad match.

All transmitters work best when connected to an antenna that responds readily to the RF voltage alternations. When the length of an antenna doesn't match the frequency, your transmitter has to work *against* the mismatched waves on the antenna. This reduces the overall efficiency of the system. Radio energy is wasted. The transmitter tries to send electrons into the antenna at the same time the last cycle of electrons is returning from its trip to the end of the antenna. The currents collide. Heat is generated in the antenna and in the cables connecting the antenna to the transmitter—and in the final amplifying elements of the transmitter itself where it can cause premature transmitter failure. This wasted energy reduces transmitter efficiency.

The best length for an antenna's radiating element is some integral fraction of a whole wavelength. If we could easily vary the physical length of an antenna, we could have a perfect match on every frequency. But, changing the physical length of a wire is not easy.

However, we *can* change the effective electrical length of an antenna by using an antenna tuner (matching network or coupler). There are several types of tuners on the market. Most of them can be used to tune your transmitter to any random length insulated wire or fiberglass whip antenna.

The transmitter is connected to the matching network with 50 or 75 ohm coaxial cable (RG–8 or RG–58 is fine). If the antenna is end-fed (an insulated backstay or whip), the network outputs should be connected between the bottom of the antenna and ground with short and direct conductors. If the antenna is a dipole or inverted-V, the outputs should be connected to the two legs of the antenna where they meet the center insulator using ⅞" twin-lead cable available at any radio supply house.

A standing wave ratio (SWR) meter should be connected between the transmitter and matching network. Some antenna tuners have an SWR meter built in. Use short lengths of coax between the meter, tuner and transmitter. By adjusting the tuner, any antenna can be matched to the operating frequency so the transmitter will operate at its optimum efficiency on any selected frequency band.

To find the perfect match, reduce transmitter output power to a minimum. Select a frequency that's not in use. Identify with your call sign and indicate that you intend to test. Listen to be certain no one is already using the frequency, then hold the code key down while adjusting the tuner. For best results, set the capacitor(s) to mid-range first and adjust the coil(s) for minimum SWR. Then adjust both capacitor(s) for the best match. Don't be disappointed if you can't get the meter to read a perfect 1:1 match. Anything lower than 1.5:1 should work nicely.

Remember: When you change frequencies, you need to re-tune the matching network. Once you find the best settings for each of the bands you intend to work, write them into your radio logbook. The next time you go back to that band, you'll be able to adjust the matching network quickly.

An antenna tuner is a must—especially on sailboats where the antenna is probably going to be a random length of wire or a whip designed for marine single-sideband.

Radio Ground

HF radio operation requires a suitable ground connection.

This is especially true where vertical antennas are used, since vertical antennas work "against" the ground. The ground is sometimes called a counterpoise because the transmitter reverses the vertical antenna's polarity with respect to the earth. Without a proper radio ground, HF operation with a vertical antenna would be poor at best.

If you have room for a dipole or inverted-V, the ground may not be as critical to your system's performance, but any radio system seems to improve when connected electrically to the planet.

However, a length of copper wire hanging over the transom in the water is not a suitable radio ground for HF work. Neither are those pretty bronze fittings so often sold as ground plates and attached to the bottom of your boat. Ground plates may work fine to prevent damage from electrolysis or shock hazard with 110 volt AC supplies, shore power or on-board generated AC, but they are not efficient at HF radio frequencies.

What is needed is more area in contact with the sea or wider conductive areas spread fore and aft, port and starboard, inside the hull. The ground counterpoise doesn't even have to get wet! It's better if it does, but the important factor is the *area* of conductor beneath the antenna.

Of course if your boat has a steel or aluminum hull, the ground connection is no trouble at all. Simply connect the radio *and* coupler to the hull with a heavy copper conductor. These connections should be made as short as possible. Wide copper strapping makes the best radio conductor. Connections should be clean and tight and sealed from corrosion with several coats of varnish or enamel. These connections should be checked from time to time, cleaned and re-painted if necessary.

If your hull is non-metallic, a radio ground for HF work can be made from bronze screen or copper strapping bonded inside the hull beneath the water line. All connections should be soldered and sealed with varnish or enamel. A minimum of 100 square feet is recommended.

If neither of the above is practicable, connect your radio ground to the engine block. Connect engine block to all through-hull fittings, tanks, bronze grounding plates, or any other masses of metal at or below deck level. Use heavy copper conductors. Make all connections clean and tight.

If you have no engine or through-hull fittings, then go ahead and hang a length of bare chain over the side. Secure the chain to a lifeline stanchion with a stainless steel hose clamp, and use the lifelines as a counterpoise. It may not be ideal, but its better than no ground counterpoise at all.

Two-Meter Rigs

For short-range communications, a 2 meter rig can be fun. If your mate gets a ticket, too, you can carry a 2 meter handheld in the dinghy when going ashore and call her at the boat should you forget the grocery list.

A 2 meter antenna need be nothing more than a 19–inch length of stiff wire mounted as high as you can get it.

Commercial antennas for 2 meters are available, but they are easy to make. An omnidirectional ground-plane antenna can be made from five 18–inch lengths of brazing rod and an SO–238 coaxial connector. One length of rod is soldered to the center pin, the other four are attached to the socket base at each of the screw holes. Coax attaches to the socket as usual, leading to the 2 meter rig.

All VHF antennas should be mounted as high as possible, atop the masts of sailing yachts or on the wheelhouses of workboats.

A 5-element beam antenna is small enough to be used on many boats. It will permit contacts where a simple whip would not get through. The gain of this antenna is about 9 db or a power ratio of about 8 times that of a vertical whip. You should be able to build it yourself. The driven element is insulated in the middle, with one side connected to the center conductor of the coax feedline and the other side connected to the shield. All elements can be made of any metal, e.g., aluminum tubing. The boom can be of wood or plastic.

Gain of this antenna is in one direction only, unlike the gain of marine VHF antennas. Don't mix your ham and VHF antennas.

Emergencies

Much has been said and written of harrowing rescues effected through the cooperation of ham radio operators. Many of these stories are marvelous accounts of efficiency and fast thinking on the part of people totally unacquainted with seagoing problems. Lives have undoubtedly been saved—but the stories don't tell all.

The publicity received by hams who have

Five-element beam antenna for 2-meter band at 147 MHz.

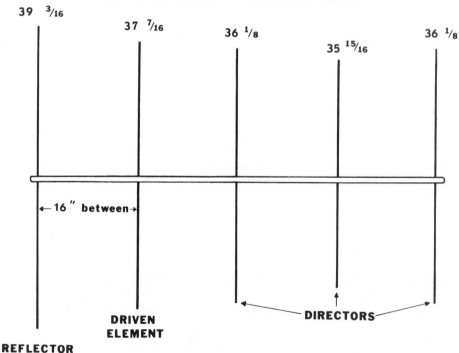

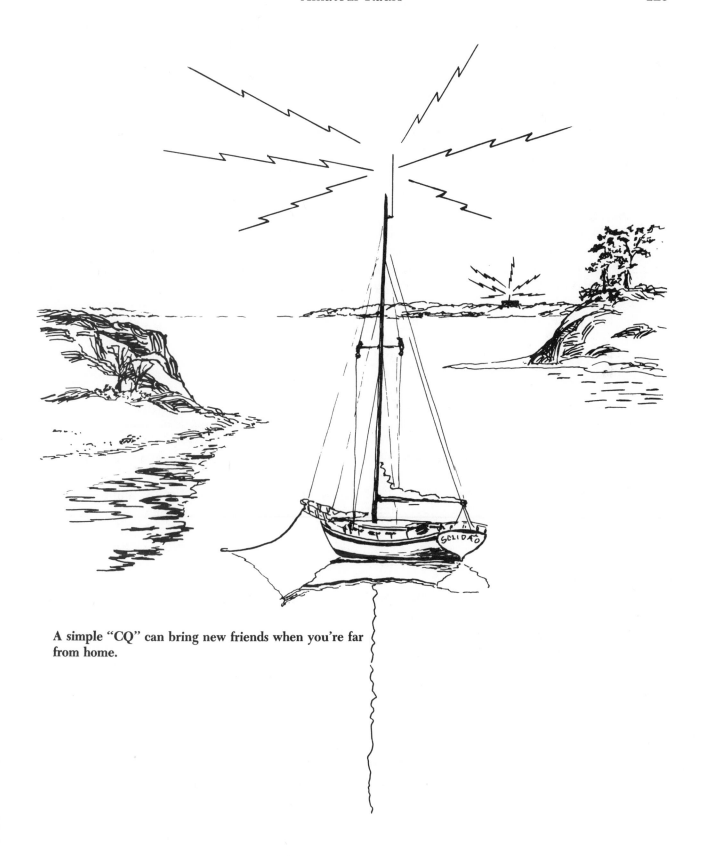

A simple "CQ" can bring new friends when you're far from home.

coordinated rescues attests to the novelty of ham radio rescues. The Coast Guard and other search and rescue units deal daily with disaster prevention without much public fanfare. When a ham in Des Moines puts a call through to Coast Guard after receiving a call of distress from a fishing vessel sinking in the South Atlantic, however, the event may be reported on the evening news. Meanwhile that same day, the Coast Guard may have rescued dozens of sinking sailors from disaster. That's their job.

My point is that there's danger in assuming too much from ham radio or from amateur radio hobbyists. Some are arguing, in the national magazines and elsewhere, that ham radio can provide your every radio need. Don't believe it. It simply isn't so.

In the first place, ham radio equipment isn't designed to survive the marine environment. Commercial VHF and marine single sideband equipment is—it has to be—the FCC requires it! Ham gear doesn't measure up, whether it's home brew or factory built. Ham gear is not required to pass the same reliability tests required of marine VHF and SSB equipment.

Equally important is the irrefutable fact that hams, though a friendly and intelligent lot, are not trained to handle traffic in emergencies, are not required to know a stem from a taffrail, and are under no obligation to monitor *any* specific frequency at *any* time.

THERE ARE NO CALL AND DISTRESS FREQUENCIES IN HAM RADIO!

If you find yourself in a jam, need help, and have nothing but a ham radio to call for help, you take your chances. Even if your rig works perfectly, that ham in Cleveland may have already closed his station and gone to bed.

Be advised. Amateur radio is a hobby, and amateur radio operators are hobbyists—not trained professionals.

Coast Guard radio operators, on the other hand, stand ready, 24 hours a day, with efficient radio systems and tested emergency procedures—competent to handle any emergency with dispatch and experience. When the chips are down, switch on your marine VHF-FM or HF-SSB radio *not* the amateur rig.

Then, if the professionals can't help you, you'll have one last chance to try that weak club station in Topeka, Kansas.

Radio is a fascinating hobby. On occasion it may be used to assist in a real emergency, providing life-saving communications. By all means, get a ham license and put a ham rig on your boat, but only after you install VHF and SSB radios. Don't put your family's safety in the hands of a radio service that is licensed solely for the use of *amateurs*.

Conclusion

This chapter just untied the dinghy. The complete story of ham radio is one for you to discover on your own.

It isn't difficult to get a license, and the reward is worth the effort. Tune in a few of the frequencies mentioned in this chapter, the Waterway Net at 7.268 MHz or the Maritime Mobile Net on 14.313 MHz. The advantages will at once become apparent.

In an extreme emergency, ham radio could save your life.

On a rainy day in the Chesapeake, it could bring you a bushel of steamed crabs and a friendly afternoon.

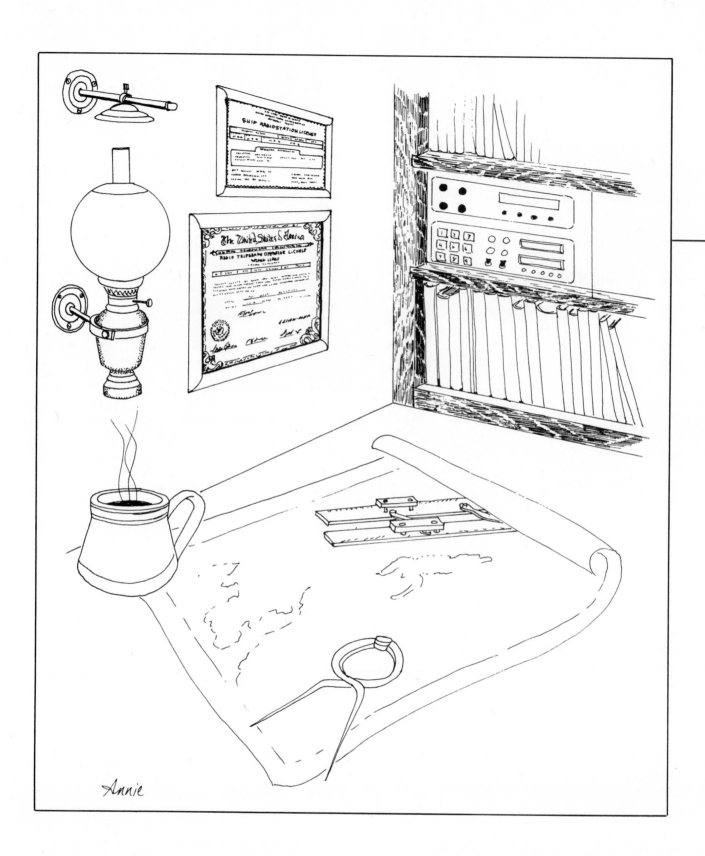

CHAPTER 8

Licensing and the FCC

General Principles

There are two vessel classifications requiring licenses from the FCC. In the first classification are cargo vessels carrying 300 gross tons or more, tugboats and vessels carrying passengers for hire anywhere within U.S. territorial waters. These craft are required by law to meet exacting license and technical standards for marine radio transmitters, radar and emergency position locating beacon equipment. They are compulsory stations. Since these craft require a licensed crew, presumed to be familiar with FCC rules, we will not further examine compulsory station licensing.

Small commercial and pleasure craft *not* carrying passengers for hire are called to a lesser standard. They are noncompulsory stations. They are not required by law to carry any type of radio or other electronic device. However, *if* they elect to do so, they must obtain at least two licenses, a ship radio station license and a restricted radiotelephone operator's permit (unless the operator holds a higher class commercial radiotelephone license). A radio amateur or citizen band license will not do.

Contact your local FCC office for further details.

Station License

Vessels intending to carry a marine radiotelephone must have a ship radio station license. Applicants must complete FCC Form 506, "Application for Ship Radio Station License". There is no fee payable with this application. This license, when granted, is only to be used from the vessel designated in the license application.

License term is five years. The license is renewed by filing subsequent Form 506 applications or by filing Form 405–B renewal. You may be assessed a fine or possibly sentenced to a prison term for operating a radio station without a station (and operator's) license or with an expired license(s). If you file for renewal but do not receive your new authorization, you may operate under

Be certain to obtain proper licenses for all radios on board *before* you transmit. It's the law!

your old license—but you should retain a copy of the renewal application form just in case. If you do not mail your renewal application before your old license expires, you are *not* authorized to operate the radio until the renewal license arrives.

No license is required for *any* radio equipment that is used to summon assistance during an emergency situation threatening immediate personal or property damage. (However, such use must not unnecessarily or maliciously interfere with other radio communications.)

If you sell your boat, you must surrender the station license to the FCC. The license does not automatically transfer to the new owner, and you may not transfer the license to a newly purchased boat for your own use. When a vessel changes hands, new licenses must be obtained by all parties.

You may operate your radio equipment after filing a Form 506 application but before receiving your license and callsign from the FCC if you complete and sign a temporary operating authority (Form 506–A). You must have *first* completed, signed and mailed a Form 506 application. The temporary authority is only good for 60 days and only if completed and signed and on board the boat.

If you move or change your mailing address, if you have your name legally changed, or if you change the name of your boat, you must notify the FCC by mail or submit Form 559–A to a local field office of the FCC. If your radio license is held in the name of a corporation, and if control or ownership of the corporation changes, you must apply for a new license.

It isn't necessary to notify the FCC if the new equipment you acquire can not be operated on any frequencies not authorized by your license. If you add equipment that is capable of transmitting on frequencies not listed on your station license, you must apply for modification using Form 506.

Operator's License

If your marine radio transmitting equipment is incapable of transmitting at carrier power ratings in excess of 100 watts (or 400 watts peak-envelope-power), you are required only to hold a restricted radiotelephone operator's permit. If your equipment can transmit at higher powers, you must obtain a commercial operator's license. Most equipment marketed for small craft requires only a restricted operator's permit.

The restricted permit is obtained from the FCC by filing a completed and signed Form 753. Applicants must be at least 14 years of age. The license is valid for your lifetime, but can not be transferred.

NOTE: No license is needed to use *any* radio in an emergency posing immediate threat to life or property.

United States of America
Federal Communications Commission

Approved by OMB
3060–0096
Expires 3/31/86

Application for Ship Radio Station License

1. NAME OF INDIVIDUAL *(LAST, FIRST, MIDDLE INITIAL)*	1A. NAME, IF OTHER THAN INDIVIDUAL

2. MAILING ADDRESS OF APPLICANT *(NUMBER AND STREET, CITY, STATE AND ZIP CODE)*

3. TYPE OF APPLICANT *(CHECK ONE)*

☐ (I) INDIVIDUAL   ☐ (C) CORPORATION   ☐ (P) PARTNERSHIP

☐ (D) INDIVIDUAL WITH BUSINESS NAME   ☐ (A) ASSOCIATION   ☐ (G) GOVERNMENT ENTITY

4. TYPE OF LICENSE *(CHECK ONE)*

☐ REGULAR   ☐ PORTABLE *(Attach Required Showings)*

☐ PLURALITY

If Plurality, indicate number of vessels _____

5. RELATIONSHIP OF APPLICANT TO VESSEL

☐ OWNER   ☐ OWNER/OPERATOR   ☐ OPERATOR

☐ OTHER *(Specify)* _____

6. NAME OF SHIP	7. CALL SIGN *(PREVIOUSLY ASSIGNED TO SHIP, IF ANY)*	8. INTERNATIONAL SELECTIVE CALLING NUMBER *(IF ANY)*

9. OFFICAL NUMBER OF SHIP (COAST-GUARD DOCUMENTATION NO. OR FEDERAL OR STATE REGISTRATION NO.). IF NONE, EXPLAIN ON SEPARATE SHEET OF PAPER.

10. CLASS OF SHIP *(SEE INSTRUCTIONS)*

10A. GENERAL	10B. SPECIFIC

11. GROSS TONNAGE/LENGTH OF SHIP *(SEE INSTRUCTIONS)*

☐ GROSS TONS _____

☐ FEET _____

12. SHIP RADIO REQUIREMENT CATEGORIES *(CHECK APPLICABLE BOX(ES) - SEE INSTRUCTIONS)*

☐ (A) RADIOTELEGRAPH STATION REQUIRED BY TITLE III, PART II OF THE COMMUNICATIONS ACT OR SAFETY OF LIFE AT SEA CONVENTION.

☐ (B) RADIOTELEPHONE STATION REQUIRED BY TITLE III, PART II OF THE COMMUNICATIONS ACT OR SAFETY OF LIFE AT SEA CONVENTION.

☐ (C) RADIOTELEPHONE STATION REQUIRED BY TITLE III, PART III OF THE COMMUNICATIONS ACT.

☐ (D) RADIOTELEPHONE STATION REQUIRED BY THE GREAT LAKES AGREEMENT.

☐ (E) RADIOTELEPHONE STATION REQUIRED BY THE VESSEL BRIDGE-TO-BRIDGE RADIOTELEPHONE ACT.

☐ (F) NONE OF THE FOREGOING *(Voluntarily equipped)*.

13. CATEGORIES OF TRANSMITTERS *(CHECK ALL TRANSMITTERS TO BE USED)*

V	VHF/FM RADIOTELEPHONE (156-158 MHz)	Q	RADAR (2900-3100 MHz)
T	SSB RADIOTELEPHONE (1600-4000 kHz)	R	RADAR (9300-9500 MHz)
U	SSB RADIOTELEPHONE (4000-23,000 kHz)	W	RADAR (14.0-14.05 GHz)
X	RADIOTELEGRAPH (405-535 kHz)	E	EPIRB (121.5 and 243 MHz) Number:
M	RADIOTELEGRAPH (2000-26,000 kHz) EXCEPT DIRECT PRINTING	S	SATELLITE (1636.5-1644 MHz)
N	RADIOTELEGRAPH (2000-26,000 kHz) DIRECT PRINTING	D	ON-BOARD (457.525-467.825 MHz)
L	SURVIVAL CRAFT (8364-kHz); NUMBER:	O	OTHER (SPECIFY)

14. **RESERVED**	15. If 121.5 and 243 MHz are requested for EPIRB'S, is the ship expected to operate in International waters beyond range of marine VHF distress coverage; or is the EPIRB required by the U.S. Coast Guard?	YES	NO

16A. Will applicant own the radio equipment? If no, give name of owner in item 16B.	YES	NO	16B. Name of owner of equipment		
17. If not the owner of the radio equipment, is applicant party to a lease or other agreement under which he maintains full control of it?	YES	NO	18. Will each transmitter be a type accepted or approved by the Commission in accordance with Part 83 of the Rules? If no, explain on reverse.	YES	NO
19. Will the ship normally communicate with foreign coast stations or make international voyages?	YES	NO	20. Will this ship be used at any time to transport passengers for hire? If yes, give maximum number to be carried per voyage. NUMBER _____	YES	NO

READ CAREFULLY BEFORE SIGNING

Certification: 1) The applicant waives any claim to the use of any particular frequency or of the ether because of previous use of same, whether by license or otherwise. 2) The applicant accepts full responsibility for the operation and control of the requested station license in accordance with applicable laws and rules of the FCC. 3) The applicant will have unlimited access to the radio equipment and will take effective measures to prevent its use by unauthorized persons. 4) Neither applicant nor any member thereof is a foreign government or representative thereof.

Willful false statements made on this form are punishable by fine and/or imprisonment. U.S. Code, Title 18, Section 1001.

SIGNATURE	DESIGNATE APPROPRIATE CLASSIFICATION	DATE
	☐ Individual Applicant ☐ Member of Partnership ☐ Authorized Representative of Corporation	
	☐ Officer who is also a Member of the Application Association ☐ Official of Government Entity	

VHF License

Marine VHF radio equipment must be approved by the FCC and designated as such by a label on the equipment chassis. If this label does not appear, do not operate the radio. It is strictly illegal to operate converted amateur radio equipment on the VHF channels.

You may install your own VHF radio without special licensing authority from the FCC or other governmental agency, however all repairs or adjustments must be made by a person holding an FCC commercial operator's license.

There is no longer a requirement to keep a VHF radio log, although every conscientious operator should do so. If you take part in distress communications, you are expected to log any and all contacts in which you participate.

When completing Form 506 for a station license, check #13-V on the form, "VHF-FM RADIOTELEPHONE (156–158 MHz)".

SSB License

Marine SSB radio equipment also must be approved by the FCC and must bear a label stating so on the equipment chassis. As with VHF, if this label does not appear, do not operate the radio.

Remember, you must have VHF on board *before* you can be licensed for single-sideband operation.

When completing Form 506 for a station license, check #13-T on the form, "SSB RADIOTELEPHONE (1600–4000 KHz)", or #13-U, "SSB RADIOTELEPHONE (4000–23,000 KHz)", or both, depending upon the frequency channels on which your equipment is capable of operating.

Radar License

If you will be installing a radar unit on board, or if radar is already installed, the frequency band must be indicated on Form 506 when applying for new station license or modification. Check #13-Q, "RADAR (2900–3100 MHz)", #13-R,

"RADAR (9300–9500 MHz)", or #13-W, "RADAR (14.0–14.05 GHz)" accordingly.

This is the only requirement for radar licensing.

Only FCC licensed commercial operators with a special radar endorsement may repair, modify or adjust a radar installation.

EPIRB License

If your boat is to be equipped with emergency position indicating beacons, check #13-E, "EPIRB (121.5 and 243 MHz)", on Form 506 and indicate how many of each type will be installed. This is all that is required.

Amateur Radio Licenses

Nearly half a million hams now operate in the United States, and about that same number operate from the rest of the countries in the world. Wherever you go there are hams. And they all hold a valid license issued by a government authority in compliance with international treaty. In the United States our authority is the FCC. Canadian authority is the Department of Communications (DOC). Some nations do not grant radio licenses to their citizens, and many do not permit American hams to operate within their borders without special permission in writing.

It was once downright difficult to get a ham license. A test of radio theory, radio law and the ability to receive Morse Code was essential. It still is. But the exams are far easier today.

The new code test is especially easy. In the old days, the code was sent by a machine for five minutes. The applicant was given a pencil and paper and asked to "copy" what was sent. The machine did not send simple text comprised of common words and phrases, either. It sent random characters, letters, and numbers, and punctuation. After five minutes elapsed, the examiner took your paper. If he couldn't find one *perfect* minute of copy among the five minutes sent, you failed the exam.

TABLE 8-1

REQUIREMENTS FOR LICENSE CLASSES

CLASS	CODE TEST	WRITTEN EXAMINATION
Novice	5 wpm	Elementary theory and radio regulations.
Technician	5 wpm	General theory and radio regulations.
General	13 wpm	Same as Technician.
Advanced	13 wpm	Intermediate theory.
Extra	20 wpm	Advanced communications techniques.

The new code test consists of a short and simple message in plain language, also sent by machine, but with a meaning you can figure out from a random word here and there. You don't even have to write it down if you don't want to! If you catch enough words to make sense of the message, you have a good chance of passing. After the message is sent, the examiner gives you a single sheet with ten multiple-choice questions about the message. If you make the right guess on seven out of the ten, you pass the code test.

The FCC has discontinued the requirement that applicants be able to send code on the old-fashioned straight key. Many now use electronic keyers or even computers to send (and receive) code, and the ability to "swing a level fist", as radiopersons used to say, is no longer thought to be important.

Receiving the code remains the single most formidable obstacle to obtaining a license. There is an energetic group lobbying the FCC for a no-code license, but Washington continues to oppose the idea—and for good reasons.

Novices can't understand why the code is so important. Non-radio people are surprised to discover that the code continues to be used by ships and aircraft on transoceanic passages, by our military, and by expeditionaries on safari. Ships transporting passengers at sea are required to carry Morse transmitting equipment and a licensed radiotelegraph operator. Automated transmissions such as radioteletype and facsimile must be identified in Morse code. Oceanic weather forecasts and navigational bulletins are broadcast in the code.

What's so good about Morse code? Two things. First, the equipment required to transmit a keyed continuous wave (CW) signal is remarkably simple to build and repair. By keying a signal, messages can be sent in International Morse code without the use of microphones or modulation circuits. An emergency CW transmitter can be built in an empty tea tin and powered with flashlight batteries. Connected to a good antenna, two or three watts can be used to communicate over thousands of miles of open sea—using Morse code.

A second advantage of using code is the wonderful way a good operator can copy a weak CW signal amid the din of ambient radio noises. An FM signal must be very loud indeed to overcome the ever-present static crashes and interfering stations. Single-sideband signals work a bit better than FM. But CW signals get through when nothing else will. That's why our government requires us to learn how to use the code—in case we or someone else may need it someday to avert an accident or summon help.

Don't be afraid of learning the code. It's only a matter of practice. Everyone who really tries can master it. Cassette tapes are available to let you listen to the code as you drive to work, with speeds from 3 to 30 words per minute. Even if you can't take time to "copy" the code from the tape, just listening to the rhythmic "dits" and "dahs" can vastly improve your learning. Soon you'll begin to recognize individual characters, and before long you'll be recognizing words and punctuation like a pro.

Be careful not to fall into the trap of memorizing the code as groups of dots and dashes. Morse code is a language, just like English or French. It's not so much a written language as it is a system of sounds. The symbols are only used as learning

Morse code equipment is still required on modern passenger liners. Note key below radio console.

tools. We never send the written message of "Hello" by writing (•••• • •—•• •—•• ———), although those are the Morse code symbols for "HELLO". Morse code isn't used to send written messages. It is used to send message in sound, messages that are copied by *hearing*. Instead of memorizing the dot and dash symbols, learn the *sounds* of the letters and symbols. Study the table that appears in the appendix. Listen to broadcast code and your tapes.

Some tapes are better than others. Tonal quality is important, of course, but a number of tape producers are now using a new method to teach beginners the sounds of the characters. Each character is sent at the goal speed, say 15 wpm, but in the first lessons spacing *between* letters is

expanded to give an effectively slower speed, say 5 wpm. In other words, rather than slowing down the sound of the letters and numbers, these tapes simply increase the time between characters, giving you more time to recognize the character before the next one is sent. Older tapes slowed down the sound of the character, keeping the space between characters proportionate. Proponents of the newer method claim that learners pick up speed faster, since the sound of the letters and numbers is sent at the goal speed initially. Of course, what works for some may not be good for others. Ask a local ham to help you pick a practice tape.

There's probably a licensed ham living within a few blocks of your home, happy to assist you anyway possible. Every ham once had someone else to help him get that first "ticket", so don't be shy. Ask for help.

Hams are easy to find. They live in houses with tall towers and strange antennas in the backyard. If there are no tall towers or ungainly antennas in your neighborhood, look in your newspaper for announcements of local amateur radio club meetings. Every town has at least one club, and many large cities have dozens of organizations. Many clubs hold special classes for beginners, teaching both the code and radio theory, preparing the neophyte to pass his novice or higher class license. If you can't find a meeting announcement in your newspaper, ask the sheriff or police chief if he knows some hams; radio amateurs often assist local law enforcement agencies in civil defense work. Someone in your local government should have a list of local hams who are prepared to provide communications during times of emergency.

FCC Bulletin PR 1035, "Study Guide for FCC Amateur Radio Operator License Examinations", can be obtained free by writing the nearest FCC field office. This publication provides a sample of the types of questions that may be asked on the exam.

Citizens Band Licensing

There are no licensing requirements for citizens band (CB) radio stations, and there is no minimum age requirement.

Callsigns issued previous to the July 3, 1983 cutoff date may continue to be used, or you may identify yourself by vessel name.

Channel authorization continues to be limited to 40 channels with the same rules pertaining to transmitter output power limits at 4 watts carrier power (12 watts peak envelope power for SSB).

Channel 9 is still reserved for emergency use.

You may not operate a CB transmitter outside the United States without express authorization from the local country. All rules not pertaining to licenses and licensing of the CB radio service remain in full effect. Fines of $2000 continue to be assessed. Out-of-band or over-power operation is automatically treated as a direct violation of the Communications Act.

Warnings

The following caveats are excerpted directly from FCC publications. Read them carefully! It is your responsibility to know the laws, treaties, rules, and regulations that currently govern any station you operate. Do not operate any radio transmitter without a valid radio station license.

As a licensed operator it is illegal for you to: (1) willfully interfere with any radio communication or signal, or (2) transmit false or deceptive signals, or (3) falsely identify a radio station, or (4) transmit unidentified radio signals, or (5) report or republish any radio communications relating to ships, aircraft, vehicles, or persons in distress without express authorization to do so.

Ignorance of the law is not an excuse. A subscription to the FCC Rules and Regulations for marine radio can be obtained from:

Superintendant of Documents
Government Printing Office
Washington, DC 20402

Ask for Vol. IV, Parts 81 and 83. Include check or money order in the amount of $24, along with your name and mailing address.

Depth Instruments

CHAPTER **9**

Depth Sounders

Certainly the most useful and least expensive item of marine electronics is the depth sounder. Prices start at LESS THAN $90 for a sounder that can read the water's depth to 100 feet! If you've ever worked your way through an uncharted channel swinging a hand lead and counting marks on the leadline, you'll appreciate the convenience of a sounder that measures the water's depth continuously, accurately and effortlessly.

Some sounders can detect fish beneath your keel. Others have a beeper that alerts you when the water gets too shallow or too deep. Some sounders read only in feet, others read only in fathoms. A few read in feet, fathoms or meters. Increasingly, depth sounders are using microcomputers, providing enhanced options to make navigation safer and more reliable.

By far the most exciting and the most practical application of microcomputers to depth finding instruments is the development of sounders that *speak*. The boys that used to work the riverboats along the Mississippi called out the fathoms, "By the mark twain, sir!" And the pilot concentrated on tasks at hand: avoiding snags at the river's bend or answering steam whisle blasts of passing paddlewheelers. Nothing was more natural than to keep one's mind on the business of piloting,

with eyes ahead for obstructions and ears keen to the leadsman's cry.

Now, through the miracle of microelectronics, depth sounders can automatically report the changing depths—in feet, fathoms or meters—by *speaking* the numbers. The better models offer the option of turning the voice off altogether or varying the length of time between each report. All models offer a volume control. Loudspeakers can be mounted anywhere.

The voice may be a bit strange at first with its inhuman twang and soft consonants that seem to lisp certain letters. But the devices can be quite

Sounding as it used to be.

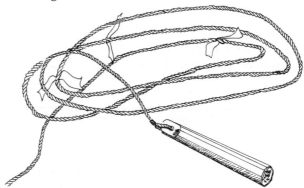

helpful—especially when piloting through tricky waters at night where glances at a digital readout can break your concentration on the range of lights ahead or the phantom shadows of unlighted floats and buoys bobbing on the darkened waters off your bow.

Another trick of computerdom, put to good use in the latest depth sounders, is the ability to measure rates of change. As the water's depth varies, a microcomputer senses the change, compares the rate of change and present depth with the pre-set alarm depth selected by the operator. If the rate of change and present depth are such that the microcomputer anticipates the alarm depth will be encountered within a certain interval of time, a beeper alerts the helmsman. If the water continues to shoal to the alarm depth, a different beep is heard.

In other words, the sounder not only warns you when the pre-set depth is reached—it can warn you in advance!

The underlying concept of depth sounders (explained in the pages that follow) is old hat, but today's talking sounders and advance warning sounders are unique and practical.

Since the primary objective of navigation is to get from one place to another without bumping into something—especially the bottom—a depth sounder should be considered the navigator's primary instrument. One could argue that a depth sounder should be the first electronic device installed on a new boat.

Compared to other navigational equipment, the depth sounder is second in importance only to the compass and chart. With those three, you can find your way safely through chowder-thick fog or in total darkness, reading the bottom as you go.

What kind of sounder should you install? What options are important? What factors are critical to the installation? What can a sounder do other than find the depth of water?

Theory of Operation

The principle of electronic sounding is well known. A pulse of ultra-sonic energy is transmitted toward the sea bottom by a device called a

Pulses of ultrasonic energy are transmitted toward the bottom by a transducer, which then receives the echoed pulses.

transducer. Transducers are like hi-fi loudspeakers in this transmit mode but, unlike hi-fi speakers, transducers emit high frequency sound pitched above human hearing range. Typical transducer frequencies are on the order of 50–200 kHz, while the average human can not hear sounds pitched higher than about 20 kHz.

At the instant of pulse transmission, the depth sounder starts a timer. The type of timer varies. In the rotating flasher type depth sounder, the timer is mechanical. In the digital display type depth sounder, the timer is electronic.

After a few fractions of a second, depending on the water's depth, an echo reflected from the bottom (or from a fish swimming below the boat) is detected by the transducer. In this detection or receive mode, the transducer is acting as a microphone.

The echo pulse is amplified and stops the timer.

The length of time for the pulse to travel downward, reflect from the bottom (or fish) and return to the transducer is called the pulse travel time. Since the speed of sound in water is constant (more or less), the longer the pulse travel time, the farther away is the reflecting surface—

whether that surface is a muddy river bottom or the scaly back of a giant grouper.

The equation that follows can be used to calculate the speed of sound in water. This equation takes into account such factors as water temperature, salinity and depth.

$$C = 4422 + 11.25T - 0.0450T^2 + 0.0182d + 4.3(S-34)$$

where C is speed of sound in feet per second, T is temperature of the water in degrees Fahrenheit, d is depth in feet, and S is salinity in parts per thousand.

Sound travels faster in warm water than in cold water (351 feet per second faster in 90° F. tropical waters than in 30° F. arctic basins). Since the water at great depth is tightly compressed and thus denser than water near the surface, sound travels faster though deep water than through shallow water (about 20 feet per second faster at 1000 feet than at 10 feet). Sound travels faster in the salt than in fresh water (142 feet per second faster in the oceans than in fresh water lakes).

As you can see, of the three factors mentioned, temperature has the greatest effect. The figures that follow show how the speed of sound varies with temperature. The figures are based on measurements at 100 feet in seawater with a salinity of 33 parts per thousand.

deg. F.	ft./sec.
30	4717
40	4798
50	4870
60	4934
70	4987
80	5032
90	5068

The average speed of sound in seawater is about 4945 feet per second (4790 feet per second in freshwater) or about 4.5 times the speed of sound in air (1117 feet per second).

Let's apply these principles to see how depth sounders work. Suppose a sounder transmits a pulse bottomward and detects the reflected echo exactly 0.104 seconds later. Total pulse travel time is 0.104 seconds, and total pulse travel distance is

(0.104 seconds) × (4945 feet/second) = 514 feet

but, since the pulse makes a round trip down to the sea floor and back, the depth below the transducer is 257 feet or half the total pulse travel distance. In other words, the time interval between the moment of pulse transmission and the moment of pulse detection is 104 milliseconds (1 millisecond = 1/1000 second) when the depth is 257 feet. These figures, of course, are based on the average speed of sound and will vary with temperature, depth and salinity.

Rotating Flasher Type Sounders

The rotating flasher type depth sounder uses a simple method to measure pulse travel time. A neon tube and small magnet are mounted on a wheel (or counterbalanced arm) that rotates behind a dial graduated in feet (or fathoms, or meters). The wheel is kept spinning at constant speed by an electric motor. As the neon tube and magnet spin past a tiny reed relay mounted behind the wheel, the field of the magnet causes the relay contacts to close briefly and activate two circuits simultaneously. Voltage applied to the neon tube causes it to flash behind the "0" mark on the dial, and voltage applied to the transducer causes a pulse of ultrasonic energy to be transmitted toward the bottom.

Meanwhile, the wheel keeps turning.

When the reflected echo is detected by the

Rotating flasher depth sounder.

transducer, voltage applied to the neon tube causes it to flash again, but this time not on the "0" mark, but at a mark further around the dial. This second mark corresponds to the length of time it took the pulse to travel to the bottom and return again to the transducer—in other words, the depth.

The simplest rotating flasher type depth sounders increase their depth range by changing the speed of the motor that rotates the wheel. By spinning the wheel more slowly, deeper depths can be detected, i.e., longer pulse travel times can be displayed before the rotating light returns to the zero mark again. Pulse energy is also increased (necessary for greater depths) since the magnet holds the reed relay contacts closed for a longer period of time, thus increasing the duration of the pulse and its total energy. A more complex circuit could perform the same task, but a rotating wheel gets the job done quite nicely.

Some manufacturers use high-energy light-emitting diodes (LEDs) instead of neon tubes. Some units offer multi-colored LED flashers to distinguish different strengths of echoes—a red flash indicates the bottom, yellow is a large fish or school of fish, green is tiny fish or plankton.

Both LEDs and neon tubes are reliable devices. Incandescent lamps, however, can't stand up to the vibration and repetitive on-off cycles the flasher must endure.

At least one manufacturer has produced a ro-

Tri-color sounder.

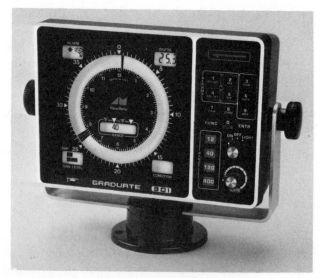

Liquid crystal display sounder. (*Aqua Meter*)

tating type sounder that uses a liquid crystal display (LCD). Current drain is minimal, but avoid mounting this one where the display can be damaged by direct sunlight.

Some older flasher type depth sounders used a microswitch to trigger the transmitter circuit as the spinning neon tube whizzed past the zero mark. Microswitches are designed so that a slight touch will close the contacts. A cam on the spinning wheel provides that touch and closes the microswitch contacts the way a magnet closes the tiny contacts of a reed relay. However, the magnet/relay method is far more reliable since there is no physical contact between magnet and relay. The relay can even be encapsulated within a small glass tube, and the magnetic field of the spinning magnet will still close the contacts just by passing near the relay, without making physical contact. Physical contact always results in some amount of wear, and wear inevitably causes failures.

No matter what discreet components are used, all flasher type sounders work on the same rotating-wheel principle.

Digital Type Sounders

Digital type sounders use the same timed interval principle that flasher units employ, except there

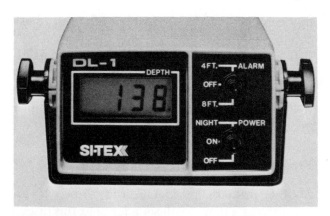

Digital sounder.

are no moving parts. A timed solid-state trigger circuit sends the sonic pulse to the transducer and simultaneously starts a digital timer/counter. When the returning echo pulse is detected, the digital counter is stopped, and its contents are displayed—as the depth.

If the reading is to be in feet, the timer/counter is set to increase by one digit each 0.404 milliseconds (404 microseconds, since 1 microsecond =1/1,000,000 second). This is the time required for an ultrasonic pulse to travel down one foot, bounce off the bottom, and travel back up one foot to the transducer.

To measure depth in other units, the speed of the digital timer/counter can be increased or decreased accordingly. If the timer/counter is slowed to one-sixth the speed used to display in feet, the least significant digit of the counter will change only every 2.424 milliseconds, or the pulse travel time equivalent to a depth of one fathom (one fathom equals six feet), and the readout will be in fathoms rather than feet. To change the readout to meters, the counter/timer is slowed to 30.5% of its rate when displaying in feet (since one meter = 3.3 feet), and the least significant digit will increase by one for each 1.333 millisecond period, corresponding to a depth of one meter.

Differences

Although all depth sounders are fundamentally the same in their essential functions, they vary widely in some particular respects. These differences are critical to the user. They should be carefully studied. The options and special features available are discussed in the next section. Here we concern ourselves with some issues common to all sounders and the decisions you should make before selecting which type of sounder to install.

Power

The first factor common to all sounders is their power drain or energy consumption. Since the depth sounder may be left on for extended periods, the battery drain may be considerable. If you are operating a sailboat without auxiliary power, excessive battery drain may be unacceptable.

Typical flasher type sounders may draw as much as 300 milliamperes (0.3 amperes) or as little as 150 milliamperes (0.15 amperes) from the battery. While this is a small drain, it can be significant over long periods of continuous use.

Digital type sounders can draw almost as much as flashers. A sounder that uses LEDs (light-emitting diodes) to display depth in glowing red digits may draw 300 milliamperes or more. An LCD display (liquid crystal) may draw as little as 50 milliamperes, but LCDs are difficult to read in the dark and may require backlighting that draws another 100 milliamperes or so to make the unit useable after sunset.

Of more importance to most of us is pulse power, one of the factors that determines how deep a sounder can detect bottom. At this time, however, manufacturers don't agree on a single method of reporting pulse power in their specifications sheets. One manufacturer may report simply, "Power Output: 450 watts"; another says, "Transmitted Power: 200 watts RMS"; a competitor adds, "Output Power: 600 watts RMS (E^2/Z)"; while another says, "Pulse Power: 1600 watts peak-to-peak". Unless we know more about how these power ratings are determined, we don't know how they differ in performance.

If two manufacturers report pulse power as "peak power" and also include pulse length, i.e., the time duration of each pulse, in the specifications, a rough estimate can be made to compare the two. Multiply peak power times pulse length. This value is a more uniform measure of pulse power. For example, if one unit has 1600 watts peak output power and a pulse length of 1 millisecond (1/1000 second), the power factor is 1.6. If another unit is advertised at 2400 watts peak output power, but has a pulse length of only 0.5 milliseconds, the factor is 1.2. In other words, the effective power depends not only upon the peak power rating, but also upon the length of time the transmitter is turned on for each pulse.

If peak power is not advertised, you can get a rough approximation of peak power by multiplying output power by 8. In other words, if a unit is advertised at 200 watts pulse power, and nothing is said about "peak power", the value given may be a so-called average pulse power figure. Oftentimes this value is equivalent to ⅛ of the peak power, so multiply the average power by 8 to get peak power, then multiply by pulse length to get the comparative effectiveness factor.

Keep in mind, however, that all of the foregoing speaks only of pulse power—and pulse power is only *one* factor that affects depth sounder performance. Transducer beam angle is important; narrower beam angles concentrate the available power more directly downward and also focus sensitivity more directly downward. Transducer mounting is critical to performance. Inexpensive transducers won't perform as well as more expensive transducers, generally speaking. And finally, when all else is equal, the receiver sections of various depth sounder units may not be equally sensitive to returning echoes. If a unit has an extremely high-power transmitter but employs only a mediocre receiver circuit, the unit's effectiveness may not compare favorably with another unit that transmits a moderate amount of power but employs a highly sensitive receiver section. We'll discuss these and other factors in following sections.

Your decision to buy one unit rather than another may rest heavily on a comparison of the convenience features one unit offers. A unit that reads depth to 3000 fathoms but has a shoal alarm pre-set to 10 feet may not be as useful as a unit

that can only read to 200 feet but offers an adjustable depth alarm.

If you require the ability to sound to a particular depth, put your requirements in the purchase contract. If the dealer is unwilling to guarantee that the sounder will perform to your requirements, talk to another dealer.

Frequency

Another primary consideration for those who are considering a new depth sounder (and this discussion applies equally to depth recorders and other sounding equipment) is pulse frequency. Pulse frequency affects sounder performance.

There are two primary pulse frequencies used by almost all manufacturers: 50 kHz and 200 kHz. Individual sounders may differ from these two figures by some small amount, but most are very near one or the other of these two values. Study the spec sheets carefully. The two are not the same!

A 200 kHz sounder will not perform like a 50 kHz sounder.

Two characteristics vary with the frequency. One is called beam or cone angle. The other is pulse range or effective penetrating power.

The 200 kHz system provides better echo discrimination and works well in shallow water. A 50 kHz system is required to penetrate greater depths but does not discriminate between small targets. The reason why lies in the length of the sound waves. Like radio waves, sound waves vary in length according to the inverse of their frequency. High frequency sound waves are shorter than low frequency sound waves.

At 50 kHz sound traveling through sea water at 4945 feet per second has a wavelength of about 1.2 inches. Each wave in the sonic pulse is 1.2 inches long. At 200 kHz, a single wave of sound energy is only 0.3 inches long.

Small waves "see" two things near each other as actually two things near each other. Longer waves may "see" the two things as one object since longer waves can't discriminate between echoes returning from targets close to each other. Short waves can see fish near the bottom without confusing the fish with the bottom itself. Short waves can also detect small fish that longer waves will miss.

But, there's a drawback to short waves that limits the range at which they can be used for sounding. Short waves interact with and are dispersed by particles in the water—air bubbles, plankton and tiny fish. Less energy is available for the reflected echo.

For deep water, select a low frequency sounder. But remember that long waves can not discriminate reflections as well as short waves. More expensive units provide for switching between high and low frequencies as needed.

Beam Angle

Beam angle is a measure of the effective area directly beneath the boat where the reflected pulses can be detected. Again, manufacturers don't agree as to how beam angle should be measured and reported in specifications sheets. The idea is to measure the effective cone of sonic energy within which reflected pulses contain a specified minimum energy. The effective region is lobe-shaped and not a straight-sided cone.

Some manufacturers measure beam angle between the transducer and the 3 db limits of the lobe. Others measure between the 6 db limits. One may report a beam angle of 12°, while another reports a beam angle of 8°, and both manufacturers may be talking about the same device—just using different measurement standards.

In general, high frequency systems produce narrow beams. Low frequency systems produce wide beams.

A depth sounder with narrow beam angle is not desirable for sailboats because it can display inaccurate depths when the boat is heeled.

Within limits, different beam angles may be obtained at high or low frequencies by the selection of specific transducers. For example, a 200 kHz transducer may be selected with a 5°, 10°, or 18° beam angle. Transducers at 50 kHz may have a 15°, 30°, or 50° beam width. In other words, at any frequency there are transducers made to provide varying beam angles—but, in general, lower frequency transducers produce wider beam angles.

A broad beam angle is desirable for finding fish. If the boat is moving at 10 knots (333 yards per minute) and a fish is swimming in the opposite direction at 5 knots (167 yards per minute), their combined relative velocity is 500 yards per minute or more than 8 yards per second! If the beam angle is too narrow, the fish can swim entirely through the beam and be missed between pulses.

A wider beam is desirable for sailboats, since wind-driven craft spend a considerable amount of time "on their ear", heeled over by the press of canvas overhead. A narrow beam angle may result in excessively deep readings, since the sonic beam is not pointing directly downward but out at an angle. Sailors beware! When close-hauled with the lee rail awash, your depth sounder may give false readings, indicating depths greater than what is actually under the boat.

For navigating in shallow water, a 200 kHz sounder and narrow beam width are adequate for most purposes. For deeper work (or for finding fish), specify a lower frequency and wider beam angle.

Sounders that permit switching between low and high frequencies may require two transducers. Transducers are matched to the sounder's output frequency. You can not use a 50 kHz transducer with a 200 kHz sounder nor a 200 kHz transducer with a 50 kHz sounder. Not only will they not work efficiently, but the sounder and/or transducer may be damaged.

If you are installing a new sounder and want to use your old transducer, ask the dealer if the new unit will work with your old transducer. If the two frequencies are not greatly different, a technician may be able to tune the new sounder to match the frequency of the old transducer. If there is any doubt, contact a factory representative for details.

For a more technical discussion of beam angles, see Effect of Beam Angle, in the next chapter, "Depth Recorders".

Transducers

Transducers also vary by shape and method of mounting. Some are round, some are bullet-shaped. Some mount on a bracket at the transom, some fit through a hole in the hull.

Shape and method of mounting can greatly affect performance. For example, a transducer's shape or its location on the hull may create bubbles or turbulence in the sonic beam. This disturbance can reduce the transducer's efficiency.

Transom-mount transducers are desirable only in small craft, such as outboard motorboats. Larger craft should always install the transducer through the hull.

Drag may be a factor in racing sailboats. A transducer that can be mounted flush with the outer skin may be desirable, but an installation of this type requires special preparation. A round transducer can sometimes be flush-mounted by building up an area inside the hull, but the method is difficult. The hull must not be weakened, and the fitting must be absolutely secure.

If limited sensitivity is acceptable, the transducer can be mounted inside the hull in the bilge area. It should be understood, however, that inside mountings reduce sensitivity and range—typically –3 db loss (50% of range) or more—and the sonic beam will be diffused. Inside mountings have worked on fibreglass, steel, and aluminum boats. Somewhat less success can be expected with wooden hulls. The hull area just outside the internal mounting should be flat and downward-facing. No struts, chines or skegs should be the beam area.

The first method of inside mounting uses a water box. The box has a removable cover, held in place with screws and sealed with a watertight gasket. The transducer is mounted through this removable cover, and the box is filled with water. The water inside the box provides a medium through which sound waves travel from the transducer to the hull and are radiated into the water below the hull.

Flush-type transducer.

Another method is to glue the transducer to the hull itself, using a two-part epoxy cement. Here the key is to ensure that all bubbles are removed from the area between the transducer's face and the inside hull surface. The bilge area where the transducer is mounted should be perfectly clean. Hold the transducer tightly in place at several positions before gluing to determine where the best returns are observed. Once the final location has been found, thoroughly dry both bilge and transducer. Apply two-part epoxy glue to both the face of the transducer and the inside surface of the hull. Then press the transducer to the hull with a rolling motion to exclude bubbles from the glue.

Note that inside mounting should only be used when external or through-hull mounting is impracticable. Reduced sensitivity is unavoidable with inside mounting methods. Also note that inside mountings will not work with a cored or sandwich material hull. If inside mounting is imperative in a cored fiberglass hull, first remove the inside skin and core material at the mounting location and build up the surrounding inner skin. Consult a marine architect or structural engineer to determine if the operation will weaken the hull integrity.

In power-driven craft and cruising sailboats, a standard through-hull fitting is preferred. Use a fairing block outside the hull to angle the transducer face parallel with the sea bottom (and sur-

face). The transducer should be located where it won't be subjected to damage from grounding and where it won't be in the flow of bubbles or turbulence when the boat is underway. Air bub-

Through-hull transducer mounting with fairing block.

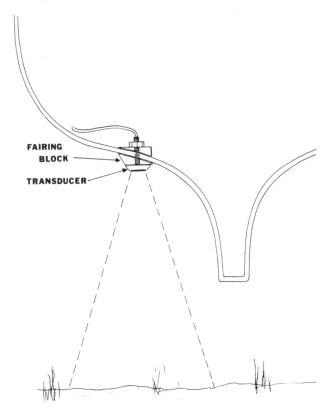

FAIRING
BLOCK

TRANSDUCER

bles are anathema to sounders. Poor results may be obtained if the transducer is mounted too far forward, where significant turbulence is created by the boat's advance through the water. Similarly poor results may be obtained if the transducer is mounted too far aft. Best results are obtained by mounting the transducer nearly amidships, or just abaft amidships.

Care must be taken in a sailboat to be certain the sounder will remain underwater at all expected angles of heel.

Displays, Range Settings and Alarms

The two basic types of displays have already been mentioned.

In some units, a rotating flasher and digital display are combined. The rotating flasher permits some limited fish finding capability (flashes above the bottom *may* be fish), while digital displays are easier to interpret.

Power consumption with LED displays may be greater than with LCD displays, but LCD displays require backlighting at night.

The availability of different ranges may be important to users who expect to navigate where water depths vary from a few feet to hundred of fathoms. Others may require only a fixed-range machine that can read depths from 0–30 feet, adequate for inland waterways, bays, lakes and rivers. For offshore work, deeper ranges are required.

Note that with rotating flashers, the total range may affect the user's ability to discriminate small changes in depth. If the 0–100 foot range is used, the difference between 8 feet and 6 feet, for example, is not discernible. If the 0–30 foot range is used instead, however, the difference between 8 feet and 6 feet is clearly displayed. This can be extremely desirable when navigating through shoals.

With the digital display, range settings may also affect the user's ability to discriminate small changes in depth, but in a different way. Even if a sounder has been carefully calibrated to the depth beneath the keel, the display may only be accurate to a change of one unit of the least sig-

This portable depth sounder requires no complex installation.

nificant digit. In other words, when the display reads 8.5 feet, the actual depth may be 8.6 or 8.4 feet, and the possible error is +/−0.1 foot. At other range settings, however, the readout may drop the decimal portion and provide accuracy to only +/− one foot or +/− one fathom, etc. Being able to select a lower range with accuracy to decimal parts of a foot makes it far easier to pilot through shoals where depth changes gradually and small depth differences are important.

Also desirable for working through shoals are depth alarms. Each different type works from a pre-set depth value. This may be fixed at the factory or adjusted by the user. Adjustable units permit the operator to set the alarm limit to any value from 1–40 feet or deeper. An advantage to being able to set the alarm to a deeper limit, such as 100 feet, can be seen in the vessel approaching the beach from offshore in a fog. With the alarm set to a deep value, the skipper is alerted well before he approaches dangerous waters. A factory-set 10 foot alarm would, of course, be useless.

Another alarm available with some units is the "deep" alarm, one that blinks or beeps when depth *exceeds* a preset limit. This may help find the edge of an offshore reef or alert the crew should the anchor drag and the boat be set into deeper water. Units with a deep alarm often advertise the feature as an "anchor alarm". The alarm beeps not only if the anchor drags into shallower water but also if it drags into deeper water.

By the way, a beeping alarm is far better than an alarm that silently blinks or flashes its display on and off.

Before leaving the topic of depth alarms, please note that a depth alarm should never be trusted as the only warning when approaching a shore in limited visibility. Actual readings of the instrument should be recorded in the log at regular intervals and compared to the chart. Moreover, *every* navigation practice should be followed to double-check the displayed soundings. Alarms don't always work!

Operation

Unlike their big brothers, depth recorders, rotating flasher and digital type sounders have very few knobs to adjust. Some digital sounders have only an on-off control—no options.

All flasher types, however, offer a gain control to adjust sensitivity. For navigational sounding work, i.e., for simply measuring the distance to the bottom, this knob should be adjusted so the zero flash and bottom flash are at about the same brilliance. Unless a large school of fish is swimming under the boat, only two flashes should be visible. If the gain is turned too high, false echoes may be detected, causing flashes to appear at random locations around the dial, or a double read-ing may be detected at twice the actual depth. If the gain is set too low, on the other hand, the bottom echo may be missed altogether. For fish finding, the gain should be set high enough to detect echoes above the bottom; this may be anywhere from slightly above the setting adequate for bottom sounding alone to a setting where a double bottom is detected, where the sounder displays the bottom at two depths, one twice the other.

Some digital sounders permit gain adjusment. Like a rotating flasher type, the gain should be set to the point where a steady bottom echo is detected. In the case of a digital display, that is the point where the reading stabilizes. If the gain is set too high, the sounder may display readings that are twice the actual depth. Many sounders adjust pulse length and gain automatically.

Some sounders may allow adjusting the displayed depth to account for the distance between the transducer and the bottom of the keel or the water's surface. If this adjustment is provided (usually accessed from the back of the instrument, often a screw adjustment), the sounder's readings can be adjusted either to show actual water depth or distance below the keel. If it is adjusted to show actual water depth, you must subtract your vessel's draft to find the available water under the keel. If it is adjusted to show the water under the keel, you must add the vessel's draft to use the readings for plotting on your chart.

If no compensation is made, the sounder's readings show the depth of water under the transducer, and both distance from keel to transducer and distance from waterline to transducer must be known to apply proper corrections.

Remember that all depths displayed indicate the distance to the bottom *straight down*, more or less (depending on beam angle and hull attitude). A rapidly shelving shoal up ahead may not be detected in time to avert running aground.

Piloting

A depth sounder can do more than tell you when you're about to hit bottom (or where the fish are). It can be a valuable piloting tool used in conjunction with chart, compass, and other navigational aids.

For example, consider the following modified chart of Cape Lookout. We've added a radio beacon on the beach of Shackleford Banks (no radio beacon exists there, and this chart should not be used for navigational purposes). Let's suppose you want to anchor inside the bight till the fog lifts in the morning. Visibility is next to nothing. The month is early January, and the ride is uncomfortably "bumpy". You could go into Moorehead City, but Beaufort Inlet can be tricky at night, even *without* a fog. The water inside Lookout

Bight makes a perfect anchorage. You decide to go for it. The tide is approaching dead low, so charted soundings should agree closely with actual depths. (United States East Coast charts are printed with soundings at mean low water.)

The beacon on Shackleford Banks is strong and clear. You steer 045° straight for the beacon and the beach, watching the depth sounder as you go. You double check the Morse identifier to make certain the radio beacon you're tuned to is the right one. Then, as long as you steer 045° toward

Following a depth contour.

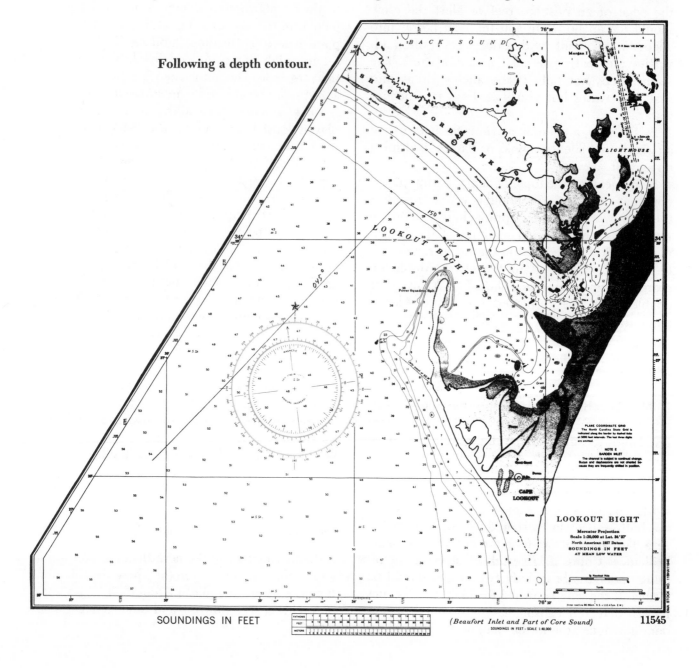

SOUNDINGS IN FEET

(Beaufort Inlet and Part of Core Sound)   11545

that beacon, you *know* you're clear of the offshore shoals at Lookout Bight. As long as the water is over 24 feet deep, you *know* you're in safe water, better than a quarter mile off the beach. (Remember, however, that radio bearings are inherently inaccurate.)

When the water depth drops to 30 feet, you reduce speed and change heading to 150°. You are inside the 30–foot contour and may now proceed gradually into shallower water. When the depth drops to 24 feet, your reduce speed again, alter course to 164°, and proceed cautiously.

If the water gets shallower than 24 feet, you steer more southerly. If the water gets deeper than 24 feet, you steer a bit to the east.

You examine the chart and notice the possible effects of tidal current. If the tide is approaching dead low, there'll be a strong ebb running out of Lighthouse Bay. Keeping this in mind, you move

in behind the bight. As you drop the hook in calm water, you notice the three submerged wrecks on the shoals inside the bight. They went in too far!

The pleasure of piloting with depth sounders is that every printed depth contour on your chart is a potential LOP. In clear weather visual bearings can be taken and used to cross with a depth contour. Often when approaching a shore only one visible landmark is charted. A single LOP does not a fix make. But a visual bearing crossed with a depth contour often will provide an adequate fix.

When there are no visual or radio bearings to cross, and no other aid to navigation is available, you may be able to find your position by keeping track of sounder readings in your log.

For example, suppose you logged soundings at regular 5 minute intervals while steering a constant course and maintaining a constant speed of 5 knots. Since 1 nautical mile is very nearly 2000

Crossing contours with visual bearings.

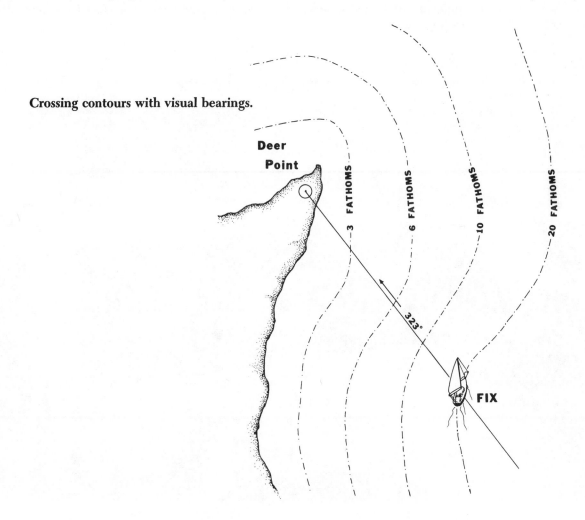

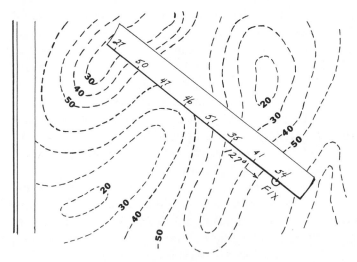

Using paper strip of soundings.

Even though this boat is equipped with digital sounder and other exotic electronic gear, its wise skipper still carries an old fashioned sounding lead.

yards, 6 knots is 12,000 yards per hour, or (dividing by 60 minutes/hour) 200 yards per minute. Every 5 minutes, then, a boat traveling 6 knots will advance 1000 yards. A record of soundings taken every 5 minutes from a vessel moving at a constant heading and making good 6 knots over the bottom will represent a string of water depths at 1000 foot intervals.

Such a string of depths can often be identified on a chart.

Cut a strip of paper one inch wide (or so) and several inches long. Find a distance scale on the chart and mark off 1000 yard intervals along the strip. Now print numbers by each mark to indicate the series of soundings taken. The paper strip is now a record of your position—soundings-wise.

At some location(s) on the chart, you may find the strip matches the charted soundings when oriented along the direction of the course steered. Admittedly, in some waters where depth changes little (like on the Bahama Banks), this method will be useless. In more rugged submarine terrain, however, there will be only one or at most two or three places where the strip matches the soundings printed on the chart. Since some other navigational information usually is available, you should be able to eliminate the ambiguity.

Remember: Whenever soundings are used to find locations on a chart, allowance for tide should always be considered. Moreover, there are ancillary factors such as wind or upland rains that can cause water levels to differ from predicted tidal levels. Always take these factors into account when using soundings to navigate.

Conclusion

The depth sounder may be the single most important item of marine electronics on your boat. If you do a lot of coastal work, it will certainly be the most used and, by all odds, the most appreciated. With a little care, any depth sounder should go on working for years, tirelessly sounding the bottom and warning you when the water gets too short.

CHAPTER 10

Depth Recorders

As its name suggests, the depth recorder (also called "chart recorder", "straight line recorder", "white line recorder", or just "recorder") is a machine that makes a record of the water's depth. The principles of operation are essentially the same as those we examined in the chapter on depth sounders—with one exception. Instead of flashing lights or blinking digits at us, depth recorders display the water's depth by drawing a picture. The picture is a permanent graph drawn on a continuously moving paper chart. It shows everything under the boat, from top to bottom and everywhere in between—especially fish.

The majority of those who use depth recorders are fishermen. Although fish can be found using rotating flashes type depth sounders (and occasionally with a digital sounder), the true fish finder is a chart recorder (or color sounder explained in the next chapter). Of course recorders cost much more than rotating flashes units but, for serious sport and commercial fishing, the recorder has no equal.

Other uses—including scientific research,

Depth recorder on bridge of modern ship.

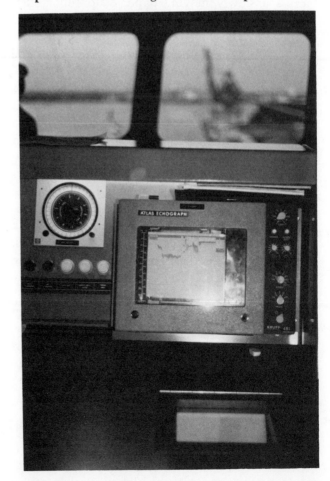

hunting sunken wrecks, finding interesting underwater formations for sport diving, dredge work, and offshore navigation—the chart recorder offers the special advantage of creating a permanent picture of the bottom, showing both what's under the boat right now and what *was* under the boat 5 minutes or 12 hours ago. Rotating flashers and digital depth sounders can only tell us what's down there right now. They make no record.

The principles of transducer frequency and beam width discussed in the chapter on depth sounders applies equally to chart recorders. Transducer mounting is the same for both units.

Principles of Operation

The operation of depth recorders differs from that of depth sounders only in the method used to display echoes. The recorder uses a moving stylus to mark a continuous strip of paper that is pulled at constant speed under the stylus, thus creating a permanent record of echoes returning from the bottom or from fish.

In the simpler units, the stylus passes down across a slowly moving paper strip repeatedly, again and again. At the start of each pass, a signal causes the transducer to transmit a sonic pulse toward the bottom, and another signal causes the stylus to mark the paper. This is called the "zero" or "transmission" mark. Every time the stylus passes the zero line on the chart paper, a pulse is transmitted into the water, and the stylus makes a mark on the moving chart. Since the chart paper is drawn from side to side under the marking stylus, the zero mark becomes a continuous line corresponding roughly to the water's surface.

If an echo is detected by the transducer, a second signal is sent to the stylus, causing it to mark the paper again. The position of this second mark depends upon the depth of the surface reflecting the sonic pulse, be it a fish's back or a muddy river bottom.

Echoes returning from the bottom cause the stylus to draw a continuous line on the paper. Where the water is shallow, the bottom line is near the zero line. Where the water is deep, the zero line is nearer the bottom of the chart. If the

depth exceeds the recorder's range, the bottom line may not be marked at all.

If an echo returns from a fish passing within the beam, the stylus marks the paper at a point representing the fish's depth. The length of this mark (i.e., its horizontal dimension) depends upon the speed of the paper transport mechanism and how long the fish remains in the beam. If the fish passes only through the edge of the beam, or if the boat is moving at a high rate of speed, or if the fish is swimming very rapidly, or if the paper transport is set to a slow rate—the mark will be shortened horizontally. If the fish passes more nearly through the center of the beam, or if the boat is moving slowly, or if the fish is a sluggish swimmer, or if the paper is moving quickly under the stylus—the mark will be elongated horizontally.

Marks caused by fish echoes have a distinctive inverted V shape. The height of the inverted V

The height of marks caused by fish depends upon the path of the fish as it passes through the beam, not the size of the fish.

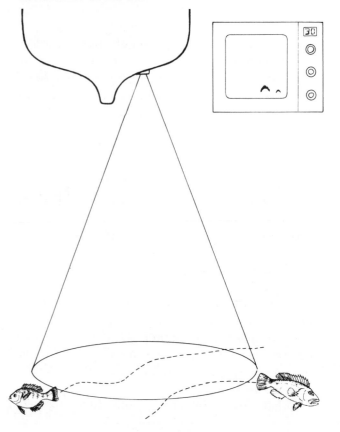

depends upon the path taken by the fish as it passes through the beam. Keep in mind that most fish swim at a constant depth. However, a fish that has just entered the beam is *farther* from the transducer than a fish that is directly under the transducer, even though both fish are at the same depth. The following figure shows why this is so.

A fish that moves through the center of the beam (or a fish that remains in one position while the boat passes directly above it) will cause a taller and wider inverted V shape to be marked on the chart paper. Taller since the distance from the transducer changes more for the fish that passes through the center of the beam. Wider, since the fish spends more time in the beam. The fish passing through the center of the beam is, at first, several feet farther from the transducer, then as the fish passes through the center of the beam it is at its closest to the transducer, and finally moves farther from the transducer as it leaves the beam—even though the fish may remain at constant depth.

If paper speed is too slow, fish may mark as vertical lines instead of inverted Vs, since the fish can cross the beam before the paper moves far enough to create the inverted V. A vertical line may also be caused by random noises. Slow paper speed works well for navigational purposes, but a somewhat faster transport is desirable for discriminating between fish, that make the distinctive inverted V mark, and noise that often causes mere vertical lines.

The depth of fish or bottom can be read by a movable clear plastic cursor marked off in feet or fathoms (or meters, etc.), or the paper chart itself may be pre-marked with horizontal lines indicating depth intervals.

Effect of Beam Angle

Since depth sounders are used primarily to find depth for navigation (with limited fish-finding capabilities), beam angle is less of a consideration than it is with chart recorders, where a picture of the bottom profile is created.

As mentioned in the chapter on depth sounders, the region of sonic sensitivity under a transducer can be measured several ways. One is to find the edges of the region where sensitivity is reduced to –3 db, –6 db, or some other value. When measured in this way, the region is found to be lobe-shaped. If the region is measured at –6 db limits, the lobe may be said to be wider than if the region is measured at –3 db limits. In fact, the lobe size is the same—only the measurement method differs.

On the other hand, if two manufacturers measure lobe limits at the same sensitivity level, e.g., –3 db, the shape of the lobe will differ from one transducer to another, depending on internal transducer structure and operating frequency. At high frequencies, the lobes are narrower (generally speaking) while at low frequencies, lobes are wider. High frequency transducers are built to have wide lobes, and low frequency transducers are built to have narrow lobes.

A wide lobe produces what is known as a wide beam angle, and a narrow lobe produces what is known as a narrow beam angle.

Manufacturers commonly ignore the fact that the shape of the sonic sensitivity region below the transducer is lobe-shaped, and they depict the region as a straight-sided cone instead. The cone is easier to draw and explain. For this reason, we will also use the theoretical cone shape for some of our discussion. Beam angle and cone angle, then, are interchangeable terms. Both describe the dimensions of the sonic sensitivity region.

Transducers with wide beam angles see larger areas on the ocean bottom than transducers with narrow beam angles. This is because the diameter of the area at the bottom of a sonic cone depends entirely upon the water's depth and the transducer's beam angle.

The foregoing table shows that the diameter of a 4° beam is only 1 foot at a depth of 20 feet below the transducer. The sonic cone is only 7 feet across at 100 feet and 70 feet across at 1000 feet below the transducer.

The diameter of a 22° beam at 20 feet is 8 feet. At 100 feet, the same beam is 39 feet across, and at 1000 feet the 22° beam sees an area on the bottom that is 389 feet across.

Transducers with a 50° beam angle can see much more. At 20 feet, the 50° beam "sees" an

TABLE 10-1

CONE DIAMETER VS. DEPTH

WATER DEPTH	BEAM ANGLE						
	4	9	18	22	36	43	50
10	1	2	3	4	6	8	9
20	1	3	6	8	13	16	19
30	2	5	10	12	19	24	28
40	3	6	13	16	26	32	37
60	4	9	19	23	39	47	56
80	6	13	25	31	52	63	75
100	7	16	32	39	65	79	93
150	10	24	48	58	97	118	140
200	14	31	63	78	130	158	187
300	21	47	95	117	195	236	280
500	35	79	158	194	325	394	466
1000	70	157	317	389	650	788	933

TABLE 10-2

SONIC CONE AREA VS. DEPTH

WATER DEPTH	BEAM ANGLE						
	4	9	18	22	36	43	50
10	0	2	8	12	33	49	68
20	2	8	32	47	133	195	273
30	3	18	71	107	299	439	615
40	6	31	126	190	531	780	1093
60	14	70	284	427	1194	1755	2459
80	25	125	504	760	2123	3120	4372
100	38	195	788	1187	3317	4875	6831
150	86	438	1773	2671	7463	10968	15370
200	153	778	3152	4748	13267	19499	27325
300	345	1751	7093	10683	29850	43872	61481
500	958	4865	19702	29675	82917	121867	170779
1000	3831	19459	78809	118701	331667	487467	683117

area that is 19 feet across. At 100 feet the area from which echoes can be detected is 93 feet across, and at 1000 feet the 50° beam scans a region that is 933 feet in diameter.

The following table shows the actual areas, in square feet, that various beam angles cover.

The table above may be more meaningful from an operational point of view since the probability of seeing a fish in the sonic cone depends upon the cone's area. In other words, a transducer with a beam angle of 36° covers more than 4 times as much as a transducer with a beam angle of 18° and is, therefore, 4 times as likely to pick up the echo from a fish swimming under the boat.

There is a tendency to assume that what the depth recorder sees is directly under the boat. This is true only with narrow beam angle transducers. With wide angle transducers, the sounding chart can be misleading since the area depicted by the markings may be quite large. With a 50° beam angle transducer, for example, a fish marking at 30 feet may be 14 feet in front of the boat, or 14 feet behind the boat, or 14 feet on either side. At 300 feet, a fish being marked on the recorder chart may be 140 feet ahead, behind, or on either side of the boat. An uninformed interpretation of the markings on the recorder chart does not reveal this truth, and an inexperienced fisherman may be frustrated by fish that mark on his machine but obstinately refuse to bite.

Dual-angle transducers are available for many makes of depth recorder. These transducers produce a beam that is flattened fore and aft. For example, a dual-angle transducer may produce a beam that's only 15 degrees front to back but is 30 degrees wide. Such dual-angle beams sweep the ocean floor with wide sonic brooms while permitting good localization along the path of the vessel's course.

Options

In addition to various beam angles, chart recorders offer a host of other options.

When selecting a unit for its options, note that options are costly and that an option-laden unit may not perform as well as a comparatively priced unit without the bells and whistles. Generally speaking, two $1000 recorders built by different manufacturers will perform equally well. However, if one of the two includes a host of extra gadgetry like depth alarms, multi-tone printing, digital depth display, event marker or similar goodies—the piper must be paid. The trade-off may very well be in basic performance.

Of course, if options are more important than sensitivity to great depths, go for the unit that provides the options you need.

Variable Paper Speed

Chart recorder paper isn't inexpensive. A 50 foot roll sells for about a penny an inch! If the machine cranks the paper through at a constant 3 inches a minute, the paper bill can run to $1.80 per hour. Moreover, each roll will last only 3 hours and 20 minutes.

Cost and convenience, however, are not the only advantages afforded by adjustable paper speed. As mentioned previously, the shape of fish echoes depends on paper speed (and other factors). Echoes also differ according to species of fish. Experienced chart recorder users can tell the difference between a red snapper and a black sea bass by the shape and size of the chart markings. The ability to increase paper speed and so extend the length of fish echoes permits greater discrimination and identification of targets.

For navigational purposes there is no need to tell the difference between a trout and a salmon. All that's needed is a slow moving chart that shows the distance to the bottom and the shape of features on the bottom. Such a chart can be invaluable to the navigator. Soundings provide positional information that can be more accurate and more reliable that any other electronic device on board. Paper speed for soundings, however, need be only a fraction of that required for fishing.

Speeds from 1/10 to as much as 3 inches a minute may be useful in different applications. A front panel control for this function may be convenient. (Some units hide the adjusting knob.)

Digital Display

Some of the more expensive depth recorders feature digital depth displays that can be operated independently of the chart. One manufacturer admits, however, that the digital displays used in some chart recorders may not work as well as digital displays in straight digital depth sounders. Although this caveat does not necessarily apply to all recorders, it is true that digital depth sounders are designed from square one with the aim of displaying water's depth in digits while depth recorders are designed with a printed chart output in mind. The two functions may not work well together in all manufacturers' equipment.

Buyers should carefully consider the value of a digital display add-on and compare the possible advantages of installing a separate digital sounder in addition to a depth recorder.

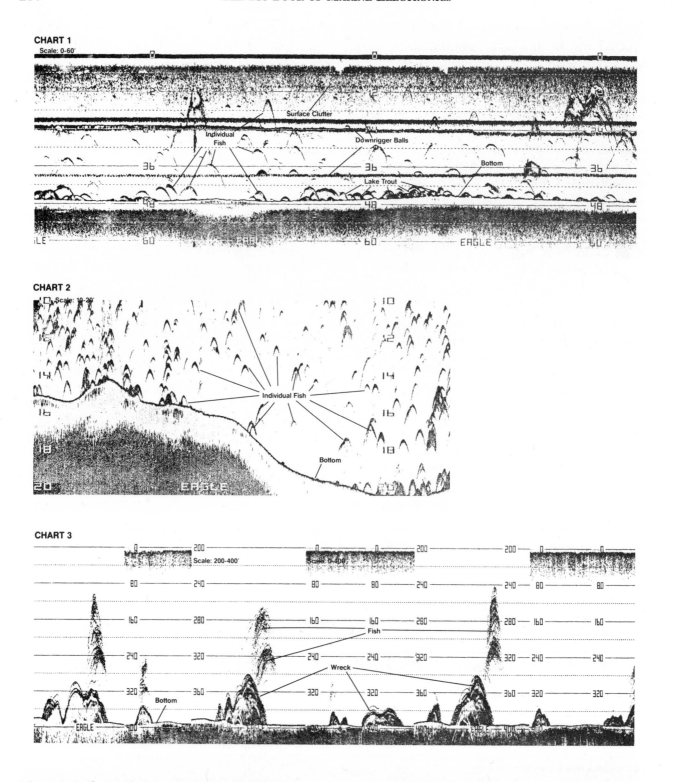

Chart 1, Eagle Mach I Computer Graph (192 kHz) shows salmon (suspended) and lake trout (on and near bottom); Lake Michigan. Graph prints three downrigger balls being trolled at 21′, 24′, and 38′. *Chart 2*, Eagle Mach I computer Graph (192 kHz) shows white bass from 10–20′; Grand Lake, Oklahoma; Ranger Boat. *Chart 3*, Eagle Mach II Computer Graph (50 kHz) prints wreck and fish off coast of Key West, Florida.

Depth recorder with digital display.

White-line recorder and chart.

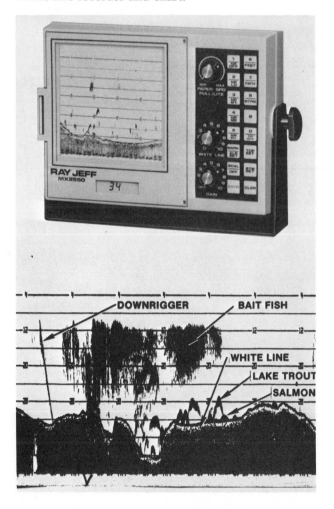

White Line

The white line function is standard equipment on nearly all depth recorders and is an imperative option if the unit is going to be used for fishing. The white line permits discrimination of targets near the bottom, such as bottom-feeding fish, that would otherwise be obscured by the strong echo from the bottom itself.

Time-controlled amplifiers in white line recorders amplify only the leading edge of returning echo pulses and display only the top of each echo. With white line turned on, the rest of the echo is ignored—and large echoes don't interfere with smaller echoes.

In less expensive units there may be only two options: white line "on" or white line "off". More expensive recorders permit fine tuning of the white line, and this can be worth the extra cost to those for whom fishing is a way of life. For navigation, the white line really isn't necessary.

Event Marker

An option that adds great convenience without adding much in the way of cost is the event marker.

At the press of a button the event marker circuit causes the stylus to mark the paper chart continuously from top to bottom. A navigator or

Recorder with cursor rule.

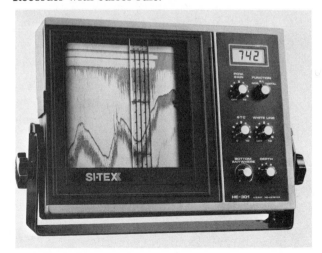

fisherman can put distinguishing marks on a chart to identify important soundings merely by pressing the event marker more than once, thus drawing one or more thin vertical lies on the chart.

The event marker takes a "snapshot" of the water profile at any given instant. A felt-tip pen can be used to mark directly on the chart paper, of course, but this is neither so convenient nor so precise as the crisp vertical line drawn by the recorder stylus at the mere press of a button. After using the event marker to precisely identify a particular position, a felt-tip pen can make notes near the marking to explain its significance for later reference.

Indeed, as explained in the next section, there are other ways to mark positions on the recorder chart!

Loran-C Interface

By interfacing the recorder to a Loran-C receiver, all event marks on the chart can be identified with the boat's precise location, printed directly on the chart next to the event mark, either in Loran-C TDs or in geographic lat/lon coordinates.

At the touch of an event button, the recorder interrogates the Loran-C for present position. The Loran-C responds by sending position coordinates to the recorder via the interface. An event mark is drawn on the depth recorder chart, and next to the mark is printed the boat's position in Loran-C or lat/lon coordinates so the operator can return to that precise location at any later time.

No special stylus is required. The recorder marks numbers or letters on the chart using the same method employed for marking fish. The Loran-C and interface do the rest.

This may be overkill for many of us, but it's an ideal option for some . . . and the added cost is far less than one might imagine. A commercial fisherman, for example, would quickly offset the additional cost by increasing his catch while reducing running time and fuel consumption. Marine research vessels will also benefit from the ability to instantaneously identify the position of bottom formations discovered by the recorder. The value to salvage operations is obvious.

Zero Line Shift

Also called "bottom anywhere", the zero line shift option permits the operator to look at any range of water below the surface. Thus one can look at the 40 foot segment from 80 feet to 120 feet down by setting the range to 40 and zero line 80. Everything above 80 feet is ignored.

If you're looking for fish that live only 50 feet or deeper, set the zero line to 50 feet and eliminate everything above that depth. With the zero line feature you can zoom in on the depths you really want to see—where your intended catch resides.

Bottom Lock

Bottom lock puts the ocean bottom at the bottom of the chart at all times, regardless of range setting or water's depth.

The bottom is visible at all times. This is great for those who fish for bottom feeders since there is no need to change the depth range to when the water's depth changes. The recorder follows the sea floor up and down, displaying it as a straight line along the bottom of the chart.

Range can be expanded to show only the first 15 or 30 feet from the bottom and nothing else. The recorder can zoom-in on bottom fish and stay locked on the bottom for a constant display.

For those interested in sunken wrecks or underwater geology, bottom lock is invaluable.

Fine Echo

Fine echo is a control that eliminates interference and false targets from the chart display. Fine echo may be achieved in several ways, but in all cases it eliminates unwanted echoes caused by other sounders operating in the area, interference from on-board electrical equipment, etc.

Sensitivity Time Control

STC limits the recorder's sensitivity to echoes returning in the brief interval immediately following the transmission of each pulse. This prevents the chart from marking echoes from targets near the surface like plankton and air bubbles that unnecessarily confuse the display.

In some units STC is automatic. In others it can be adjusted over a wide range. Still others provide three or four settings. A few use a simple on-off switch. Some have no STC at all. Perhaps the best STC is tunable, permitting the operator to obtain the best markings at all depths.

Care should be exercised when using STC. Since sensitivity is reduced near the surface, shallow obstructions may be missed. STC should be reduced or switched off altogether when operating near shoals.

STC is also available on some depth sounders.

Power Reducer

Nearly all recorders offer some means of adjusting receiver gain. A few also permit operator adjustment of output power, i.e., the amount of energy transmitted in each sonic pulse.

Sonic pulses from a deep-water recorder may be so powerful in shallow water that the returning echoes overdrive the receiver amplifiers, causing marks to be blurred or indistinct. Overly strong signals can also reflect from the surface of the water and appear on the chart as unwanted noise.

By reducing power, sharper, more distinct echo markings are possible in shallow water.

Conclusion

The chart recorder is a fisherman's friend. It has limited application for sailing enthusiasts who don't fish, but may be an invaluable aid to divers, research oceanographers, or other who need to differentiate bottom structures. It can also be helpful in determining what type of bottom you're over when selecting the best anchor for optimum holding power or the best location for the anchor to bite in.

As a navigation tool, the chart recorder provides a record of water depths that later can be compared to charted contours to obtain a fix or line of position. (See the preceding chapter for an explanation of how to use depth readings for navigation.)

Although chart recorders have been in use for decades, many are now being replaced by newer devices that make old depth recorders obsolete for finding fish. One of these, the color sounder, is described in the next chapter. Color sounders do not, however, provide convenient records of bottom contours and, where a permanent and convenient record is desired, the depth recorder continues to be a useful piece of gear.

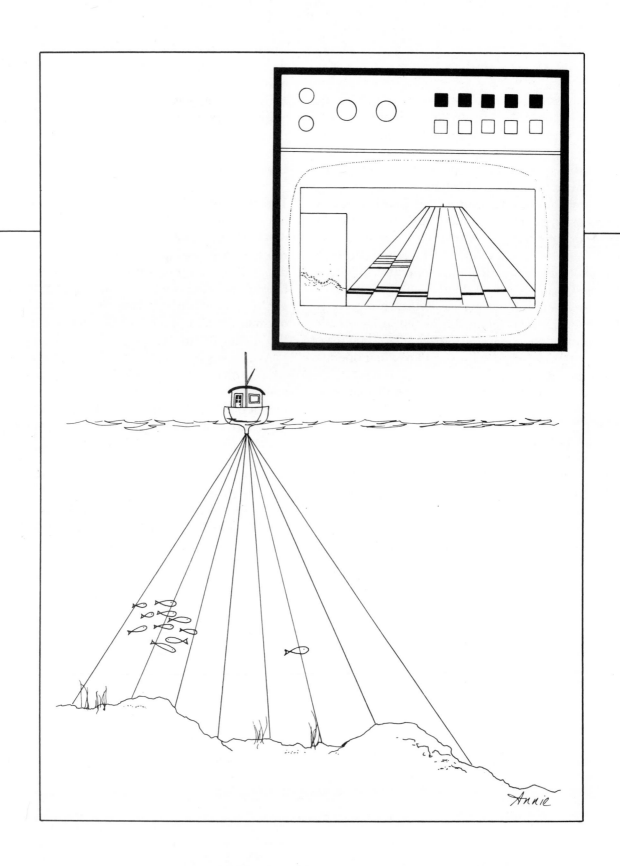

Color Depth Sounders

General

If you fish, you should seriously consider a color sounder. There's just nothing like it for finding fish!

Instead of a dull grey chart, these miraculous machines paint vivid color pictures of the bottom and all creatures in the water underneath your boat. Echoes of varied strengths are displayed in different colors so, with experience, it's possible to tell both size and species of fish at all levels. The use of contrasting colors is especially useful in detecting the presence of fish located very near the bottom and to distinguish between a cloud of drifting plankton or useless weed and a school of tasty fish worth thousands in the boat.

Color sounders use most of the technology of recording sounders. Everything that's been said in this book about transducers, power in the pulse, beam angle and so forth, applies to color sounders. Fixed bottom display modes, adjustable depth windows, power adjustment, and other functions are identical. At first glance the only difference is that the color sounder has a color CRT where the chart recorder has a paper transport.

But, the color sounder is much, much more.

Color depth sounder with bottom indicator. Note arrow at 72 feet. (*Si-Tex*)

Theory of Operation

The options possible with a color sounder are far more versatile than those available with depth recorders. They are far more fantastic, too! The microcomputer makes it all possible.

The transmitters and receivers built into color

165

sounders are essentially the same as those used in depth recorders, but what's done with the received signals after they've been bounced off watery targets under the boat is amazingly different.

The signal intensity of each returning echo from an underwater target is coded and stored in the computer's memory. Echoes within the range selected by the user are displayed on the color screen as dots of light. The color of each dot depends upon the strength of the returning echo.

Noise Elimination

Successive pulses are sampled so false echoes caused by random noise or other phantoms can be eliminated before the color dot is painted on the CRT. The number of pulses sampled before the microcomputer paints a trace on the color CRT may differ from one sounder model to another. In general, however, the process is quite simple.

The microcomputer measures the intensity of each received pulse and the depth of the target, storing the composite of these values into its memory as a single "byte" of data. (The term "byte" refers to a binary coded element of computer information, a single computer word that can be stored in memory.) Each stored byte contains a code for depth and intensity of a single pulse or series of pulses.

If an echo does not recur at the same depth (or nearly the same depth) with the next pulse, the microcomputer tags that byte as a possible false echo and, if the echo does not recur with the third pulse, the computer erases the byte.

False echoes clutter the screen and can be confusing.

However, if an echo does recur a statistically significant number of times, say 4 out of 5, the byte containing the binary code for depth and intensity is moved to an area of data storage called video memory and is displayed.

Video Display

The picture on a color CRT is actually composed of thousands of tiny dots that glow when bombarded with electrons. An electron gun inside the

Low-density block pixel display. (*Techsonic*)

CRT tube scans rapidly across the screen in closely spaced horizontal lines called rasters. If a dot needs to be illuminated at a particular point on the screen, the gun fires electrons at it as it scans past that point. The gun is aimed by electromagnets that bend the stream of electrons in response to varying currents in the magnet coils. There are no moving parts. The raster scan is faster than the eye can detect.

On a color sounder CRT (or personal computer with a color display), groups of color dots make up tiny blocks of color called pixels. The number of pixels on a screen is a function of the microcomputer device driving the video display—not the CRT tube itself. All color CRT's are pretty much the same in this respect. The factor limiting the number of pixels on the screen is frequently the amount of memory available to store pixel data. Where many pixels are desired, there must be many memory locations to store each byte of pixel data. Large amounts of memory increase cost.

The designers of one color sounder may decide that a screen of 65,536 color pixels is detailed enough for the purposes of finding fish—that's a screen measuring 256 by 256 pixels. Another designer may insist that 262,144 pixels give better resolution—that's a screen measuring 512 by 512. The fact is, however, that other factors may be more important than pixel size. Display options can vary widely from unit to unit. The manner of arranging a display on the screen may more than compensate for lack of pixel density.

The best way to determine which works best is to see for yourself. Many fishing partyboats (headboats) are putting color sounders on board. Ask the skipper if she or he will let you visit in the wheelhouse to observe first-hand how the color sounder marks fish. You may decide the higher pixel density just isn't worth the added cost . . . or not.

Here's how the color video display works.

Many video circuits have their own dedicated microcomputer, separate from the microcomputer that measures depth and intensity of returning echoes and stores pixel data. The video

High-density pixel display. (*Wesmar*)

circuit microcomputer has but one task, to read current values stored in video memory and display them on the color CRT. The two microcomputers may communicate with each other, the main computer telling the video computer when to shift the color picture to the left and paint another vertical line at the right edge of the color CRT—just as the depth recorder does on its paper chart.

The video computer labors silently, reading video memory and updating the screen as new memory is added, shifting the image to the left on command from the main computer. The result is a color image of the water's profile under the boat—an image that moves slowly to the left, just as a depth recorder chart image moves to the left as new soundings are made.

The depth data stored with each pixel byte tells the video computer where to paint that pixel. The returning echo intensity data, also stored with each pixel byte, tells the video computer what color to paint the pixel. Thus the position and color of the pixel on the screen is a function of depth and echo strength, respectively.

Each pixel, every single point of color on the screen, is same size. Large, persistent targets may mark as a large group of pixels, while small, transient targets may use only a few pixels.

Options

If that were all a color sounder could do, it would still be a pretty fantastic piece of gear—since fish and bottom and floating plankton and even thermoclines (regions where the water temperature changes rapidly with depth) are displayed in vivid colors in accordance to the target's echo intensity.

But, that's not all.

Color sounders can do almost everything depth recorders can do—except make a permanent paper record you can file away in a scrapbook. However, color photographs can easily be taken of any screen at any time, and some manufacturers offer a data cassette option that allows you to record, on a standard stereo cassette recorder, the sonic images of the bottom. The audio cassette

Color depth sounder with convenient control access.

all or part of the display with the sea bed always at the bottom of the screen. The microcomputer keeps track of the position of the bottom and adjusts the display accordingly, making the bottom appear as a straight line at the lower edge of the screen. There are no humps or bumps on the bottom—even when the boat is tossing around on the surface. The bottom remains a straight line. Fish just above the bottom are clearly visible without bottom irregularity confusing the picture.

If some form of depth expansion option is available, you can zoom in on a region 15 feet from the bottom, or a region that begins at 80 fathoms and extends to 120 fathoms. Or you can look at the 20 foot depth window located between 400 and 420 feet.

The most common use of depth expansion mode is to examine the window that includes the bottom and the first 20 or so feet above the bottom. That's where many species of fish, like grouper, spend most of their time. Another operator may be interested in the range from 10 to 40 feet. A depth expansion option makes this possible.

can be played back at any later time so you can review the images and make plans for future trips to that fishing ground.

You can insist on the same performance from a color sounder that you would expect from a depth recorder. The important point to note is that, like personal computers, differences between models and manufacturers can be tremendous. This field is just beginning to take off. The market hasn't yet been saturated, and new ideas are added daily. Some ideas are useful. Other ideas cut costs. Shop around, and try stick with reputable manufacturers.

Depth Functions

Make certain the unit you select offers all the depth ranges you can imagine ever using. Some manufacturers, in an effort to keep prices down, may offer units with limited depth capability and limited depth flexibility.

Depth expansion features are extremely valuable. With them you can look closely at any range of depth below the keel, excluding those depths in which you have no interest.

Bottom lock may be useful. This feature fixes

Lateral Display

A real bonus available only with color depth sounders is the ability to display a dual image of the depth profile. In addition to the familiar advancing chart display, a lateral display can be shown simultaneously to tell where fish are from *side to side*.

With a conventional chart recorder or color sounder with only the conventional chart-type advancing display, you don't know whether marking fish are directly under the boat or off to one side. Now, with the lateral display color sounder, a separate depth profile shows the side view as well as depth and echo intensity! When you begin marking fish near the bottom, you know at once which way to turn when doubling back to get over the fish again. With the color sounder in "stereo mode", showing vertical and lateral views simultaneously you might, for example, see fish marking just above the bottom and off your starboard side. With that information, you

Lateral and vertical "stereo" display. (*Si-Tex*)

know you must turn to starboard to get back over the fish.

Without a lateral display, all you know for certain is that fish are down there. If you are running west and mark fish that are swimming north, circling back to port might cause you to miss the school entirely—since by the time you get back to where the fish had been, they may have moved away farther to the north. There's now no way to find them again except to resume searching. The result, of course, is time and fuel wasted—with no fish.

The lateral display is certainly worth considering if you're serious about catching fish.

Conclusion

As state-of-the-art microelectronics continues to be applied for the benefit of fishermen, we'll be seeing even better devices for finding fish and determining their size and species.

It's conceivable that future sounders will be able to detect food within a fish's digestive tract, probing the *insides* of the fish with varying frequencies and analyzing the responding echoes for particular wave patterns characteristic of an empty stomach or a stomach filled with varied kinds of food—other fish, shrimp, squid, etc. A high-speed microcomputer could easily convert such data into consistently accurate predictions of the fish's hunger and consequent tendency to bite into a chunk of juicy bait lowered down to him on a barbed hook. Knowing what the fish's last meal consisted of, we may even be able to predict which bait will have the best results.

Far-fetched? Not really! Today's gear is already miraculous.

Why should the future be any less incredible?

PART **IV**

Miscellaneous Equipment

CHAPTER 12

EPIRBs

Who Needs 'Em?

Emergency Position Indicating Radio Beacons aren't just for sailors crossing lonely oceans. They are for anyone operating any kind of boat in *any* waters.

Even a ski boat, out on an inland lake for a day of fun, can collide with a submerged obstruction, catch fire and sink beneath the surface in the space of a few frightening seconds. Passengers and crew may find themselves bobbing helplessly in the water with no way to summon help. Even where accidents occur within sight of shore, lives may be lost when injury or the rush of time prevents the use of life jackets. Wind, current, or cold water can make swimming impossible. Darkness or fog may delay or prevent rescue.

EPIRBs are not costly. Typical prices range from $200–300.

Even if your vessel is equipped with VHF and SSB radios, a radio beacon that can be operated apart from the boat's battery and antenna system is imperative. An EPIRB can summon help when electrical malfunctions disable other communications gear, making it your only contact with the world.

EPIRBs are designed to perform one function: to save lives. They should only be used in true distress situations where a life is in jeopardy or substantial property damage is threatened. Misuse, even misuse resulting from simple negligence, can result in criminal charges. You can be sued if you or a member of your crew is found to have intentionally and maliciously activated an EPIRB when you were in no immediate distress, and if rescue crews are diverted away from a legitimate emergency to assist you.

So take precautions to ensure your EPIRB can only be used in true distress situations.

There are several types of EPIRBs available. Select the one best suited to the type of boating you do.

Types Available

EPIRBs were first developed for use by downed aircraft, and units transmitting on frequencies monitored by aircraft are still available. More recently, however, the FCC has approved EPIRB use on marine VHF frequencies. Some older units still transmit on 2182 KHz, the LF call and distress channel (not recommended).

Class A and Class B EPIRBs

Class A and Class B EPIRBs are designed to be used by vessels operating offshore.

Both transmit simultaneously on two emergency frequencies: 121.5 MHz, an international distress frequency monitored by commercial aircraft (and many private aircraft as well), and 243 MHz, an emergency frequency monitored by military aircraft. Both types also can be heard by some recently deployed satellites, depending on your position and that of the satellites. Both are equipped with batteries capable of powering the units for several days.

The range of class A and B EPIRBs can be hundred of miles.

Class A EPIRBs activate automatically when they come in contact with the water. They will deploy without assistance in the event of sinking. Class A EPIRBs are required aboard certain commercial vessels.

Class B EPIRBs do not deploy automatically. They require an operator to turn them on manually. This type EPIRB is popular among pleasure boat operators.

Class C EPIRBs

Class C EPIRBs are designed to be used near the coastline or on inland waters. They transmit on marine VHF Channel 16, the call and distress frequency. Like Class B units, they must be manually activated.

The range of class C EPIRBs is limited to about 15 miles.

Which to Choose

If you are crossing oceans far from shipping lanes, an EPIRB that transmits on channels used only by ships won't do much good. On the other hand, if you do all of your boating along the coast, an EPIRB transmitting on aircraft frequencies may not get results as quickly as one using VHF frequencies that can be received by nearby boats and shore shore stations. Speed is of the essence in the event of marine disaster.

Offshore, the better choice may be an EPIRB that transmits on frequencies that will be heard by passing aircraft or orbiting satellites.

The problem with Class C EPIRBs is that in certain areas of the briny blue, hundreds of miles from shore and perhaps just as far from the nearest VHF equipped boat, you may never be heard on Channel 16. The range of an EPIRB transmitting on VHF frequencies is severely limited by the height of its antenna. Since most EPIRBS are used by persons in the water or in rubber rafts, antenna height is no more than two or three feet at best. Most EPIRBs are limited to about one watt of transmitted power. The range of one watt VHF waves radiating from an antenna only a few feet above the water may not exceed 10 or 12 miles. (You who have sailed across an ocean will remember how many days the only boat you saw was the one under your feet.)

Class C EPIRBs are strictly for those who operate near shore and near other marine traffic where chances are good their distress signal will be heard by another VHF-equipped boat or shore-based Coast Guard station.

On the other hand, Class A and Class B EPIRBs can be heard at far greater distances than Class C units, since the receiving station may be an airplane flying at 35,000 feet or an artificial satellite whizzing through space many miles above the earth's surface.

Class C EPIRBs transmit *only* on VHF channels. Class A and B EPIRBs transmit *only* on aircraft frequencies.

Offshore, away from traffic, your best bet is Class A or B.

Near shore and traffic your chances are better with Class C.

Emergency Flasher

Some units offer the additional safety of a flashing light.

But, the question arises whether or not you need a flashing strobe light to drain battery power from the EPIRB transmitter.

Clearly if you get dumped in the drink at high noon, a flashing light won't do much good. It will not be visible, but it will drain precious amperes from the battery.

On the other hand, if you're bobbing helplessly in the waves at midnight, within sight of a fishing vessel on which the crew are all on deck busily tugging on their nets, but with no one in the wheelhouse to hear your distress call on the VHF, a brilliant strobe might catch their attention.

Perhaps the better choice is to carry two units—an EPIRB and a flashing strobe—each relying on its own batteries.

Maintenance

Like every other electronic device on board, and perhaps in some sense *more* than any other device, your EPIRB needs care and maintenance so it can be counted on to perform in an emergency.

Batteries for EPIRBs should be replaced each year or before each offshore passage.

If the gaskets show signs of deterioration, replace them.

Since even brief EPIRB signals can summon search and rescue teams, units should never be activated for test purposes. If your EPIRB has no self-test, have a qualified marine electronics shop test it before you head offshore. In fact, it's a good idea to have the unit tested in the shop rather than rely on a self-test. The shop test makes certain the unit is transmitting properly on the correct frequency. A self-test may do no more than verify that the batteries are good.

Oh, by the way, if the tiny EPIRB antenna breaks off in an emergency situation, you can jury rig a substitute with any wire. The substitute should be precisely the same length as the portion broken off, and the antenna should be straight. If all you have is a flimsy length of wire that won't stick up in the air, simply turn the EPIRB over and let the wire hang straight down. EPIRBs work almost as well upside down.

Mounting

The EPIRB should, of course, be mounted where it will be handy in an emergency. However, it should not be mounted where it is going to be kicked or bumped or possibly knocked overboard. Although most manufacturers build their EPIRBs to withstand the harshest oceans environment, you should not mount an EPIRBs where it will be unnecessarily exposed to direct sunlight or continuous dousings from rain or spray.

EPIRB upside-down. This one floats and activates automatically as soon as it is turned antenna side up. Most of the unit is filled with batteries. Generally, bigger batteries mean longer calls for help—and that can make all the difference.

Of course the units are designed to be out in the weather, but why expose them to more weather than necessary? If it's possible to mount an EPIRB where it will be handy and protected from the hot sun and damp air, then by all means mount it there. On the other hand, if the EPIRB isn't accessible, it won't be much good to you when you need it in an emergency.

If you elect to stow your EPIRB in the life-raft cannister, remember that a heavy boarding sea can carry life raft *and* EPIRB over the side, leaving you and crew clinging to the wreckage with no way to summon help.

Similarly, the man overboard pole and horse-shoe bouy can be torn away as greybeards growl across the decks. Attaching your only EPIRB to these intentionally detachable devices may also prove to be a most regrettable mistake.

Stowing one in the abandon-ship bag is a good idea, provided you can lay your hands on the bag before you abandon ship.

Since one can never foresee every possibility—especially when planning for emergencies, the most prudent will have more than one EPIRB on board—one on the man-overboard pole, another in the life-raft cannister, still one more in the abandon-ship bag, and perhaps a fourth mounted safely on a bracket just inside the companionway where it can be grabbed at a moment's notice.

Sometimes a moment may be all you have to work with.

CHAPTER 13

Autopilots

An autopilot can make long passages pure pleasure, providing time for the helmsman to make a sandwich or a cup of coffee, to examine the chart carefully, to reef or change sails, to secure a loose piece of gear on deck, or to jump below and pump the water rising curiously in the bilge.

A spare and able hand at the helm is frequently welcome.

But let it be said at once: Autopilots can not replace the alert watch of a human helmsman and, single-handed sailors notwithstanding, they are not intended to steer while you snooze. Countless accidents have resulted when sailors have assumed, "No ships are in these waters. It's safe to nap for a few hours." It's true that thousands of such naps have been taken without unhappy consequences, but it's equally true that lives needlessly have been lost due to careless and undisciplined watchkeeping.

Many ships cruise at speeds from 12 to 18 knots. A few exceed 20 knots! Simple mathematics shows that a vessel making 24 knots can travel 10 miles in 25 minutes. Even a large ship can be obscured by haze or mild rain showers at 10 miles. The 30 minute napper may be rudely awakened by the rending sounds of his hull's

being plowed beneath the waves by the bow of a charging container ship.

To compound matters, the preceding possibility assumes your craft is sitting dead in the water. If, on the other hand, you are making 8 knots to-

This autopilot mounts easily on any steering wheel shaft and can interface with Loran-C to steer to a waypoint or series of sequential waypoints automatically. (*King*)

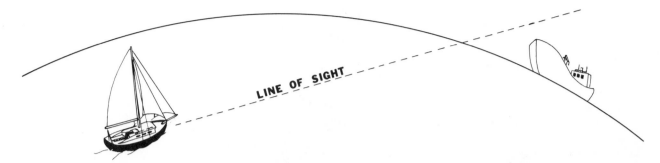

Why you shouldn't leave your autopilot "on watch".

ward an oncoming ship, your combined speeds further reduce the time before collision. If you absolutely must nap off because injury or illness (or choice) has left you short on crew, set an alarm and limit sleep periods to brief catnaps.

So, having emphasized the danger of using your autopilot to catch Zs, let's examine the device itself.

All autopilots are the same in a few respects. Obviously, all have some type of control to actuate the automatic circuitry. All have some type of compass or other sensing unit to detect the vessel's heading in true, magnetic, radio or other reference. And, of course, all have some type of power unit to change the boat's heading either by turning the existing rudder or an accessory rudder. These components may be combined in one device, or they may be three distinct modules, mounted at different points in the boat and connected by wires and cables.

Power Units

Although power units vary widely, there are three basic types: linear mechanical, rotary mechanical, and hydraulic. It is essential that you select the proper power unit for the type of boat *and* the type of boating you'll be doing. An offshore commercial powerboat, for example, may stay on autopilot control 90% of the time, while an afternoon sailor may only need the occasional extra "hand" when out by himself when a sudden squall calls for a change of headsails.

Another consideration is how your boat handles. A boat that handles easily may steer well under the control of a lightweight, low-cost autopilot. A crank craft with an outboard barndoor rudder may require greater force to keep the old gal on course.

Which power unit is best for you may be determined by consulting others with similar type vessels who have used one or another type of power unit. Ask around. But remember, what works well on one boat may not work at all on another.

Linear Power Unit

The simplest autopilot power unit consists of nothing more than an arm or bracket that attaches to the boat's tiller, pushing it from side to side as required. Typically, these are worm-gear driven by a low current electric motor powered by the main batteries. The complete autopilot is contained in one housing that mounts across the cockpit footwell. The control panel and direction sensing device are both contained within the simple (and inexpensive) mechanism. The entire unit can be removed at the end of the day and stowed safely below or packed up to be used on another boat. Delivery skippers sailing shorthanded find these simple autopilots adequate to assist them when making long and tedious offshore passages with limited manpower, since they can use the autopilot on practically any boat with tiller steering.

After initial adjustments are made to fit these simplest of autopilots to the cockpit seats or coamings, all that's required is a simple connec-

Autopilot at the tiller of a Westsail 32.

tion to the boat's battery supply using a two-conductor cable with wire gauges heavy enough to provide the required DC voltage and current to the device. (Consult the sections on voltage drop in the basic electronics chapter. Also consult the wire tables in the appendix and the manufacturer's specifications for voltage and current requirements of your individual unit.)

A second type of linear mechanical power unit is permanently installed in the boat. It is substantially more powerful, and it is significantly more expensive. These power units connect directly to the steering quadrant on the rudder shaft by

means of a push-pull rod similar to that used by the economy models—but the thrust required to control the rudder by direct connection to the rudder quadrant is several times that needed to force a tiller from side to side in the cockpit. These units should be installed by a professional.

Permanent power units operate by means of a stout pushrod. The power unit must be securely attached to the hull or some immovable structure, with minimal play between the power unit and rudder quadrant. Above all, there should be no flexing anywhere. Flexing can result in loosened fastenings or fatigued fittings.

The electrical power cable should be routed

Linear power unit connected to rudder quadrant.

directly to the voltage source (with a fuse or circuit breaker at the voltage source, of course). The wire used to supply electrical current to the power unit should be as short as possible and heavy enough to prevent dropping more than a few tenths of a volt. (Consult the chapter for electrical theory and the appendix for wire sizes and resistance tables.)

The position on the rudder quadrant at which the pushrod attaches to the quadrant affects the amount of force necessary to control the rudder. The further out from the rudder shaft the force is be applied (the longer the arm) the greater the torque on the rudder shaft. At the same time, however, a longer arm requires greater pushrod travel. This tradeoff must be considered when determining how to connect the pushrod to the quadrant.

Pushrod quadrant control is most effective within the first 20° or so either side of neutral rudder. As more rudder angle is applied, more force is required to further increase the rudder angle.

Rotary Power Unit

Rotary power units are, perhaps, the most common type used in small boat autopilots. Most are chain and sprocket driven, although a few newer units are providing direct drive to the shaft at the steering wheel, with self-contained control and direction sensing components in one package.

Torque from a sprocket on the power unit is transmitted to a second sprocket on either the rudder shaft itself or on the steering wheel shaft by means of a bicycle-type chain. The torque available for turning the helm can be multiplied or divided, as needed, by selecting different sprocket sizes for the power unit and for the helm or rudder shaft sprocket. If both sprockets have the same number of teeth, the torque ratio is 1:1. If the sprocket on the helm has twice as many teeth as the sprocket on the drive unit, the torque ratio is 2:1, and torque is multiplied by two.

The installing technician can determine the amount of torque required to turn the helm when the vessel is underway and select a suitable

sprocket combination. It must be kept in mind, however, that at high speed or in heavy weather, considerably more torque may be required to control the helm. The higher the torque ratio, the slower the helm will respond to the autopilot. In some cases, adequate torque can only be achieved by means of a beefier power unit.

The same rules about firm mounting used with linear power units apply equally to rotary power units. The power unit must be secured so its mountings cannot flex. The unit must be bolted, not screwed, in place—and lag bolts are not acceptable.

The power unit sprocket and the sprocket mounted on the helm or rudder shaft must be carefully aligned and in the same plane, so the chain travels fairly. A mounting should provide some means for adjusting chain tension. Consult the instructions for chain slack. Over-tensioning

Autopilot adapted for pedestal steering.

can cause premature chain failures. Chain and sprockets should be kept clean and well lubricated. Make certain the entire assembly is mounted where it can't get fouled by loose gear tumbling about in heavy weather.

Carry a spare chain and extra master link clip.

Hydraulic Power Unit

Larger craft with hydraulic steering use autopilots with hydraulic power units that connect directly to the vessel's hydraulic steering control lines. This is the best installation where hydraulic steering is used, since there are no moving parts and the system (properly installed) can not interfere with the manual steering system. Hire a competent shipyard or marine electronics technician experienced in installing hydraulic power units.

Do not use ordinary copper tubing for hydraulic lines. Special hydraulic lines are designed for the purpose; use them. Soft copper tubing can easily be punctured or may be weakened by unsuspected corrosion or electrolysis. Any potential for hydraulic fluid leaks must be prevented. Use hydraulic plumbing supplies only, and enlist the labors of an experienced technician unless you are confident in your own abilities as a plumber.

Compass Unit

Also called the sensor or sense unit, this part of the autopilot detects direction.

There exist three principal types of compass units: gyro, magnetic card, and flux gate. The gyro compass is, perhaps, more precise and reliable than the other two types, but it is also far more expensive and is commonly found only in commercial craft and the most luxurious world-class yachts.

The magnetic card compass is similar in function to the card compass you steer by. The principal difference is that the entire compass is enclosed so you can't see the card. Instead, a system of optical sensors electrically determine the card's position. These compasses are subject to the same characteristic problems that plague other card compasses. The jewelled support bearings wear out. They must be checked regularly for loss of fluid and topped-off if necessary. They must be mounted away from sources of magnetic interferenc, preferably near the vessel's center of motion to minimize errors caused by mechanical accelerations on the card.

The flux-gate compass must also be located free from nearby magnetic influences and near the vessel's center of motion. But flux-gate compasses have no moving parts (other than gimbals that hold the compass level). There are no optical sensors to burn out or be knocked out of alignment. The flux gate compass is entirely electronic—and thus maintenance-free.

Whichever type compass is selected, the principal problem is to mount the compass where it won't be subjected to wild motions. Autopilot compasses do *not* belong in the forepeak.

Autopilot with magnetic compass.

Autopilot control located within easy reach on flying bridge of cabin cruiser. (*IMI Southwest*)

Control Unit

Locating the control unit depends entirely on convenience and intended use. It is possible to have several control units located at various positions on the boat. In addition, hand-held controls are available to permit the operator to move about.

The most important factor when considering autopilot control units is the degree or variety of control desired. Some inexpensive units only allow the operator to change the vessel's heading. For the serious user, this is not enough.

Course Change

There are several ways to change course using an autopilot. One is to select the desired course by setting some sort of dial control or digital readout to indicate the heading in degrees (usually uncorrected for deviation or variation). Another is to disengage the autopilot, manually steer the vessel to the desired heading, and re-engage the pilot. A third is to push a button for port or starboard and wait until the vessel comes around to the new

heading, before releasing the course change button.

Clearly, some methods may be more suitable to your boating needs. Check the specifications before you buy.

Deadband

This control may have different names (e.g. sensitivity), or it may be combined with other controls

Control unit. Note rudder override buttons left and right.

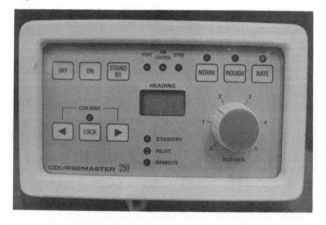

Wheelhouse of the
motorsailer *Aegis*.

and thus not be available separately. Deadband permits the vessel to wander off course by a certain adjustable amount before the autopilot attempts to turn the rudder. When running before a steep, following sea, for example, it may be desirable to limit the amount of rudder action and permit the vessel to deviate somewhat from an exact heading, rather than cranking away needlessly at the rudder in a vain attempt to keep the boat constantly on course. Many craft tend to average a steady course, even when the head is swinging to port and starboard as waves roll up and under the transom from astern. A deadband control minimizes needless oversteering, conserves batteries, reduces strain on the steering gear, and may provide a shorter passage time in the long run by letting the vessel follow its natural path through the water.

Under millpond conditions, on the other hand, it may be desirable to limit the amount of port or starboard deviation that is tolerated before the rudder angle is changed by the power unit. This is accomplished by setting the deadband control to its minimum.

Rudder Angle

Rudder angle controls, like deadband, may have many names or may be combined with deadband into a single control.

The rudder angle control simply limits the amount of rudder angle applied to correct an off-course condition. In extremely heavy weather, where steering is difficult and waves tend to throw the vessel's head from side to side, more rudder angle may be needed to hold her on course. In milder circumstances, there may be less need to so forcefully alter the vessel's head, and rudder angle can be set to a minimum to reduce wear and tear on the steering gear and conserve battery current.

The very latest autopilots are able to compute the amount of rudder angle to apply at any particular moment by an ingenious application of electronic memory and logic circuits based on rate of turn, last command to the power unit, etc.

Other autopilots employ a rudder feedback module to tell the control unit how much rudder angle is applied. The module should be adjusted precisely and should be secured firmly. The control cable should be routed to avoid damage.

A combination of microcomputer circuitry *and* rudder feedback may provide somewhat better overall steering response than either technology operating alone.

Some autopilots use rudder angle limit switches to prevent the autopilot power unit from forcing the rudder beyond its stop. The switches should be positioned and adjusted so the rudder can not turn beyond the autopilot manufacturer's recommendations. In most applications, rudder angle should be limited to no more than 45° either side of neutral amidships. Consult the owner's manual for technical specifications.

Dodge

A convenient control for operating in congested waters is the dodge. Activating this control causes the vessel to turn to port or starboard to avoid obstructions. When the dodge control is released, the autopilot once again brings the vessel back on its original heading.

This feature is especially useful on handheld control units. For example, an operator can use the dodge feature to con through dense fog while perched out on the bowsprit, crouched behind the forepulpit, or standing lookout in the rigging.

Loran-C Interface

Many autopilots are capable of accepting course correction information from a Loran-C receiver via an interface cable. Several interface "standards" exist in the industry at this time. However, if you want to take advantage of this technology, you must scrutinize the manufacturers' specifications before buying either Loran-C or autopilot to make certain the two are going to speak the same language. Interface protocols and data syntax are beyond the scope of this book. Ask your marine electronics dealer which language the units talk, and insist on knowing if the language is going to be compatible with other gear—like speed log, satnav, etc. Some manufacturers created their own interface language, so their autopilots only understand their Loran-C units.

Other manufacturers see the wisdom of adopting an industry-wide standard. However, only a few manufacturers have agreed to a standard. The National Marine Electronics Association's proposed standards have not met the approval of all the manufacturers, and some of the dissenters are leaders in this technology.

With a Loran-C interface, it's possible for an intelligent autopilot to correct for cross-track

error and follow any pre-selected course (or set of courses) between waypoints. (See chapter on Loran-C for explanation of waypoint programming.) If the vessel wanders off the desired courseline, the Loran-C sends a coded message to the autopilot, and the autopilot immediately alters the vessel's heading to bring the boat back to the desired track.

This option can result in tremendous savings in fuel for powerboat owners, and may reduce passage times for sailing craft as well (assuming fair winds).

Before opting for this function, however, consider the need. Unless you intend to perform some type of oceanographic survey or have some other reason to follow a precise path over the bottom, this interface may not be needed. The old-fashioned human interface performs the same function quite nicely, and at a fraction of the cost. If, for example, your Loran-C shows cross-track error of 3/10 mile to port, while the autopilot is steering 108°, it's a relatively simple matter to reach over and manually change the autopilot heading to 112°, bringing the vessel back on track. No expensive interface required.

In fact, there may be more total wandering with an interface system when the autopilot has to constantly keep up with changing information from the Loran-C. On the other hand, if mere mortals make occasional changes to the autopilot setting as needed, the total distance sailed may, in fact, be much shorter—with less wear and tear on the steering gear.

The decision depends primarily on your intended use.

Features

The trend in autopilots, as with all marine electronics, is toward increased use of microcomputer circuits. Certainly, an autopilot that can "think" has countless advantages over one that relies on older, more mechanical technologies. Automatic steering offers countless challenges to engineers hoping to beat out the competition and provide more machine for less money.

Some autopilots use their smarts to perform dy-

Autopilot control with digital/analog compass readout. Note self-test display in window.

namic self-tests on internal circuits, power units, direction sensors, and feedback modules. These state-of-the-art autopilots may not malfunction any less often, but they can tell you what's wrong when they do! (Well, at least so long as the self-test circuits continue to operate properly.) Digital code displays correspond to various internal failures. Office copiers have been performing this amazing feat for years, and we may expect to see much more of this practical application in the months to come.

An off-course alarm is offered on some of the spiffier units, alerting the crew if the autopilot is no longer able to continue tracking the selected course.

Conclusion

Autopilots vary widely in performance and cost. Commercial operators (and small boat sailors with extra cash) may insist on the most powerful, the most exotic, the most expensive. The rest of us won't demand nearly so much.

It needs to be said, however, that there may come a time when you'll wish you had a first-rate autopilot to take over the helm while you shorten sail or secure a liferaft cannister that has broken loose and threatens to be washed away by the next boarding greybeard. A spare hand in a storm can make all the difference. In heavy weather,

however, an inexpensive autopilot may be more hazard than help. If you anticipate sailing where the weather can kick up to a stiff Force 7 on occasion, it is well worth the price to install a beefy unit you can count on.

An improperly installed autopilot can cause more problems than it relieves—in some cases resulting in damage to the manual steering functions so the boat cannot be steered at all! Proper installation is imperative.

Finally, autopilots have no eyes. They are not intended to replace the human lookout. Only in the most extreme emergency should the pilot be relied upon to steer your boat without an alert crewperson on watch.

Autopilot control in cockpit of modern sailboat.

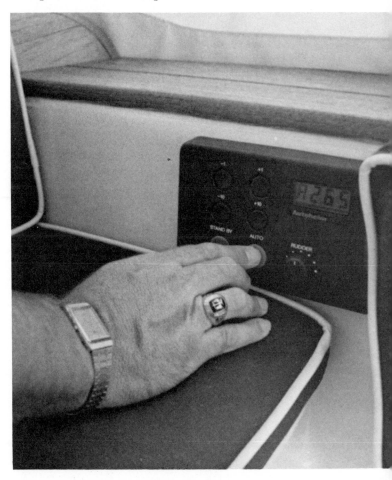

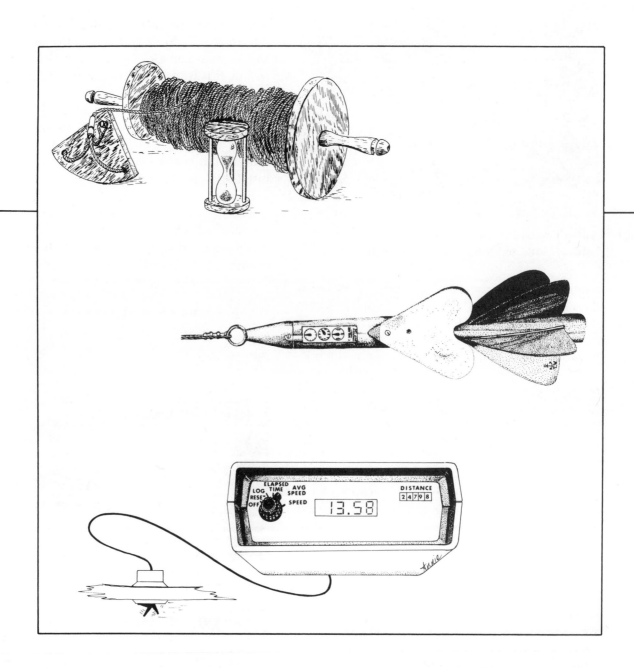

CHAPTER 14

Speed–Distance Instruments

Not many years ago the only speed-distance instruments for small craft were mechanical devices. Knotmeters operated just like the speedometer in your car. A pointer and resettable trip log were driven by a small propeller under the hull connected to the dial with a mechanical cable. The propeller suffered from fouling, and the cable was prone to rust. Accuracy was always questionable. Reliability was equally uncertain.

Taffrail logs using a heavy torpedo-like spinner towed behind the boat on a braided line were preferred by serious offshore sailors. The spinner was towed well aft and deep below the surface away from wake turbulence. The best are costly but provide accurate distance measurements—except where sargassum or other floating weed fouls the spinner or where sharks and other ichthyian creatures attack the spinning "bait". Today's wise offshore skippers keep a mechanical taffrail log on board as a reliable backup—insurance against electronic log failure.

With the advent of transistors in the fifties,

Early mechanical impeller speed log transducer. This spinner drives a mechanical shaft attached to a dial in the cockpit.

Modern speed log impeller.

electronic logs began to be seen in small craft. A magnetic impeller, in the shape of a propeller or paddlewheel, extends into the water. As the boat moves through the water, the impeller is set spinning. The spinning magnet, in turn, induces an alternating current in a pickup coil built into the through-hull unit. This current is measured and displayed on a meter calibrated in knots. Wires, not mechanical cables, connect the impeller with its dial. Reliability is improved.

The principle of the spinning magnetic impeller and pick-up coil, sometimes called a speed transducer, is still used. Modern pick-ups don't measure voltage, however. They count pulses caused by the spinning magnet. Digital circuits convert the pulse count directly into speed. Accuracy is far greater.

Many other improvements have also been made.

Today's logs have better spinner designs, reducing fouling and errors caused by slippage and impeller cavitation. The latest spinners grab the water better as it flows around the hull. The result is improved accuracy at all speeds.

Battery drain is minimized through the use of complementary metal-oxide (CMOS) integrated circuits and low-power liquid crystal displays.

Interfaces to other equipment are already a re-

ality. By the end of the century, central processing computer modules will be commonplace in small craft. A master "brain" will monitor the vessel's speed, course, current position, fuel economy, effect of sail trim, distance to destination, and anticipated time of arrival. Weather instruments will be interfaced to predict the likelihood of fog or unfavorable winds, and the central computer will suggest course modifications or send direct commands to the autopilot to change course to take advantage of favorable weather and tidal current conditions.

An elegant voice will speak to you in the language of your choice while color pictures will appear on glowing panels, showing wind direction, subsurface obstructions, current, buoy positions, and quality of the helmsman's steering. At the heart of it all will be some type of speed log.

By interfacing logs to flux-gate compasses, devices available *today* yield far more than speed and distance! They provide a constantly updated display of your dead-reckoning position—no matter how many times you tack back and forth. Give it the coordinates of your present position and the coordinates of your destination, and an internal computer can calculate the great-circle or rhumbline bearing and distance to go. If you're tacking to windward, the computer interrogates the log to determine speed through the water and interrogates the flux-gate compass to determine

Low-current liquid crystal dual display of boat speed and engine tachometer. Such combination displays can aid in finding the optimum speed for power boats. (*Aqua Meter*)

Integrated speed log, depth sounder, and wind instrument. Upper display is remote readout that can be mounted anywhere on board. (*SR Mariner*)

heading, constantly updating your actual position on its display. Bearing and distance to any selected waypoint are available at the touch of a button.

Some units provide automatic correction of DR position to account for errors resulting from an unknown current. The operator inputs his coordinates at known positions when fixes are available. The computer notes the difference between the computed DR and the fix coordinates. The computer then calculates current set and drift to account for the difference. The computed values are stored in the internal memory. The operator can request computed DR with or without correction based on estimated current—or he may input current predictions based on tabular or charted data.

Sailors especially benefit from these new devices since they we spend so much time "zig-zagging" from place to place. Distance made good means little when that distance was sailed in umpteen different directions. Through the miracles of microcomputers and the flux-gate compass, DR position corrected for set and drift is constantly available.

Doppler Log

The most accurate (and most costly) speed logs operate on the Doppler principle, reading actual speed over the bottom.

They are, however, limited by depth. Logs capable of operating beyond the continental shelf are egregiously expensive. Some Dopplers, however, are within the price range of small craft operators.

Doppler logs operate by transmitting pulses of sonic energy to the bottom by means of directional transducers. Large ships (and world-class yachts) use quadri-directional transducers so vessel speed is known axially, i.e., not only forward or reverse speed but lateral velocity as well. Doppler speed measurement remains accurate

Multi-display unit.

even when operating at docking speeds. In fact, some large ships use two transducers, one forward and one aft, so the pilot can give commands to the docking tugs based on minute motions of the ship.

Doppler logs and flux-gate compasses can be interfaced to satellite navigation equipment, greatly improving the accuracy of sat-nav positions between transits. Sat-navs don't know where they are between transits. The Doppler log gives speed made good over the bottom. If this information is combined with compass data, the computer in the satellite navigation gear can provide a fairly accurate DR position between transits.

Some units automatically compute current set and drift, correcting values at each transit fix. The differences between DR positions and fixes obtained by satellite transits are used to determine the values for set and drift used in subsequent running fixes between transits, providing even greater accuracy.

Other logs can be interfaced to satellite equipment also. If the sat-nav computer is programmed with the latest algorithms, it can correct for errors due to current (after several transits) so a standard log can provide performance nearly equal to that of an expensive Doppler log. The computer merely adjusts to compensate for the through the water readings.

Accuracy

The latest impeller-driven speed logs have vastly improved accuracy over their predecessors. Logs on the market today use speed averaging, under microcomputer control, cancelling errors in speed due to the vessel's pitching and yawing motion.

Without microprocessor averaging, speed measured through a heavy sea would differ from that over a millpond. Water molecules don't just move up and down as waves roll by. They follow elliptical paths, moving forward at the crests, backward in the troughs. As the waves get higher, this effect becomes more pronouced. Water atop a big wave is moving forward, while water in the trough is moving backward. The problem is that the total forward motion is greater than the total

Log with speed averaging.

motion aft—resulting in an overall transport along the direction of the wind.

A microcomputer can analyze incredibly small changes, almost infinitessimal intervals of time, and determine an average speed, based on measurements taken when your boat is on top of the waves and measurements taken when you were wallowing in the troughs.

Calibration

All speed logs require some amount of calibration.

Differences between impeller locations and variations in hull shape make it impossible for manufacturers to pre-calibrate their units for every shape and type of boat.

The purpose of calibration is to determine how the speed log readings compare with known speeds. If a speed log is adjustable, it can be compensated for errors. If not, a table can be prepared to convert measured speeds to true speeds.

Remember: Except for Doppler logs, speed measurements are referenced to the water, not the bottom. Readings don't reveal the effect of leeway. If a current exists, speed over the bottom is in error by the amount of current plus any leeway. Corrections for current and leeway are always needed.

Calibration is easy. Select two points between which the distance is accurately known. Calibration ranges erected for the purpose are so-marked on some charts, but any two points will do if you know the exact distance between them. Distance

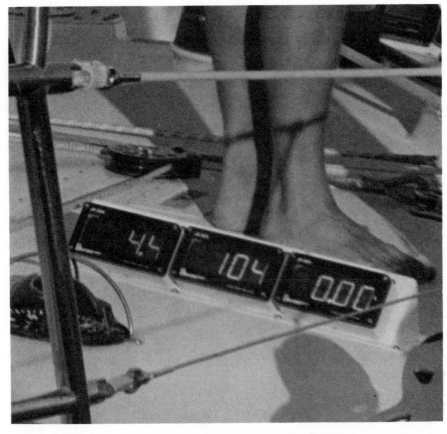

Wind and speed log displays mounted at deck level.

can be measured by the chart, radar, or any reliable method.

Be wary of buoys. They move.

Unless you're absolutely certain no current is running at the time of your test, you should make reciprocal runs to cancel effects due to current. Measure the time required to go from one point to the other; then use the following equation to calculate your speed. Also make a note of the speed log reading.

Multiply distance run (in nautical miles) by 60, then divide by time of run (in minutes) to get speed in knots.

$$\text{Speed} = \frac{60 \times \text{Distance}}{\text{Time}}$$

If the two reciprocal speeds aren't the same, add the speeds together and divide by two.

Average the speeds, not the times.

For best results, run the measured course several times, in both directions, and at different speeds. Compare the calculated speeds with the measured speeds per the speed log. If the log is adjustable, make small changes between runs errors remain at *all* speeds. If the log cannot be adjusted, make a table of the differences between the log readings and actual speeds at each speed. Keep this record as a conversion table to correct speed log readings to true (through the water) speed.

Installation

The most important point to keep in mind when installing a speed log is the location of the impeller or transducer. It should be mounted well below the waterline where it won't be exposed when the vessel rolls and pitches in a heavy sea.

It should be mounted where total vessel motion is minimized, i.e., near the center of the boat. If mounted too far forward, the impeller will pick up errors due to the plunging bow. If too far aft, errors due to wake turbulence may be introduced.

Another consideration is access from the bilge.

Speed log through-hull transducer located below sole where it can be cleaned and serviced from inside the boat. Notice similar plug in bracket? It's used to keep water out when transducer is removed for servicing.

Many units can be removed from inside the boat for cleaning or inspection. If the dinette has to be disassembled to get to the transducer in the bilge, the unit is in the wrong location.

The transducer cable should not be routed through greasy bilgewater. It should be routed up and away from the bilge, preferably up under the side decks and thence to the control/display unit.

Mounting the display unit requires only common sense, since most are totally waterproof. Mount the display where it is easily seen from the helm. A small awning or brow coaming can be fitted to the display to reduce glare.

See the chapter on general installation techniques for more details and tips on mounting brackets, cable connections, etc.

Console with instruments for depth, wind speed and direction, and speed through the water. (*Coastal Navigator*)

Conclusion

Next to a compass and depth sounder, a speed log is probably the most useful navigation device.

With interfaces to flux-gate compasses, satellite equipment, and other electronic gear, extremely precise and reliable data is available to the navigator.

Finally, one of the most practical applications of speed log and flux-gate technology is the interface to wind instruments, an option discussed more fully in the next chapter.

CHAPTER 15

Wind Instruments

Once upon a time, the most practical wind instruments were a few strips of lightweight fabric tied to shrouds and backstay. Strips cut from nylon stockings worked quite well and required no batteries. If the strips stood out, nearly horizontal, one knew the wind was strong. If the strips flew off to one side or the other, one knew the wind was right for a reach.

Electronics soon displaced these durable friends with costly dials and guages to show wind speed and direction by positions of meter needles or little boat-like shapes that turned behind round windows. Some of us were not impressed. We kept our wisps of rag.

Accuracy and readability were not exceptional. A good sailor could tell where the wind was by the feel of it and the sounds it made in his ears as he turned his head from side to side. Guages,

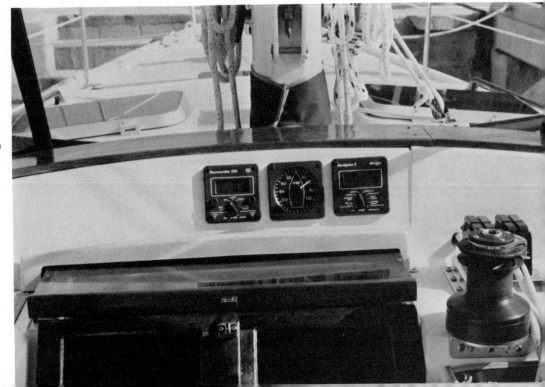

Digital depth sounder, wind indicator, and speed log displays at companionway of center-cockpit motorsailer. (*IMI Southwest*)

Wind instrument mounted atop coffee grinder.

Wind speed and direction indicators with masthead unit. (*Ray Jefferson*)

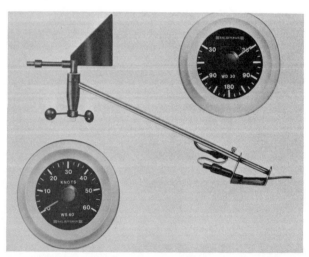

dials, and meters couldn't compare with the skill of experience.

That has changed now.

The Technology

Today's wind instruments are valuable counselors, providing essential information for cruising sailors as well as those who enjoy competing.

Accuracy is so improved that zephyrs can be detected. Minute changes in wind speed and direction can be sensed and displayed. Optical sensors detect the rate of rotation of tri-cup spinners and the position of the direction vane. Mechanical and magnetic interference is minimized, since light beams are used to detect the motions of the tri-cups and vane. In the old days, magnetic sensors were used to detect the wind. The sensitivity of these devices was limited in that a significant amount of force was needed to overcome magnetic friction. By using infrared sensors, the only friction left is in the bearings supporting the devices. There are no magnetic fields to overcome. The result, of course, is greatly improved sensitivity and accuracy.

But accuracy is just the beginning.

Microcomputers are now interfaced with speed logs and flux-gate compasses to provide such invaluable readings as true wind direction, wind direction relative to ship's heading, velocity made good to windward, or velocity made good along a pre-selected course!

Sailing at top or optimum speed is just as important for the cruising sailor as it is for racing enthusiasts. In the long run, it may be more important. Obviously, cruising folks needn't mount great long-armed coffee grinders on deck to sheet in ten-acre headsails, but where a simple sail change now and then or a slight tweak on the mainsheet can improve velocity made good to the next gunkhole anchorage—why not?

Today's latest wind instruments provide the information needed to confidently make those sail adjustments.

The optimum course to steer when sailing close-hauled is not necessarily the closest course to the wind! Many beginners believe that the

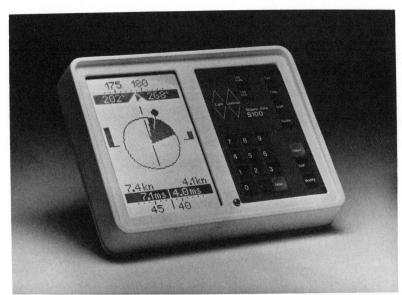

Integrated wind computer.

Hand-held wind speed instrument. (*Sims*)

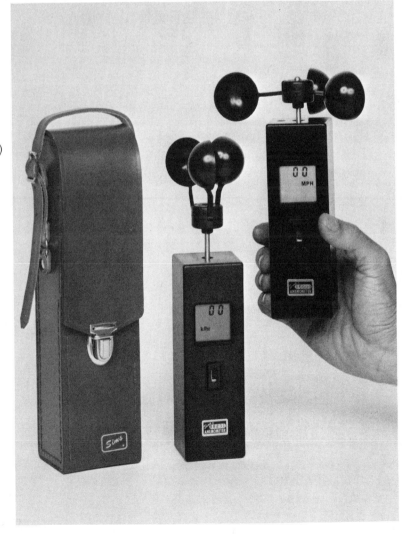

This single display shows wind speed digitally with apparent wind angle indicated by a meter needle. (*Kenyon*)

closer they sheet their sails and the closer they point into the eye of the wind, the better their windward progress. In fact, that is seldom the case. Obviously, if one sails too close to the wind, the boat slows down or stops altogether.

Of course, sailing too far off the wind adds extra distance.

Somewhere in between is the optimum course for optimum speed to windward. Sail higher on the wind or farther off the wind, and that efficiency is lost.

Sailing downwind offers a similar problem. It's not always faster to sail dead before the wind, even if your destination is straight downwind. With the wind a bit on the quarter, the total efficiency of most spreads of canvas is increased, making tacking downwind as important at times as tacking upwind.

Today, however, thanks again to the marvels of microcomputer technology, wind instruments can tell you when your progress to windward or leeward is at its peak. You can quickly find the best course to steer and trim your sails for maximum speed—without using seat-of-the-pants technology or some other arcane indicator of sailing efficiency.

Installation

Installing wind instruments is pretty much the same as any other piece of gear. Power is usually no problem, since today's units need so little of it. However, a few special considerations deserve attention here.

You might think the top of your mast is the best place for the anemometer and windvane because it's free from turbulence and in the wind flow. Actually, wind flow on the very truck of a mast is quite complex and confused. Updrafts blast along the sails, mixing with surrounding flow.

Wind sensor mounted on boom ahead of mast to avoid turbulence. Note VHF antenna at masthead where it belongs.

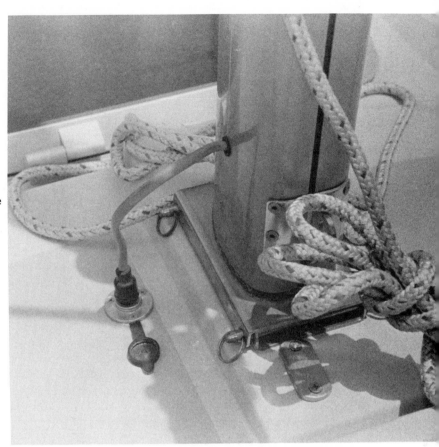

Waterproof plug makes mast removal easier. Note cap to cover receptacle when plug is not installed. This type of step required the socket to be mounted beside the mast. Some stepped-on-deck masts permit the socket to be mounted directly under the hollow mast to minimize exposure to moisture. Other masts are stepped through the deck, of course, and the cable can be led out through a slot at the base of the mast inside the boat.

The best location for your wind instruments is ahead of the mast on a boom. Most manufacturers provide such a boom.

The instruments should be securely mounted, of course, and some particular care should be taken to align the base of the vane unit with the vessel's fore-and-aft line. If the base is not lined up during installation, vane readings will be in error.

If cable connectors are provided near the masthead unit so the vane and anemometer can be removed from the mast without pulling the cable up through the mast (and pulling it back through again later), servicing the masthead unit will be easier. Using connectors in cables to masthead devices is good practice with all types of gear. The connector must be absolutely impervious to weather. Use silicone grease on pins and sockets. Wrap the connector with waterproof tape. Secure the cables so water will run away from the connectors, not into them.

Masthead installations proceed much more quickly and safely with the mast sturdily supported horizontally on the ground. It's hard to concentrate when you're trying not to fall out of a bosn's chair.

Ideas for routing cables inside your mast are offered in the installation chapter.

PART V

Fundamentals

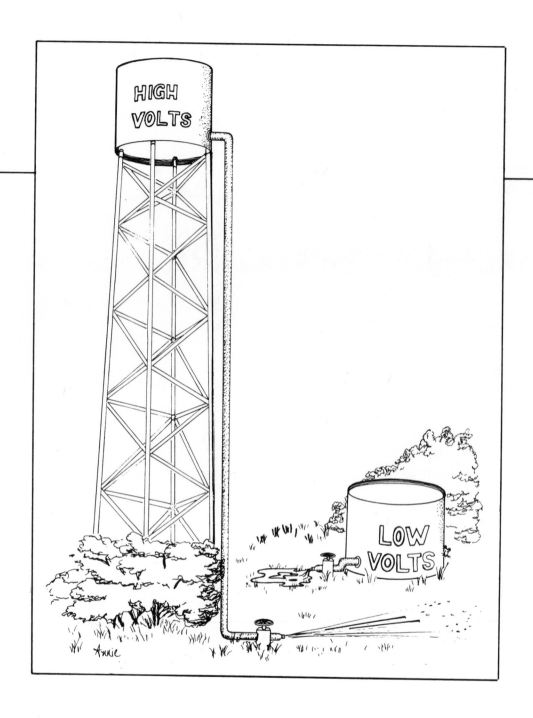

CHAPTER 16

Circuit Fundamentals

Introduction—The Electron

All electronic equipment depends on the predictable behavior of tiny particles of matter called electrons.

All electrons are identical. There's no real difference between them. Each is a discrete unit, actually an atomic sub-particle, carrying a negative charge, and possessing a rest mass of 1/100,-000,000,000,000,000,000,000,000 grams.

Since electrons have such small mass, they're easy to get moving. The slightest force sets them in motion. They move through wires, through integrated circuits, through transistors, through speaker coils, through microphones, through depth sounder transducers, through radar scanners—predictably obeying simple laws—doing work for us.

Everything around us contains electrons. In most materials the electron content is balanced by a proton complement that cancels the negative charge, leaving a net charge of zero. When you rub a rubber rod with wool, you transfer excess electrons to the rod. Since electrons don't move about easily in dry rubber, they tend to stay

All electrons behave pretty much the same.

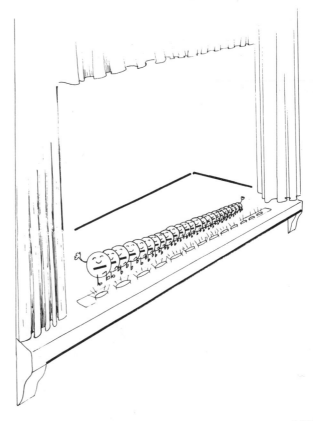

205

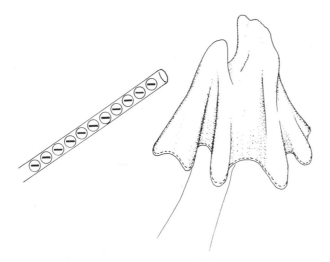

After rubbing with wool, the rubber rod has an excess of electrons and an overall negative charge.

natural distribution, driving them away from the rubber rod and onto the opposite side of the cork. The net charge on the cork remains neutral (since the number of electrons in the cork is unchanged) but the near side of the cork has a temporary electron deficiency, creating an area of positive charge. This area of positive charge is attracted to the negatively charged rubber rod.

But, if the cork ball touches the rubber rod—*BINGO!*

It jumps away. Some of the excess electrons in the rubber rod move over to the cork ball, giving the cork more than its normal complement of electrons. Now the cork is negative—just like the rubber rod.

The result? Like charges repel. So the little cork ball jumps away.

This simple experiment proves that electrons have charge, that electrons exert a force on other electrons, and that electrons are able to move readily from place to place.

Electrons (and all the other sub-atomic particles) are special, almost mystical, entities. For example, all apples are apples; but some are red, some are yellow, some are green. All electrons are electrons; but every electron is *precisely* the same. There's no real difference between them. Their essential nature is as yet unknown and unlikely to be understood anytime soon. They are certainly unlike anything we can observe in the visible world around us, things we can touch and examine with our senses.

Instead, we must content ourselves with ob-

in the rod once you put them there (instead of flowing back into your hand). So, for a few minutes at least, the rubber rod has an excess of electrons and a net negative charge.

If the charged rubber rod is brought near a cork ball, its extra electrons repel the natural electrons in the cork ball, forcing some of them to move to the far side of the cork. The effect is to leave a net positive charge on the near side of the cork. A positive electrostatic charge is induced on the near side of the cork ball. The negative field surrounding the excess electrons on the rubber rod interacts with the negative fields surrounding the electrons on the cork, interfering with their

Induced charge on rubber rod.

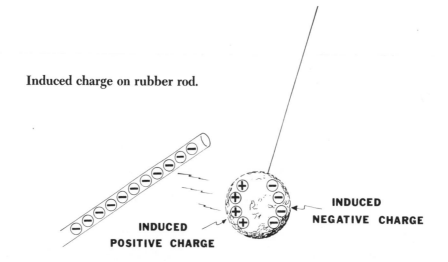

INDUCED POSITIVE CHARGE

INDUCED NEGATIVE CHARGE

Electrostatic force.

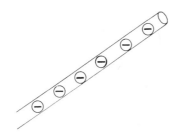

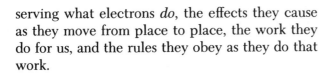

serving what electrons *do*, the effects they cause as they move from place to place, the work they do for us, and the rules they obey as they do that work.

Electrical Values

So, we need to understand the ground rules, the changeless laws that electrons inviolably obey.

Before we can take advantage of the marvelous work electrons do, we must first exert a force to make them move. Left to themselves, electrons tend to stay in one place. Trillions of dollars are spent each year as steam turbines, diesel power plants, solar panels, nuclear generators, hydroelectric dams, and even windmills work day and night to force the little fellows from one place to another.

Electrons move easily through materials we call conductors, a little less easily through materials we call semiconductors, and almost not at all through materials we call insulators. Gold is the best conductor of all. Silver is second. Copper is third. Aluminum is inferior to copper and should not be used as an electrical conductor when copper can be used instead.

Silicon and germanium, the substances transistors and diodes are made of, are examples of semiconductors. Semiconductors offer the advantage of being adjustable conductors. Their utility comes from the fact that a vast flow of electrons can be controlled by a tiny electrical impulse.

Glass, rubber, epoxy, dry wood, air, and vacuum are examples of insulators—under most conditions. But moisture, especially the salty damp so common to the marine environment, can render an otherwise safe insulator totally ineffective. A three-foot length of dry fir might be a suitable insulator to pick up a fallen wire on a farm in dusty Kansas, but the same board used for a similar purpose down at the dock may conduct just enough electrical power to stop your heart.

Whether electrons move through conductors, semiconductors, or even insulators (lightning is a striking example of electrons moving through an insulator), their rapid motion results in work being done on the environment. Invariably, there is some amount of heat released within the material through which they move. Heat is usually an unwanted waste of energy in electric circuits, but in some applications it may be the result desired—like heating an iron to press your shirt or raising the temperature of a tungsten filament in your bunk lamp to provide enough light to read by.

Two other effects of electrons on the move are the creation of magnetic and electrostatic fields. These are essential to the functioning of radio, radar, and other marine electronic equipment.

To make electrons work for us—either creating heat in a filament or force fields in an antenna or electric motor—we must apply an outside force. This force is called electromotive force or EMF. It is measured in volts.

Remember this: voltage is the force applied to

Sometimes electrical energy is wasted as heat.

the electrons in a circuit. It is neither work nor energy. It is only force. If an extremely high voltage is applied to a circuit , but electrons don't move—no work is done, and no energy is expended.

Voltage can be likened to water pressure in a pipe. Pressure for city water systems is created by storing water in a tank atop a high tower or building. The tank is like a battery. Water force (voltage) depends upon how high the tank is. A higher tank exerts more pressure on the water in the pipes of your house, just like a higher voltage battery exerts more pressure on electrons in the wires of your marine radio or spotlight.

If we replace the water tank (battery) with a motor-driven pump, our analogy is that of an electrical generator. Both apply pressure.

The speed at which electrons move does not depend upon the electromotive force (voltage) applied to the circuit. In fact, electrons travel at a relatively constant speed in any given conductor material. That speed is nearly the speed of light.

What does happen when the voltage is increased is that *more* electrons move, i.e., the amount of electron current increases.

Electron current is measured in amperes or amps. The amount of work done, and the amount of energy used, depends upon how many electrons are moving and how much pressure is pushing them. If a given number of electrons move through a conductor past a particular point in the circuit in one second, we say that one ampere of current is flowing. The number of electrons used to measure one ampere is quite large. The number is so large, in fact, that it has a special name of its own, the coulomb.

One coulomb = 6,250,000,000,000,000,000 electrons

$$\text{or } 6.25 \times 10^{18} \text{ e}^-$$

When six quintillion two hundred fifty quadrillion electrons flow through a circuit in one second, we say there is a current of one ampere. Fortunately, believe it or not, the flow of electrons is always impeded by the materials—even gold—through which we make them move. Impedance to one-way (DC) electron flow in circuits is called resistance and is measured in "ohms". If electrical circuits had no resistance at all, we'd have no way to limit the amount of current flowing. Our circuits would run wild.

Resistance limits current—voltage tends to increase it.

These three parameters—voltage, current, resistance—are the principal measurements used in electrical calculations. Voltage is the force or pressure that makes electrons move. Resistance is the factor that tends to impede their motion. Current is the amount of electrons actually on the move, the rate of electron flow (in coulombs per second). Increase the voltage, and the current increases. Increase the resistance, and the current decreases. It's that simple.

Ohm's Law

A simple but useful and inviolable law that anyone can use to predict the behavior of electrical circuits is Ohm's Law, named in honor of Georg Simon Ohm (1787–1854) who first wrote about the unchanging relationship between voltage, current, and resistance. If we know the electromotive force applied to a circuit in volts and the electrical resistance of that circuit in ohms, we can easily calculate the amount of current that will flow in the circuit. On the other hand, knowing the current and resistance of a circuit, we can find the applied voltage. We can calculate the resistance, of course, if we know the applied voltage and how much current is flowing.

In other words, if we know two of the values, we can readily calculate the third.

Ohm's Law is expressed by the following equation:

$$E = I\,R.$$

Electromotive Force (E in volts) equals current (I in amps) times resistance (R in ohms). If you remember this one equation, noticing that the letters are in alphabetical order, you can rearrange the terms using the rules of algebra to derive two other equations.

$$\text{since } E = I\,R$$
$$\text{therefore } I = E/R$$
$$\text{and } R = E/I$$

Let's apply it.

For example, suppose you plan to connect some electrical device directly to the ship's DC voltage supply. The device requires 10 amperes at 12.6 volts (the nominal voltage of a 12V lead-acid storage battery at full charge). What is the internal resistance of the device? Let's use Ohm's Law to find out.

$$E = I\,R$$
$$\text{so, } R = E/I$$
$$\text{and, } R = 12.6\,/\,10 = 1.26 \text{ ohms}$$

Knowing the resistance of a device is extremely important when you're laying out a new circuit and need to know what wire size is suitable. Let's examine a slightly more complex situation.

Imagine you're installing a new gadget that needs a minimum of 4 amperes to function prop-

erly. Let's assume your boat is a sailboat. You don't run the engine or stay plugged into the dock to keep your batteries fully charged, so you can expect battery supply voltage to drop as low as 12 volts from time to time. The new gadget you're installing has an internal resistance of 2 ohms. If the wires from the battery are perfect conductors, the only resistance in the circuit is that of your new gadget: 2 ohms. Using Ohm's Law we can calculate how much current will flow through the gadget if we connect it to the battery using perfect conductors.

$$E = I\,R$$
$$\text{so, } I = E/R$$
$$\text{and, } I = 12\,/\,2 = 6 \text{ amperes}$$

With 6 amperes, the device will work just fine since we said the gadget needs only 4 amperes to function properly.

But you don't have perfect, resistance-free conductors. Suppose all you have is a reel of 28 gauge wire. Does this make a difference?

The answer is *Yes*! It makes a critical difference. The 28 gauge wire is quite small. It offers a resistance of 65 ohms for every 1000 feet. If, after routing the wire around bulkheads and under the cabin sole, the length of wire required for the round trip is 50 feet, then the resistance of the 50 feet of 28 gauge wire itself is

$$(50\,/\,1000) \times 65 = 3.25 \text{ ohms}$$

Add this 3.25 ohms to the 2 ohms of your new gadget, and you have a total circuit resistance of 5.25 ohms.

Now what happens when you throw the switch?

The battery's 12 volts tries to push electrons through the wire's 3.25 ohms and the gadget's 2 ohms. The amount of current that can be delivered through the unit by the push of 12 volts is found by using Ohm's Law again.

$$E = I\,R$$
$$\text{so, } I = E/R$$
$$\text{and, } I = 12\,/\,5.25 = 2.3 \text{ amperes}$$

That's not enough! Your new gadget needs at least 4 amps to operate at peak performance. You'll have to shorten the length of 28 gauge wire or use bigger wire. Remember, the resistance of a wire counts going to and from the battery.

Let's see how short we need to make those power leads, if all we have is 28 gauge wire (about the heft of speaker wire).

First, what is the maximum total circuit resistance that will permit 4 amperes to flow when the battery is pumping only 12 volts instead of its fully charged potential of 12.6 V? To find out we use Ohm's Law again.

$$E = I\,R$$
$$\text{so, } R = E/I$$
$$\text{and, } R = 12\,/\,4 = 3 \text{ ohms}$$

You'll remember that your new gadget has an internal resistance of 2 ohms. That means the wire we use to connect it to the battery can have no more than 1 ohm of resistance *in the total circuit*—coming and going. The resistance of 1000 feet of 28 gauge wire is 65 ohms. (Tables of wire sizes and resistances are included in the appendix for your convenience.) Using algebra we can solve for the length of 28 gauge wire that has a resistance on only 1 ohm.

$$l = 1000\,/\,65 = 15.4 \text{ feet}$$

So, if you use only 15.4 feet of 28 gauge wire to connect your new gadget to the battery, the gadget will work fine even when the battery voltage drops to 12 volts.

Again, however, the 15.4 feet is the total allowable length of wire permitted, so the gadget can be no farther than half of 15.4 feet from the battery. Maximum length of the paired power cable, using 28 gauge wire, is then 7.7 feet. If you try to defeat Ohm's Law, you'll find your gadget will either work poorly or not at all.

This practical application of Ohm's Law is critical when you are connecting marine electronics equipment to the battery. Many problems with marine electronics equipment can be corrected by replacing the DC supply lines with larger wire. The wire size and resistance table appear-

ing in the appendix gives standard copper wire sizes and their resistances in ohms per thousand feet. Refer to this table when deciding what size wire to use for connecting lights, radios, or any device requiring a known minimum value of electrical current.

Corroded contacts and connections are a common source of unwanted resistance in electrical circuits on boats. Only clean, bright metal surfaces provide zero resistance. Any corrosion between the mating surfaces of a wire and screw, between two wires, or between the base of a light bulb and its socket serves to impede the flow of electrons—thereby increasing resistance. A section of the trouble-shooting chapter addresses the problems of corrosion and electrolysis.

Electrical Power

Electrical power is measured in watts. Two simple equations allow us to calculate the amount of power a device (or connecting wire) can dissipate. In the first equation, power (in watts) equals the product of the EMF (electromagnetic force in volts) times the current (in amperes).

$$P = I\,E$$

In the second equation, power (in watts) equals the square of the current (in amperes) times the resistance (in ohms).

$$P = I^2\,R$$

Suppose 12.6 volts are applied to a device with a resistance of 2.1 ohms. How much power will be generated in the device? We can find the answer by using either power equation. First, however, we need to know how much current will flow through the device when the voltage is applied. To calculate the current when we know the voltage and resistance, we use Ohm's Law

$$E = I\,R$$
$$\text{so, } I = E/R$$
$$\text{and, } I = 12.6\,/\,2.1 = 6 \text{ amperes}$$

Now that we know how much current flows through the device, we can use a power formula to determine how many watts are dissipated by the device. Let's try the first formula.

$$P = I\,E$$
$$\text{so, } P = 6 \times 12.6 = 75.6 \text{ watts}$$

Do we get the same answer using the other equation? Let's try it and see.

$$P = I^2\,R$$
$$\text{so, } P = 6^2 \times 2.1 = 36 \times 2.1 = 75.6 \text{ watts}$$

Let's try another example. You want to put a reading lamp in your bunk, but you're worried about the drain on your batteries. The bulb is marked 25W. How much current will it require at 12.6 volts? The answer is found using simple algebra again.

$$P = I\,E$$
$$\text{so, } I = P/E$$
$$\text{and, } I = 25 / 12.6 = 1.98 \text{ amps}$$

If you were interested in the operating resistance of the lightbulb, you can refer again to Ohm's Law.

$$E = I\,R$$
$$\text{so, } R = E/I$$
$$\text{and, } R = 12.6 / 1.98 = 6.4 \text{ ohms}$$

The digital meter shows 7.5 volts are applied to the circuit containing a 2000 ohm resistor. The analog meter shows 3.75 milliamperes are flowing through the resistor, just as Ohms Law decrees! The 9-volt battery used for this demonstration is nearly dead, hence the 7.5 volt reading.

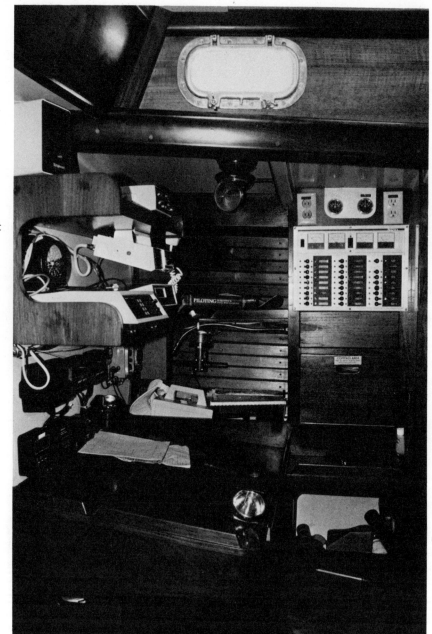

A compact and convenient electronics installation.

Voltage Drop

When resistance is present in a circuit conducting current, there will always be a voltage difference between the point where current enters the resistance and the point where current comes out of the resistance. This difference is called voltage drop.

The current flowing into a circuit element must equal the current coming out the other side, but the pressure (voltage) causing the flow is reduced by the element.

The amount of voltage dropped by a circuit component depends on the component's resistance and the amount of current flowing through it. If the current increases, the voltage drop across

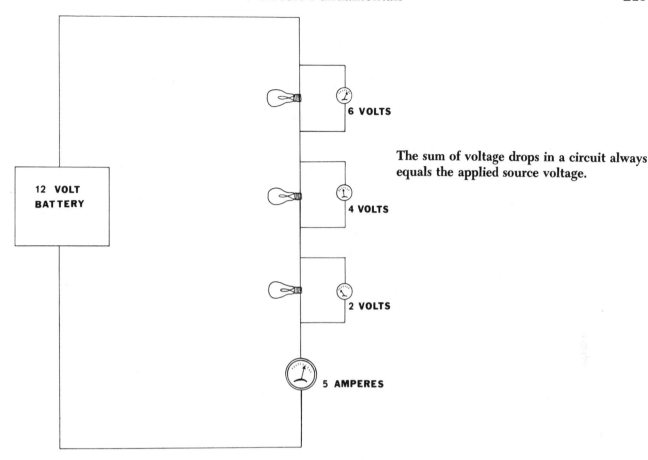

The sum of voltage drops in a circuit always equals the applied source voltage.

the element also increases. If several elements are connected in series so the same amount of current flows through each, the element with the greatest resistance will cause the greatest voltage drop.

The measurement of voltage drops can be used to advantage in many situations—especially when you're sleuthing out a problem in a faulty circuit. If you know a circuit component's resistance and can measure the amount of voltage drop across that component, you can calculate the current flowing through the component using Ohm's Law. If there is no voltage drop at all, you know how there is no current in that component.

Voltage drop is measured in volts. It is the difference in EMF (voltage) potential between any two points in a circuit. The sum of voltage drops in a circuit always equals the applied source voltage.

Thus, if three different light bulbs are connected in series with a 12V battery, each will cause a proportional voltage drop in the circuit, and all the drops will equal the source voltage.

We can read the individual voltage drops by attaching a voltmeter across each of the circuit elements.

In a series circuit, the rate of current through each of the circuit components is equal to the rate of current through each of the other components—including the source.

Note: Since we know how much current is flowing in each of the bulbs in the above circuit, we can readily find the amount of power (in watts) that is radiated by each of the bulbs. We can even calculate the operating resistance of each bulb.

In a series circuit carrying 5 amperes of current, the bulb causing a 6V drop dissipates 30 watts and has a resistance of 1.2 ohms.

$$P = I\,E$$
$$\text{so, } P = 5\times6 = 30 \text{ watts}$$
$$E = I\,R$$
$$R = E/I$$
$$\text{so, } R = 6\,/\,5 = 1.2 \text{ ohms}$$

Likewise, the bulb causing a 4V drop dissipates 20 watts and has a resistance of 0.8 ohms, and the bulb causing a 2V drop dissipates 10 watts and has a resistance of 0.4 ohms.

Here's another useful application of what we now know about voltage drops. Remember that wherever there is resistance in a circuit, *carrying current*, there will be a measurable voltage drop across that resistance. We can use this fact to test for faulty connections, i.e., connections with unwanted resistance such as those which all too often result when terminals on power cables corrode or when contacts in a switch are burned. (Again, refer to the section on meters in the troubleshooting chapter.)

Conclusion

The rules and laws of electricity *never* change. Rely upon them. Work with them. Look over the examples again. Memorize Ohm's Law and at least one of the power equations. They'll come up again and again as you work with electricity.

It bears noting that the principles above apply strictly to direct current (DC) circuits—the kind that are powered by batteries. Alternating current (AC) has some special rules of its own, but that's beyond the scope of this book. Several reference books are listed in the bibliography for the reader who wants to dig a little deeper in the mysteries of circuit analysis.

CHAPTER **17**

Batteries

Your boat's storage batteries are essential to the reliable operation of every electronics device on board. You could say the batteries form the backbone of your boat's electrical system.

Even when the engines are running, your batteries play an important role in the boat's electrical supply circuits, serving to maintain voltages at constant levels—keeping voltage up when heavy

Wind-powered generator to keep the batteries of this ocean cruiser charged.

loads are added to the circuit and absorbing transient high-voltage "spikes" caused by relaxing inductive fields such as those created by solenoid valves or electric motors. This ability to regulate voltage is extremely important. Should your batteries be disconnected by mistake, so that the only source of electrical power is an engine-driven generator or alternator, the resulting voltage fluctuations may be so extreme that sensitive electronic equipment may function improperly or be permanently damaged. Batteries are not just storage devices. They are active components, essential to the proper operation of every electrical and electronic device on board.

Reliable battery performance depends on routine service. Applying simple, common-sense battery fundamentals can extend a battery's life well beyond the manufacturer's warranty period. Longer life means fewer purchases and added savings.

It's important to install the proper type of battery to meet the needs of your boating needs. Boat manufacturers may deliver a new boat without batteries, or with only one. On boats with in-

Running a battery down until it's stone dead is the worst thing you can do to it.

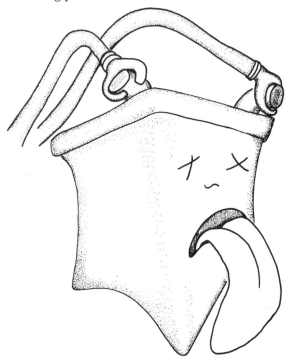

board engines, most experts agree that two batteries are the minimum—one to be kept in reserve for engine starting, the other to power lights and gadgets while the engine isn't running. As you begin to add electrical and electronic equipment to your boat, you'll find greater need for reserve battery power. When you replace the original batteries, you may decide to install heavier batteries with additional reserve power. The larger batteries may cost more initially, but they'll last longer in heavy use.

Keeping the batteries charged is another critical factor. If you allow your batteries to repeatedly run down between charging, you may find yourself complaining in only a few months about that five-year guarantee the salesman offered. Batteries are not designed to be completely discharged, *ever*. Running a battery down until it's stone dead is the worst thing you can do to it. Even a recreational vehicle (RV) battery that is intended to be used for long periods between charging will suffer if it isn't recharged before its voltage drains away to nothing.

Overcharging can be equally damaging if the battery's water level is allowed to drop below the tops of the plates inside the battery or if the temperature inside the battery is allowed to rise until the plates buckle. Charging must be controlled. The battery should be kept charged, but it should not be overcharged. Chargers, charging rates, and methods to monitor a battery's state of charge are included in the pages that follow.

Safety

Batteries can be dangerous.

The electrical power stored in a fully charged battery can melt solid iron, start a fire, or completely destroy an expensive electronic device. If a steel wrench is accidently dropped across the terminals of a 12V battery, the resulting current flow through the wrench can release enough heat to literally melt the wrench in two! There's always the danger of fire when live electrical connections are made, especially when a battery cable is connected to the terminals. To avoid sparks, all electrical loads should be switched off before connecting battery terminals. If a battery is accidentally connected backwards, i.e., with reversed polarity, to an unprotected solid-state device, the components in that device may be *immediately* destroyed. Batteries contain tremendous power and should be treated with respect.

Batteries also generate two highly hazardous gases: hydrogen and oxygen. Individually these gases are relatively harmless, but in combination they are highly explosive. Batteries should be installed where there is ample ventilation to prevent the buildup of these gases. Fortunately, both gases are lighter than air and will not accumulate in the bilge as gasoline vapors do. However, they may accumulate just under the overhead, or in pockets under the deck in the engine room, or under the lid of a tightly fitting battery box. A few cubic inches of the mixed gases can do serious damage if ignited by a spark or open flame. Avoid this danger. Ventilate the battery installation.

Most dangerous of all, perhaps, is the heavy liquid inside the battery—the sulfuric acid electrolyte. Sulfuric acid, even the dilute solution used in batteries, is an extremely corrosive substance. If it splashes on your clothes it will eat holes in them. If it splashes on your skin it will cause deep and painful burns. If it splashes in your eyes it may cause permanent blindness. The immediate antidote for contact with sulfuric acid is liberal and continuous flushing with water or any water-base liquid—fresh water, seawater, milk, soda pop— anything to wash away the acid will work. Use lots of it. A solution of baking soda, baking powder, milk of magnesia or any antacid will neutralize the electrolyte. But keep flushing the contaminated area while you make up an antacid solution. Flush immediately and continuously. If the acid is in your eyes, summon a physician *at once*. Force the eyelids open and flood the surface of the eye with cool, clean water for at least five minutes. Use no neutralizing solution in the eye without the doctor's advice. Even if you feel no discomfort, there may be tissue damage that deserves immediate medical attention.

If a child should swallow battery acid, force the child to drink large quantities of milk or water. Follow with an antacid liquid or salad oil. Again, summon a doctor *at once*!

When diluting concentrated sulfuric acid to make electrolyte solution, ALWAYS ADD ACID TO WATER, and not the other way around. Sulfuric acid has a chemical affinity for water. When the two are mixed, tremendous heat is released. If water is added to the acid by mistake, the water may be heated into steam, pop and sputter, causing acid to be thrown violently from the container. Remember that "A" comes before "W", so add Acid to Water. And add small amounts while stirring constantly to disperse the heat. If the solution gets noticeably hot, allow it to cool before adding more acid. Do not use metallic or metal-lined containers (lead is an exception to this rule).

Store replacement battery acid where it can't be spilled, where children can't play with it, and where it won't be exposed to excess heat or direct sunlight.

Use a battery carrier to lift and transport batteries. If you must transport a battery by hand, lift from opposite corners. Never lift a battery by pressing against the sides or ends as the walls of battery cases are not built to withstand pressure. Using the walls as lift points may cause the case to fracture or result in forcing acid from the cell caps on top of the battery.

Never lean over a battery that is being charged or one that is being used to start or jump-start an engine. The charging process releases explosive hydrogen gas. A tiny spark can cause the hydrogen to explode, bursting the battery case, and drenching you with battery acid. The rapid discharging process of starting an engine (or powering any low resistance circuit) creates enough heat to boil the electrolyte, possibly rupturing the battery case or causing acid to spew from the cell caps. Wear eye protection.

When attaching a battery charger or adding a circuit, make certain the charger or circuit is turned off before connecting the wires to the battery terminals. It takes just one spark to ignite the hydrogen in a battery and cause an explosion. Keep all open flames and sparks away from the battery at all times. Always shut down the battery charger and all other circuits before disconnecting from the battery.

Ventilate the battery compartment to prevent hydrogen buildup. Vent caps are available to re-

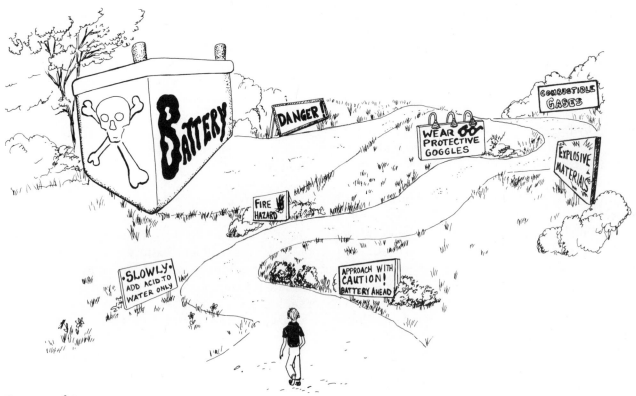

Battery safety.

duce the risk of explosion by providing a flame barrier between the inside of the battery and the world outside. Keep caps in place when charging.

If dense fumes or smoke arise from the battery at any time, shut down all circuits and disconnect the battery cables at once. Wear eye protection. Keep a fire extinguisher handy.

Battery Fundamentals

Most boats today use 12V lead-acid storage batteries similar to the batteries used in automobiles. Marine batteries are built more ruggedly than auto batteries and are recommended if available, but an auto battery will work as a replacement if it's all you can find.

An exception is the sailboat or other craft that doesn't use an engine or shore power to keep its batteries constantly charged to their full voltage level (12.6 volts). These vessels may drain the battery nearly dead between rechargings. Such deep discharges can damage regular batteries—even

marine batteries. If this is the type of use you anticipate, you may decide to install special recreational vehicle (RV) or golf-cart batteries. These special batteries are built specifically to withstand deep discharges and long periods between recharging. More on this later.

A few boats use 32V batteries, and only rarely does one find a 6V system. Most use 12V systems. Nearly everything in marine electronics is built to run on a 12V supply. The technology of 12V battery construction is established—hence 12V batteries cost less and are more widely available.

There is an advantage to higher voltage systems, however, especially for powering running lights, deck lights, interior lights, etc. Remember the power equations?

$$P = I\,E$$
$$P = I^2 R$$

Suppose you want to power a 48 watt light bulb from a 12V battery. Using the first power equation you can find the amount of current that must flow through the bulb under a pressure of 12V to yield a power output of 48 watts.

$$P = I\,E$$
$$so,\ I = P/E$$
$$and,\ I = 48\,/\,12 = 4\ amperes$$

Now let's try it with a 32V system.

$$I = P/E$$
$$so,\ I = 48\,/\,32 = 1.5\ amperes$$

But, you may argue, a watt is a watt is a watt. That's certainly true. But don't forget that the wires between the battery and the bulbs at the top of the mast or up in the chain locker offer resistance to the flow of current, and that resistance to current causes a voltage drop and lost energy due to heating of the wire. The more current that flows, the more energy loss due to heating. By increasing voltage, we can deliver the same amount of power to the lightbulb but with less current and less wasted energy.

Suppose the distance from the batteries to the masthead light and back is 150 feet. Also suppose that the light is wired with 14 gauge copper wire with a resistance of 2.5 ohms per 1000 feet. The resistance of 150 feet can be found as follows.

$$R = (150\,/\,1000) \times 2.5 = 0.375\ ohms$$

That certainly doesn't seem like much. However, let us use the second power equation to find out how many watts will be lost due to heating the wire, comparing the power lost using 12V to the power lost using 32V.

$$P = I^2 R$$

$$so,\ P = 4^2 \times 0.375 = 6\ watts\ for\ the\ 12V\ circuit$$
$$and,\ P = 1.5^2 \times 0.375 = 0.84\ watts\ for\ the\ 32V\ circuit$$

The 32V circuit is seven times as efficient as the 12V circuit.

Please notice, before we leave this subject, that lower voltage circuits require heavier gauge wires (lower resistance) to deliver the same power. To deliver 24 watts at 6V, 4 amps must flow. To deliver 24 watts at 12V, only 2 amps must flow. But notice that power dissipated in a resistance varies as the square of current, so 4 amps dissipates four times as much wasted energy as 2 amps flowing in the same length of wire.

Still 12V batteries are the standard in most boats. The essential principles are pretty much the same for all batteries; only the specific numbers change. Much of what we discover in this chapter applies equally to 12V, 32V and 6V systems. The principles of lead-acid storage batteries, do's and don'ts, preventive maintenance routines, and the causes of premature system failure are independent of voltage ratings. Charging rates and voltages given in the following pages are specific for 12V batteries. More data on batteries in general or other types of batteries in particular is available from: Battery Council International, 111 East Wacker Drive, Chicago, IL 60601. Telephone 312/644–6610. The Battery Council publishes some excellent technical manuals. This organization has been compiling data on batteries since 1924.

Battery Chemistry

Batteries store electrical energy by means of chemistry. As the battery discharges, one set of substances is chemically converted into a second set of substances. When the battery is recharged, the second set of substances is reconverted back into the original set of substances, and the process is ready to take place again.

Fundamentally, the battery consists of two sets of plates immersed in a solution of sulfuric acid (H_2SO_4). One set of plates, the plates connected to the positive battery terminal, is composed of a paste of lead dioxide (PbO_2) pressed into a matrix frame that holds it in place. The other set of plates, the plates connected to the negative battery terminal, is composed of sponge lead (Pb) with traces of other metals to increase the plates' strength. The H_2SO_4 solution dissociates into H^+ ions and HSO_4^- radicals. (A radical is just another name for an ion that is composed of more than one atom. Ions and radicals carry an electrical charge.) In the fully charged battery, then, we find a set of Pb plates, a set of PbO_2 plates, a number of H^+ ions, an equal number of HSO_4^- radicals, and water.

When these ingredients combine, the following reaction wants to occur:

$$Pb + PbO_2 + 2H^+ + 2HSO_4^- \rightarrow 2PbSO_4 + 2H_2O$$

The chemical tendency for this reaction to occur determines a battery's voltage, the force exerted on electrons in a circuit connected to its terminals. In the lead-acid storage battery, the electromotive force created by each fully charged cell is 2.1 volts. Cell voltage is thus 2.1 volts per cell. In a 12V battery, there are six such cells connected in series, hence the total battery voltage equals 12.6 volts (when fully charged).

In order to convert the Pb and PbO_2 into $PbSO_4$, the Pb must transfer electrons to the PbO_2. This it cannot do directly. The electrons require a path between the Pb plates and PbO_2 plates, i.e., between the negative and positive terminals of the battery. We supply this path when we connect external circuits between the battery terminals: running lights, Loran receivers, bilge pumps. The chemical tendency of the discharge reaction causes electrons to flow through any circuits we connect *outside* the battery. The electrons are forced to move from the negative Pb plates, out the negative battery terminal, through any external circuit connected to the battery, back into the positive battery terminal, and finally to the PbO_2 plates where the chemical action is complete.

Notice that the Pb and PbO_2 convert to $PbSO_4$, lead sulfate, in the process of discharging the battery. At the same time, the concentration of H_2SO_4 decreases. As the amount of $PbSO_4$ builds up, and the concentration of H_2SO_4 goes down, the battery potential (voltage) drops. If too much $PbSO_4$ builds up on the plates, as will happen when a battery is completely discharged, the battery can be permanently damaged. This is why a battery should always be recharged before it goes completely dead. If you want a battery to last beyond the manufacturer's warranty period, keep it charged to within 10% of its fully charged state whenever possible.

The discharge process discussed above is the same for all lead-acid batteries and essentially the same as that which takes place in any kind of battery regardless of type—flashlight batteries, hearing aid batteries, spacecraft batteries, even rechargeable nickel-cadmium batteries like the ones in your electric shaver. The only difference is the chemistry inside.

In order to pump a charge back into a lead-acid battery, we force the substances inside the battery to revert to their original identities. They don't want to do this, so we apply work to the battery and *make* it happen. What's needed is some external electrical force (voltage) to pump electrons away from the PbO_2 plates and back to the Pb plates. This electrical work can be done by connecting the battery to an engine-driven or wind-driven generator, to solar panels on deck, or to a shore-powered battery charger like those used in engine shops or automotive service stations.

The chemical equation for recharging a lead-acid battery is just the reverse of the discharging equation shown above.

$$2PbSO_4 + 2H_2O \rightarrow Pb + PbO_2 + 2H^+ + 2HSO_4^-$$

When the charging process is complete, all of the substances have been forced to return to their original state, and we say the battery is fully charged. We simply force electrons into the battery terminals in reverse order, converting all the $PbSO_4$ back into Pb and PbO_2. Since these original substances still tend to be $PbSO_4$, the battery has regained its *voltage*.

Unfortunately, the charge/discharge cycle can not be repeated indefinitely. Subtle physical and chemical changes take place with each cycle. If the battery is discharged rapidly and completely, not so subtle changes may take place; the battery can be permanently damaged by the intense chemical activity and heat created by the rapid discharge process. The damage may make it impossible for the battery to be restored to its original charged condition. If a battery is allowed to sit for long periods without charging or replacement of lost water, it can discharge itself, dry out, and be rendered forever useless. Bad batteries can be replaced with new ones, or they can sometimes be rebuilt. Contact a battery specialist (not a service station attendant) to find out if rebuilding is possible with the type of batteries you're using. If you decide to replace with new batteries, ask for an exchange credit on your old batteries.

Testing and Charging

In general, lead-acid storage batteries last longer if they are discharged slowly and not deeply. For long battery life, keep your batteries charged—but do not overcharge.

The state of charge in a battery can be determined two ways: by measuring cell voltage with a digital voltmeter (See chapter on trouble-shooting for tips on using meters.) or by measuring specific gravity (density) of the electrolyte with a hydrometer. A needle movement type meter is not accurate enough to measure state of charge.

Refer to the following table to determine state of charge in your battery using a digital voltmeter. The leads of the voltmeter should be connected across the terminals of the battery. The temperature of the battery should be between 60° and 100° Fahrenheit.

TABLE 17-1

STATE OF CHARGE BY OPEN-CIRCUIT VOLTAGE

OPEN-CIRCUIT VOLTAGE	STATE OF CHARGE
12.6 and up	—full—
12.4–12.6	75–100%
12.2–12.4	50– 75%
12.0–12.2	25– 50%
11.7–12.0	0– 25%
below 11.7	—dead—

By permission of Battery Council International

The voltages listed in the table above must be measured with no circuit drain on the battery. Measurements should not be made immediately after the battery is taken off charge or immediately after it has been subjected to a high current load. Allow 10–15 minutes for settling before testing.

Since the difference in voltage between a fully charged battery and one that's stone dead is only 9/10 volt, the measurement must be made with a calibrated digital voltmeter (or a voltmeter with an expanded scale).

The digital voltmeter method of measuring state of charge gives only an approximate indication of battery condition, but is far easier to accomplish than the hydrometer method that follows. With a calibrated digital voltmeter mounted in the chartroom bulkhead and connected across the output terminals of your main battery switch, you can keep tabs on your batteries' condition with ease.

When you want to take a more accurate assessment of battery condition, the hydrometer can be used (requiring a trip to the battery compartment). A hydrometer is an instrument for measuring the specific gravity (density) of liquids as compared to water. Water weighs precisely one gram per cubic centimeter. Its density is 1.000 g/cm^3. Its specific gravity is 1.000.

The specific gravity of any other liquid can be measured by comparing its density to that of water. The acid electrolyte in a fully charged battery is 1.265 times as dense as water, so we say its specific gravity is 1.265 (at 80° Fahrenheit or 26.7° Celsius).

The hydrometer is nothing more than a glass or plastic tube with a weighted float inside and a rubber bulb on top. A flexible hose at the bottom is placed into the opening of a battery cell, and the rubber bulb draws the acid electrolyte up into the hydrometer. As the liquid rises in the hydrometer, the weighted float may rise with it, floating at a particular level depending upon the specific gravity of the liquid. If specific gravity is high, the float will ride higher in the tube. If specific gravity is low, the float will sink lower or perhaps not rise at all.

A calibrated scale shows the specific gravity of the liquid being tested. This scale is made for readings at 80° Fahrenheit. At other temperatures, the reading requires a correction. Note that we're concerned about electrolyte temperature. Some hydrometers include a built-in thermometer to measure the temperature of the electrolyte. If yours does not, you can use any glass bulb thermometer.

You can see from hydrometer temperature corrections chart in the appendix that for every 10° rise above 80° Fahrenheit (or 5.5° rise above 26.7° Celsius), you should add 0.004 to the measured specific gravity to get a corrected reading, and for every 10° drop below 80° Fahrenheit (or 5.5° drop below 26.7° Celsius), you should subtract 0.004 from the measured specific gravity to get a corrected reading.

Glass hydrometers are easier to see through than their less expensive plastic counterparts, but glass is far more susceptible to breakage. Plastic hydrometers tend to become cloudy with time, and they are more easily scratched. The real cheapies with little colored balls that float or sink depending on the state of charge of the battery are not accurate enough for serious battery care.

Plastic or glass, the hydrometer should be kept clean and in a protected location near the batteries where it won't be lost or damaged. A convenient storage device is a short length of plastic pipe, capped at the bottom and mounted vertically on a bulkhead near the batteries. The pipe protects the hydrometer from damage and contains any droplets of acid that might otherwise get mixed in with your tools and cause unwanted corrosion and/or burns.

TABLE 17-2

STATE OF CHARGE BY SPECIFIC GRAVITY

SPECIFIC GRAVITY	STATE OF CHARGE
1.265	—full—
1.225	75%
1.190	50%
1.155	25%
1.120	—dead—

By permission of Battery Council International

Batteries are rated by their electrical capacity as measured in ampere-hours (A.H.). If a battery is rated at 100 A.H., it can deliver 100 amperes for 1 hour, or 10 amperes for 10 hours, or 1000 amperes for 6 minutes. Of course these are ideal figures, but the principle remains: the higher the ampere-hour rating, the more electrical energy that can be stored in the battery.

Now suppose that a 100 A.H. battery is 50% discharged and needs recharging. Fifty ampere-hours are missing and must be replaced. This we do with the charging system. We can pump 50

amperes back into the battery for a period of one hour, or we can pump 10 amperes back into the battery for 5 hours, or we can pump 5 amperes back into the battery for 10 hours. However we go about it, we need to replace 50 ampere-hours of electricity (plus 20% due to efficiency losses).

Notice, however, that a 50 ampere charging rate could cause damaging temperatures within the battery. When we are charging a battery, we have to be concerned about the battery's internal resistance and the heat that is released whenever current flows through an electrical resistance. Remember that the amount of heat released increases as the square of the current so that a 10 ampere rate of charge releases four times as much heat as a 5 ampere charge, and a 50 ampere rate of charge releases 100 times as much heat as a 5 ampere charge. Electrolyte temperature should not be permitted to exceed 125° Fahrenheit (51.7° Celsius).

Engine-driven charging systems, generators or alternators, should deliver approximately 14.4 volts to the batteries. In higher temperatures, however, this may be too high a charging voltage, and at lower temperatures 14.4 volts may not be high enough to keep a good battery fully charged. Many charging systems have fixed voltage regulation. Others permit adjusting the charging voltage to suit climate or other variables. If a battery will not charge higher than 75%, the charging voltage should be increased. If the battery is using excess water so that more than one or two ounces per cell must be replaced each 50 hours of charging time, reduce the charging voltage. Refer to manufacturer's literature for complete information on adjusting charging voltages.

So-called low water-loss batteries do lose water if charged too rapidly. However, these batteries are built so lost water can not be replaced! Either don't overcharge or don't use low water-loss batteries in your boat.

Remember that amount of charge is measured in ampere-hours and is calculated by multiplying the rate of charge in amperes by the duration of charge in hours. Add 20% for inefficiency.

Whenever possible, it is always best to charge with low current for long periods, rather than at high current for short periods. Of course, if you're

For longer life, protect cockpit instruments with a plastic cover when you aren't using them. Sunlight can ruin them.

charging with the engine-driven alternator or generator your only control over charging rate is to adjust the charging voltage at the voltage regulator. But, if you're using a battery charger connected to shore power or on-board AC, you do have a choice.

To avoid overcharging, first check the state of charge with a hydrometer (or a digital voltmeter) to determine percentage of ampere-hours still in the battery. Second, subtract the state of charge percentage from the battery capacity. If a 100 A.H. battery is 40% charged, you need to replace 60 A.H. plus 20% or a total of 72 A.H.

Batteries are sometimes rated in terms of reserve capacity, rather than ampere-hours. Reserve capacity is the number of minutes a battery can deliver a constant current of 25 amperes. A battery rated at 200 reserve minutes can deliver 25 amperes for 200 minutes. This rating is used for automotive battery sales—representing the approximate length of time the battery can continue to supply electrical energy to your automobile after the alternator or generator quits. The 25 ampere rating assumes a worst condition with windshield wipers, low-beam headlamps, and ignition all drawing energy from the battery.

Reserve capacity can be converted roughly into ampere-hours by converting to ampere-minutes then dividing by 60. Thus, a 180 reserve minute battery is roughly equivalent to a 75 A.H. rating.

Charging rate depends in part on your charger. Inexpensive chargers rely on the battery's rising voltage to reduce charging current. As the battery takes a charge, its voltage increases and opposes the charger's voltage thus reducing the charging current. These chargers supply a fixed output voltage near 14.4 volts when connected to 110 volt AC supply. If the AC supply voltage is high or low, the charging voltage will be high or low accordingly. The only regulation is that which the battery provides. If you leave one of these chargers attached to the battery, it will continue to pump reverse charging current through the battery, even after the battery is completely charged. The battery can be damaged by overheating or by excessive water loss.

The battery electrolyte will bubble when fully charged. This is called "gassing". When all the $PbSO_4$ has been reconverted to Pb and PbO_2 by the reverse charging current, the charging current begins to decompose the water (H_2O) in the electrolyte, releasing hydrogen and oxygen (the gases that form an explosive mix!). If a battery is allowed to continue gassing for an extended period, enough water may be lost to expose the tops of the plates to air, causing permanent damage. The plates must remain covered with electrolyte at all times. Water must be replaced as it is lost.

The best water for battery work is distilled water. However, almost any water fit to drink may be used unless it contains large amounts of minerals.

Incidentally, inexpensive chargers can be quite dangerous! All chargers use some type of transformer to reduce shore power voltage to battery voltage. The very cheapest transformers won't isolate the shore power circuit from the charging circuit.

Notice that the non-isolating transformer ties one leg of the shore power to one side of the charging circuit. Result? One side of your 12V system may be "hot" with respect to the 110 volt shore power! This can be both hazardous to your health *and* result in rapid electrolysis damage. Look for an Underwriters Laboratory seal. Avoid chargers with non-isolating transformers.

If your charger permits adjusting the charging current, you can change the rate of charge to suit your needs. A totally dead battery can be put on quick charge, but quick charge should not exceed 60 amperes and should be reduced if excessive gassing or high temperature results. The duration of quick charge depends on the battery's rated reserve capacity. A table of recommended charging rates and times appears in the appendix. This table gives the recommended charging rates and durations to restore a totally dead battery to 70–90%. Choose the slower charge whenever possible.

A good rule of thumb for slow charging is to charge at a rate equal to one ampere for each positive plate per cell. If the battery has 11 plates per cell, 5 of them will be positive plates (in most batteries) so 5 amperes is the optimum slow charge rate. If 50 ampere-hours must be replaced by charging, plus 20% for inefficiency, you can leave the battery on charge at 5 amperes for 12 hours (60 ampere-hours total).

To make certain you don't overcharge, test the electrolyte at one-hour intervals. When an hour

NON - ISOLATING

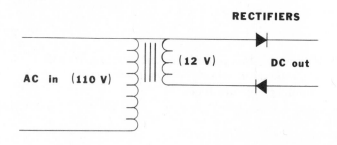

ISOLATING

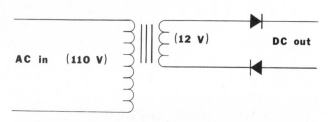

Isolating and Non-isolating transformers.

on slow charge results in less than a 3 point (0.003) increase in specific gravity, and gas is being evolved from each cell, the battery is fully charged. Further charging will only deplete the water level and result in overheating.

If the electrolyte temperature rises above 125° Fahrenheit (51.6° Celsius) or if the amount of gassing seems extreme, reduce or stop charging until the battery cools.

Automatic chargers include special sensing circuits that monitor the battery voltage and reduce the charging rate according to the amount of charge in the battery. As the battery becomes more fully charged, the automatic circuitry reduces the amount of charging current until at full charge the charger turns itself off.

Beware of imitations, however. The term "automatic" may mean the charger automatically switches from 12V to 6V if used on a 6V battery. A true automatic charger adjusts the charging rate to suit the amount of charge still needed by the battery, reducing the charging current as the battery voltage increases.

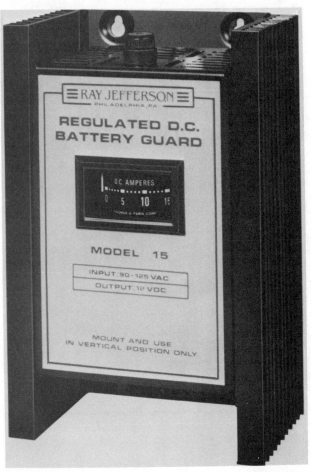

Automatic battery charger.

Do not attempt to charge a frozen battery. Bring the battery temperature to 60° Fahrenheit (15° Celsius) before charging. A fully-charged battery will not freeze until the mercury drops to *71° below zero* Fahrenheit (–57° Celsius), but a dead battery can freeze at 19° Fahrenheit (–7° Celsius). Keep your batteries charged—especially when cold weather threatens.

Maintenance

Batteries need lots of care to provide long and dependable service. You may trust the local garage or gas station to service your automobile's battery, but the care of your boat's batteries depends on you. Routine service will save you money by extending the life of your batteries.

It is essential that the batteries be secured so they can't be tossed around in heavy weather. Lead-acid storage batteries are heavy objects and can do serious damage if permitted to bounce about. The batteries should be mounted in plastic or lead-lined boxes to prevent acid spills from reaching wood or metal.

Better yet, keep the acid cleaned up. A small amount of acid on the top of a battery case can provide a path for current leaks that can drain the battery dead. Keep the battery clean. A mild solution of baking soda or baking powder does a good job of neutralizing acid spills. A toothbrush will let you scrub away at the acid-soaked dirt. Use eye protection!

Keep the battery filled. Cover the plates with about ½ inch of water. To prevent spills, do not fill to the rim. If the battery has level indicators in the cell filler openings, fill to these indicators and no higher.

Keep terminals and cable connectors clean and tight. Special terminal cleaning brushes are available at auto supply stores. Some models can be chucked in a drill motor for effortless and thorough cleaning.

Inspect the battery cables often. Acid and ubiquitous marine corrosion erode the cable where it meets the connector. Individual wires in the cable may break at this point, increasing resistance and decreasing the current-carrying ability of the cable. If this occurs, it is not necessary to replace the entire cable. Many battery service companies sell cable repair kits. The kit includes a new battery terminal connector on a short length of heavy cable with a special adaptor that can be attached to your old cable using a pair of wrenches. Just cut the old connector off using a hacksaw (better than bolt cutters) and attach the repair kit.

Selecting the Right Battery

Manufacturers offer many types of batteries for different applications, including so-called "marine batteries". As a top executive of one battery manufacturer admits, however, a marine battery may be nothing more than an automobile battery with wing-nut terminals and a carrying strap! The

Notice DC monitor panel. Such instruments indicate battery condition and amount of load on the DC system.

insides may be identical to an ordinary automobile battery with the same capacity rating.

Batteries differ primarily in two respects: ability to deliver current and ability to be deeply discharged between charges. These are the parameters you should look for when buying a battery. If you aren't going to be hauling the battery down the dock each time you use the boat, you don't need a fancy carrying strap. Besides, battery carriers exist that will work with *any* battery. And adaptors are readily available to convert an automobile battery terminal for use with wing-nut connections.

Cold-cranking capacity is a rating sometimes given for a new battery. It is the number of amperes the battery can deliver for 30 seconds with-

out dropping below a certain cell voltage. Higher cold-cranking capacity means better engine starting. Diesel engines need more cranking capacity than gasoline engines. An eight-cylinder engine needs more cranking capacity than one with four cyclinders. Read the literature supplied with your engine or starter motor. If the answer isn't there, consult a marine mechanic.

In addition to the engine starting battery, you may want one or more deep discharge batteries for powering the radios, lights, refrigeration, or other electrical devices while the engine isn't running. These batteries may *not* have high cold-cranking capacity but should have a high ampere-hour or reserve capacity since they are not going to be used (and should *not* be used) to start the engine(s). They are for powering moderate electrical loads for long periods between charging.

But, again, beware. Batteries sold for recreational vehicles (RV batteries) may not be true deep-discharge batteries. Examine the literature closely. What you want are deep cycle batteries to provide continuous power when the engines are not running. Deep cycle batteries *will* be damaged if you repeatedly drain their every last electron before recharging, but they last much longer than regular automotive or marine engine-starting batteries in an identical deep-cycle service. It is never a good idea to let *any* battery run dead. Even deep-cycle batteries should be recharged daily if possible.

Always switch to your engine starting battery to fire up the engines. Deep-cycle batteries may be damaged if used to crank big diesels or high-compression gasoline engines.

A word about no-maintenance batteries. These batteries have no filler holes for adding water. Do not be misled, however, into believing that such batteries can be used on their sides or upside down. There are openings in the top of these batteries to release pressure caused by gassing, and the batteries must be kept upright.

Troubleshooting Batteries

If a terminal connection smokes when the battery is being charged or subjected to a heavy load, chances are the connection is not clean and tight. Resistance, remember, creates heat when a current flows through it. Remove the connector, clean, retighten, then coat the terminals with high-temperature grease. Take care not to get grease on the terminal connections *before* tightening as it may interfere with the electrical contact.

If your batteries have connecting straps on top of the case (most newer batteries have internal connecting straps), you can measure the open-circuit voltage of individual cells. Each cell should show 2.1 volts when the battery is fully charged. If one cell shows a markedly lower (or higher) voltage than the others, expect trouble. Test the

cells again with a hydrometer. If the same cell shows more than 50 points difference in specific gravity, that cell may be bad.

Always put the battery on charge before pronoucing it dead. A prolonged charge may restore life to a problem battery. Even if charging does not bring the voltage or specific gravity up right away, the battery may still be salvageable. A long, slow charge at 2–3 amperes for a period of several days can put new vigor in a battery that has been left discharged for a long time.

Restoring a Dead Battery

A build-up of $PbSO_4$ (a process called sulfation) can reduce a battery's effectiveness. In time, sulfation will ruin any battery. A long, slow charge may convert the sulfate back to lead and lead dioxide, the original battery materials. However, if the sulfate collects at the bottom of the battery case, it can short the sets of positive and negative plates together. If this occurs, the cell will indicate a low open-circuit voltage or no voltage at all, the cell will not take a charge, and the specific gravity of its electrolyte will read lower than the other cells.

All may not be lost. After trying a slow charge, *carefully* drain electrolyte from all the cells into a plastic or rubber container. Fill the battery with clear tap water (distilled is not required). *Gently* bounce the battery on a soft wood board to loosen the accumulation of sulfate. Take care not to break the case or dislodge the internal plates from their mountings. Now dump the water. (The water stills contains sulfuric acid so take care where you dump it.) Repeat this process two or three times to clear all loosened sulfate accumulation. Allow the electrolyte now in the container to sit for several hours so the dirt and other contaminants will settle to the bottom. You can filter the acid through a wad of glass fiber stuffed into the bottom of a plastic funnel or simply pour off the clear acid and leave the dirty acid at the bottom of the plastic container. Do not overfill the battery. The plates should be covered by no more than ½ inch of electrolyte. If you need more electrolyte, add water, not acid.

Put the battery back on a slow charge and test again after several hours. If all cells now show a relatively equal charge, about the same specific gravity, but the charge is not quite 100%, keep charging. If after two or three days at 2–3 amperes the electrolyte is still not 1.265, add acid. You may have to remove some electrolyte to make room; if so, use the hydrometer or rubber syringe. Add the acid slowly. Wear eye protection. When the electrolyte specific gravity is again 1.265 and the open-circuit battery voltage is again 12.6 volts, the battery is ready for service.

You can't expect another lifetime from this battery, but you may be able to keep from junking it before its time.

It has been said by some that adding certain salts of active metals can remove the harmful effects of premature sulfation. Advocates of this process recommend a mix of epsom salt [$MgSO_4$], alum [$KAl(SO_4)_2$], and borax [$Na_2B_4O_7$]. The worth of these chemical additives is questionable. But! If everything else fails, it won't hurt to try one level tablespoonful in each cell. That's the recommended dosage. Good luck!

Annie

CHAPTER 18

Installation

General Installation Notes

Anyone with an average amount of common sense and a moderate degree of skill with simple hand tools should be able to install most marine electronics equipment.

This chapter offers some tips to get you started and to help you avoid some of the more common errors.

Even if you don't intend to do the work yourself, review the pointers included in this chapter so you can better supervise the technician you're paying to do the job. It's perfectly proper to ask questions. Everyone makes mistakes. If you see one, call it. After all, *he* isn't staking his life on the job—*You* are.

The first section of this chapter provides some pointers that should be useful with all types of marine electronics installation work. Subsequent sections deal with some individual considerations that apply to particular types of equipment.

Making The Connection

Voltage is the life's blood of marine electronics. Make certain all connections are clean and tight,

Doing your own installations can be fun.

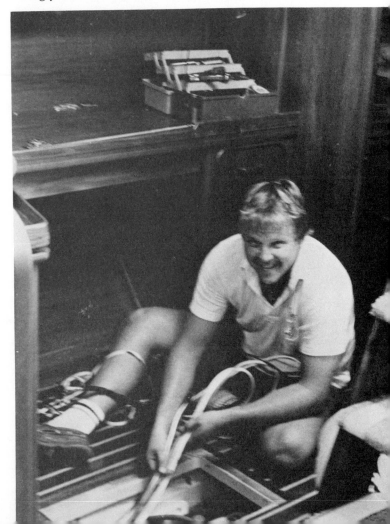

The proper way to attach
crimp-on terminals.

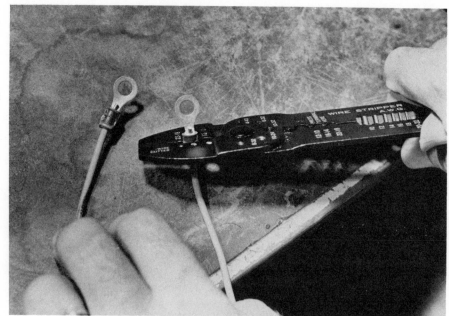

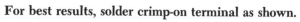
For best results, solder crimp-on terminal as shown.

and that wires are short and heavy enough to meet the equipment's current demands.

Never rely on connections made by merely twisting two wires together—unless the connection is also soldered and securely covered with insulation to seal out moisture and prevent contact with other conductors.

Whenever possible, where a wire is to be connected to a another wire or screw post, use crimp-on terminals. Crimp-on connectors can be simply crimped or crimped and soldered for extra integrity between the conductors. To protect the connection from corrosion, the barrel end of the terminal may be painted with epoxy paint or varnish to seal out moisture. Be certain to use a terminal with the correct diameter barrel. The barrel should be only slightly larger than the wire.

Crimp tightly, in at least two places, side by side.

Heat the work—not the solder.

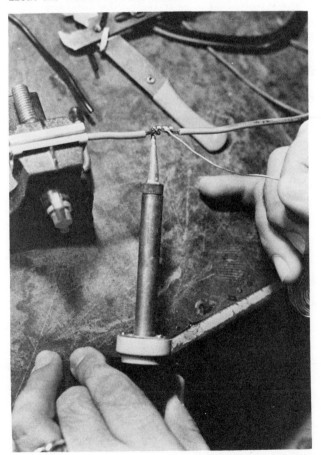

Use a crimp-on tool. Don't use pliers, and don't beat on the terminal with a hammer.

Soldering

The trick to soldering is using the right solder, the right soldering iron, and heating the *work*, not the solder!

There are two grades of solder suitable for marine use. Each is an alloy with different ratios of tin to lead. The 50:50 alloy melts at 425 degrees Fahrenheit and is somewhat stronger than the 60:40 alloy that melts at 371 degrees. The 60:40 alloy is best for work with components that can be damaged by excessive heat. The 50:50 alloy is best for work where strength is important.

Do *not* use acid-core solder. Use only rosin-core solder for electrical connections. Acid-core solder contains corrosives that attack copper. Acid-core solder should be used for non-electrical connections only.

Soldering irons vary by temperature, power, and style. For component soldering, a 30–watt pencil iron is recommended as its small tip is less likely to transfer large temperatures to heat-sensitive components. For soldering large conductors or attaching structural parts, use a 200–watt iron. For general use, a two-speed soldering gun may be best; the low speed is suitable for general component work, and the high speed is hot enough to heat large work areas for structural soldering.

Before soldering, make a sound mechanical joint capable of withstanding mechanical stresses *without* the solder.

Keep the soldering iron tip clean and freshly tinned. Wipe the tip often with a damp rag to remove burnt rosin and old solder. Then lightly cover the tip with fresh solder. This process is called "tinning the tip". A freshly tinned tip will transfer heat to the work much more quickly than a burnt tip, and will not weaken the new joint with impurities.

Using a freshly tinned tip, heat the work while touching the solder to the work surface. Do not touch the solder to the soldering iron. The solder should be melted onto the work—not onto the soldering iron tip. When you heat the solder so it

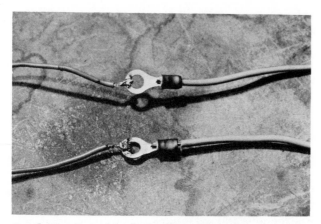

Good ("hot") and bad ("cold") solder joint.

runs off the iron onto the colder work surface, you get a cold solder joint. Since the work surface is cooler than the melting point of the solder, the solder is not welded to the work surface. Coating a joint is not soldering it! Heat the work *first*.

In a properly soldered joint, the work surface is hot enough to melt the solder. After the solder seems to "wet" the work, remove the solder but continue to hold the soldering tip in place for just a second longer to allow the melt to flow *into* the joint. Then pull the tip away. Allow the solder to cool. If the joint flexes during cooling, cold air may be drawn into the space between the surfaces, causing uneven cooling and another type of unreliable cold solder joint.

The surface of a finished solder joint should be shiny, not dull. If the solder surface is dull, re-heat the joint until the solder flows into the joint again. Do not add extra solder.

If you aren't fully confident about your prowess with a soldering iron, call in an experienced radio technician. A bad solder joint can cause total failures or intermittent operation. An improperly soldered connection may work for weeks—then fail suddenly . . . possibly with disastrous consequences.

Insulation

Tape does not make the best insulation—especially when it is constantly exposed to heat and moisture. Never use ultra-cheap plastic electrical tape found in those 39–cent tool sale displays in discount department stores. Its adhesive softens quickly, and the plastic quickly becomes brittle. If you must use black plastic electrical tape, buy the best.

Joints that may be subjected to chafe or friction should be first wrapped with fabric electrician's tape, then covered with plastic electrical tape.

Also, if you insist on using electrical tape, stretch it as it's applied—just as you stretch an elastic bandage when you wrap a sprained ankle. Start at one side. Wrap slowly and neatly. Overlap each previous turn by about half the width of the tape. Apply the last wrap without stretching.

If you have the time to do a better job of insulating a wire joint, use plastic shrink tubing. It is easy to apply. Just cut a length of tubing 50% longer than the exposed conductor you want to protect. Use the smallest diameter tubing that

These terminal strips were installed behind the bulkhead of a navstation. The large strip supplies ground (two leftmost terminals connected to heavy wire) and six 12VDC power leads. The smaller strip provides connections to wind sensor. The technician will connect instruments and radios of navstation to these strips using short leads.

will slide over the wires and the finished joint. Slide the tubing onto one of the wires before making the splice, then slide the tubing over the splice and heat. Use a hair dryer (or industrial air heater). If hot air isn't available, gently and evenly heat the tubing over any open flame.

Shrink tubing may be used anywhere. It's available at many hardware or electronic supply stores and may be purchased in a handy assortment of lengths and diameters.

Remember: Use the smallest diameter that will fit over the conductor to make the tightest seal.

If you need to insulate a splice but no tape or shrink tubing is available, do *not* use masking tape, surgical adhesive tape, or band-aids. Instead, wrap the joint with fabric. Lightweight canvas is good. Denim or stout linen also work well. Secure the fabric in place with lashings of light cord (unwaxed dental floss or sailtwine works nicely), then varnish (or paint) to exclude moisture. Where carefully done, this work can produce very serviceable results.

Screw contacts on the back of an electrical distribution panel, for example, can be painted with varnish or sprayed with a clear acrylic *after* the screw connection has been tightened. This prevents the corrosive, moist salt air from entering the space between the metallic surfaces of the conductors under the screws.

Mounting Hardware

When mounting expensive electronic devices, the object is to insure that they stay where you put them—under the very worst possible conditions.

Do not trust metal-tapping screws in fiberglass. Metal-tapping screws (also sometimes called self-tapping screws) will not hold in fiberglass when subjected to vibration or shock.

It is far better to secure gear in place with through-bolts. When the unit to be mounted is particularly heavy and susceptible to serious damage if the mounting should fail, through-bolting is required. For lighter gear, flat washers can be used on the back of the mounting surface to spread the load. But, for heavy gear, back up the nuts with a metal plate drilled for the bolts. Do

not use plywood except when mounting the very lightest gear, and use flat washers whenever the back up material is not metal. For gear that's susceptible to magnetic interference (e.g., a compass unit for an autopilot) use aluminum back up plates and non-magnetic fasteners.

Test stainless steel with a magnet. Some stainless is magnetic.

Lock washers are recommended wherever an installation is subjected to vibration. Split washers are probably better than star washers in most cases, especially with larger bolts—although star washers work well where the mating surfaces are soft metal into which the star washers' teeth can

Instruments on S.O.R.C. contender mounted where they can be read by the helmsman.

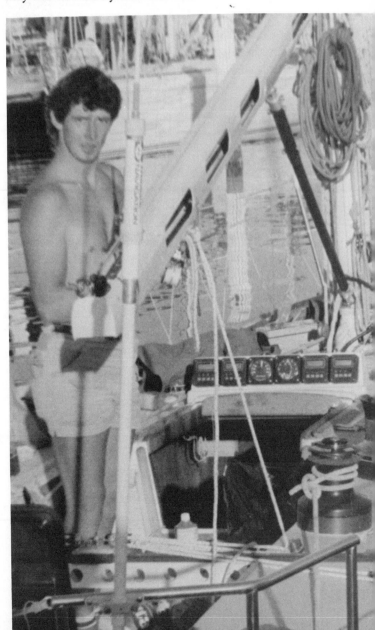

penetrate sufficiently well to resist loosening. With hard stainless steel parts, use split washers.

An alternative to lock washers is the self-locking nut, with nylon inserts that grab bolt threads and resist loosening. Where absolute security against loosening is required, use self-locking nuts *and* lockwashers. For semi-permanent installations, use a thread locking compound (available at automotive supply houses).

Aluminum screws tend to freeze in steel, even stainless. The same is true of steel screws used in aluminum. Avoid the combination.

An alternative to metal screws is the nylon screw. For a few applications, nylon hardware works quite well. It doesn't conduct electricity and will not rust or corrode, but it is not as strong as steel or aluminum.

Wood screws are for wood. Metal tapping screws are for metal. Use the proper screw.

Some ship's carpenters insist that wood screws can be driven in with a hammer, saving both time and elbow grease. This fact is indisputable, but the best joint results when wood screws are screwed in. If elbow grease is in short supply, use a variable speed power drill and screwdriving bit. Don't use push-type "Yankee" screwdrivers for driving screws into finish woods as they tend to slip and gouge the wood beneath. For best results, pre-drill before starting wood screws. Drill-sizes can be found in tables, but good results are possible by holding the screw in front of the drill bit and up to the light. If the drill bit can be seen in the threads, it is too big. Better too small than too big.

Wood screws will turn more easily if you first rub the threads across a bar of soft soap.

Routing Cables

Never run cables through the bilge! The only exception is cable specially manufactured to be submerged in oily bilgewater. Some wires *are* classified as waterproof. Most are not. Waterproof cable costs far more than standard cable. Ordinary insulation, though it appear impervious to water and/or oil, cannot withstand soaking. In time, bilgewater penetrates to the wire inside,

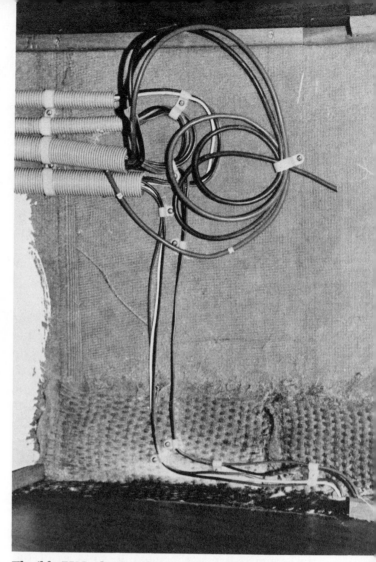

Flexible PVC plastic tubing used as conduit protects wires from moisture and is easier to install than rigid conduit.

corroding the copper and increasing cable resistance. The best place to route cables is up under the side decks.

Avoid running cables through seat lockers where they may be banged about by shifting cargo. Plan your installation so that all wiring can be routed through PVC pipe. The pipe protects the wire from moisture and physical damage. If you are ordering a newboat, insist on plastic conduit. Specify conduit large enough to accomodate additional wires in the future. If you run a double-length, continuous loop of stout cord through your conduits, from end to end, you'll have a "fish" ready in place to pull new wires through as you need them.

Nylon lock-ties work well to bundle cables where wires can't be enclosed in conduits. Some

View through aft hatch of S.O.R.C. competitor showing SSB radio and other instruments safely protected.

ties have a screw lug so the cable can be wrapped, the tie pulled tight, and the bundle secured with a screw. Alternatively, the lock-tie can be wrapped around a pipe or other fixture to hold the bundle securely. Use wire cutters to snip off excess nylon tie.

Don't use electrical tape to hold wire bundles in place. If nylon lock-ties aren't available, use light cord. Do not pull the cord too tightly around the wire bundle as some wire insulation is soft enough to be easily damaged.

Installing SSB

Getting the bill for an SSB installation can be a stunning surprise. A proper installation can represent at least one-third of the total cost of the system.

Why is installation so important?

SSB installations are called systems because their several parts—transmitter, receiver, ground, antenna, and power supply circuits—are so intimately dependent upon each other. The weak link theory applies, and proper installation is essential to tie together the separate parts.

You can save money by picking up a set with only one or two frequency bands and installing it yourself. But, if you want the system to perform at all hours of the day, at short range and long, you'll shell out the beans for a system with more channels, then shell out still more to hire a marine electronic specialist to install it. In the first instance, you'll be lucky if you can talk beyond the harbor, in the second you may find it possible to talk to Europe or the South Pacific on a regular basis.

It pays to supervise your unit's installation. A sharp eye can detect careless connections and shortcuts taken by an irresponsible radio technician doing the job for you.

Selecting the Location

If your vessel is a ship or yacht with a wheelhouse, then an obvious location for the SSB radio is near the wheel. Watch out for the mike cord, though. It will stretch with use. If you mount the radio directly over the wheel, the cord may be in the way or even catch the spokes.

By the way, stretched microphone cords can be re-tightened by reversing the twist of each coil. Detach the microphone cable by unplugging the microphone connector if provided. Start and one end of the cable and work toward the other. If the cord does not attach to the unit by means of a detachable plug, start at the unit end of the cord and work toward the microphone. The object, either way, is to reverse the turn of each coil so tension is returned to the cord. The process can be repeated as necessary.

Many good installers mount SSB radios on the bulkhead either below the dash or behind the helmsman. The microphone should be accessible to the person at the wheel.

In a sailboat, where the steering station is out in the wet, the SSB should be installed below. Although some manufacturers offer waterproof remote control units with special microphones designed to withstand occasional drenching, even these units may be ruined if exposed continuously to the raw marine environment.

Mount your SSB where it will stay dry.

Avoid locations where the crew may be disposed to use it for a coffee table. If a drink spills into *any* item of electronic gear, chances are it'll be ruined. If the radio is mounted on the topside of a console or under a shelf, for example, chances are that sooner or later someone will stow his coffee cup over it. If the radio is hung from the overhead, on the other hand, it'll be difficult to spill coffee or other drinks into it. This may seem obvious, but countless gadgets are brought into elec-

Excessive wire length can cause unwanted resistance, but transducer or Loran-C antenna cables should not be cut unless the manufacturer specifications permit shortening these cables as some equipment is designed to work with an optimum length cable.

Mount electronic gear where it can not be damaged by accidental spills.

tronics shops for damages resulting from spilled drinks.

If you must mount a control console on a flying bridge or in a sailboat cockpit, tuck it away under a coaming or beneath a cockpit seat to prevent physical damage and frequent dousings. In no circumstance should the radio be mounted where it can be kicked, sat on, or soaked by a boarding wave.

Moreover, when choosing a location for the

transceiver, keep wire lengths as short as possible. Keep power leads, ground leads and antenna leads to a bare minimum. The more wire you run—under seats, through galley lockers, behind bunks—the more energy you lose to stray radiation and resistance—and the more interference you pick up from other gear.

Make the installation convenient—but pay attention to the electronic necessities discussed in the next sections.

Power Supply

Modern radios are uncompromisingly voltage-conscious. Many of the new integrated circuits won't work at all unless they are supplied with precise voltages. Moreover, an SSB transmitter may draw more than ten amperes—ten times the current required by a VHF or CB radio. Unless adequate current flow is available, the radio can not transmit effectively.

Leave only enough wire to permit servicing the unit.

Optimize the route of power cables from batteries to radio. Wires should be short and as heavy as practicable. Finally, make certain each connection is tight and clean.

A tiny bit of corrosion in an SSB power cable or connection can reduce transmitted power. Use heavy wire. Seal all contacts. Use anti-corrosion battery grease on exposed terminals. A liberal coat of varnish does a fair job, but varnish tends to crack when the joint is flexed. Make certain metal surfaces are shiny clean *before* tightening connections. Do not connect dissimilar metals; electrolysis will result.

Again, where possible, mount the radio near the batteries so the power cable is as short as possible.

Don't coil excess cable. Cut it off! Leave only enough wire to allow the service technician to remove the radio from its mounting bracket with the cables connected so he can make tuning and other adjustments to a live set.

Grounding

The radio ground is the most important part of an SSB systeminstallation. It is critical to both transmitting *and* receiving.

Without a good ground, your SSB radio can't work well, no matter how powerful its transmitter is, how high or how efficient the antenna or how supernaturally sensitive the receiver may be.

So, what's a proper radio ground?

Perhaps it will be clearer at first to focus on what is *not* a proper radio ground. An effective ground in DC voltage or shore power AC voltage circuits won't work at 16 MHz. In other words, a through-hull valve or length of bare chain hanging over the side does not provide an effective ground for radio frequency energy.

Some manufacturers advertise porous bronze grounding plates, designed to be attached to the bottom of your hull. Their makers say the plates' porosity increases their surface area, but they don't make an adequate radio contact with the sea to optimize SSB performance.

The ground counterpoise system for a marine SSB installation should provide at least nine

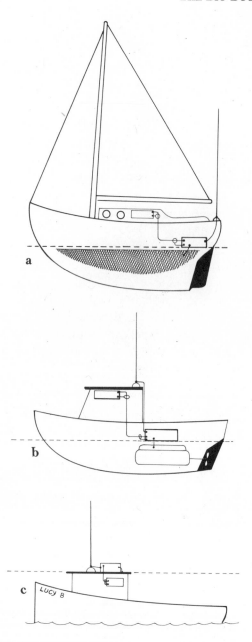

Three grounding arrangements. In "a" the tuner is grounded to a copper screen mesh bonded inside the hull and is mounted just below the antenna and connected to both the antenna and ground system with short leads. In "b" the tuner is grounded to the engine; the lead from tuner to antenna is "hot" and should be installed so personnel can not get burned from contact. In "c" the ground counterpoise is the wheelhouse roof itself, and the tuner is again connected to it by a short lead. Connections from the tuner to ground in each case should be made with heavy copper strap rather than wire.

square feet of highly conductive surface (copper mesh screening, aluminum plate, steel deck, etc.). Many authorities claim nine square feet is not enough and insist that 100 square feet is minimal! Everyone agrees: The more conductive counterpoise you connect to the ground side of the SSB radio, the better the radio will work.

Any radio conductive material will do—aluminum sheeting, copper strap, bronze wire mesh, or simply lengths of heavy gauge wire run throughout the bilges, behind bunks, in the engine room, above the headliner, or wherever room and ingenuity can get it.

Wire mesh laid in the deck of a fibreglass boat makes a good ground—even though no part of it is in contact with the sea! A new boat can be built with copper mesh bonded between the headliner and deck. Two heavy copper straps should be soldered to the mesh and brought out to connection points—one near the anticipated position of the radio unit, another at the location of the antenna tuner. Both tuner and radio should be connected to the counterpoise with short leads of heavy copper strap—not wire.

Broad copper strap or copper mesh screening can be laminated under the innermost layer of material in a molded hull to make an effective ground. Joints should be soldered, and heavy copper strap should be run up to the radio and antenna tuner locations.

The ideal radio ground is a steel or aluminum hull and deck. All connections should be tight, waterproof, and treated for electrolysis prevention. Copper to aluminum contact, for example, is certain to deteriorate over time. A sealant like that used on automotive battery terminals may be effective against corrosion.

Heavy copper conductors should be used throughout. Copper is the best conductor for the job. Six-inch strap is recommended.

The antenna coupler and the transceiver should be intimately bonded together and to the vessel ground system.

Installing VHF

The VHF is not nearly so difficult to install as the SSB. It requires neither an elaborate grounding system nor antenna tuner. A few points do need your attention, however.

Mounting Location

Many of today's VHF radios are virtually waterproof and can be mounted out in the weather. Don't do it!

If so much as a teensy-eensy drop of salty water gets inside *any* marine electronics device, it will malfunction—sooner or later. Salt water is highly corrosive to copper, and copper is what wires are made of. Even moist salt air inside marine electronics gear can ruin it in a matter of weeks. Keep the water out.

Mount the VHF—waterproof or not—where it'll stay dry, not in the companionway or out in the cockpit.

And don't mount it down near the cabin sole. Mount it high on a bulkhead or on a special shelf as far above the bilge as you can get it. Mount all radios (and batteries) high, where they'll stay dry and continue to function—with water in the cabin.

Mount your radio where it won't be kicked or sat upon, where the direct rays of the sun won't beat down on it, away from engine heat and vibration.

If you simply must talk on the radio from the flying bridge, or from the sailboat cockpit, or down in the engine room, install remote handsets. These are a small fraction of the cost of a new VHF. Mount the radio where it will be protected.

When selecting a mounting location, remember to keep the power cable as short as possible to reduce losses caused by resistance. Route the cable as directly to the voltage source as possible.

The cable should be fused or connected to a circuit breaker at the voltage source, not at the radio. If a power cable becomes shorted at any point along its length, the fuse or circuit breaker at the voltage source should blow. If no fuse or circuit breaker is installed, the shorted power cable could cause a fire.

Pay particular attention to the power connections. The power output of VHF transmitters depends more on supply voltage than on any other factor. Keep the voltage up. Shorten power cables. Make connections clean and tight.

VHF Ground

VHF is not as sensitive to ground system efficiency as SSB.

But, VHF antennas get hit by lightning from time to time. In fact, tiny lightning discharges may hit the VHF antenna dozens of times during an electrical storm. If the VHF is not properly grounded, these static discharges can damage the radio—and this is especially true of units with microprocessors, frequency synthesizers and other integrated chip circuits. Even the weakest static discharge can destroy integrated circuits. Good grounding reduces the likelihood of damage.

Grounding won't improve transmission much, but it may reduce the effect of atmospheric noise and other interference.

Porous bronze grounding plates are adequate grounds for VHF. If your hull is aluminum or steel, of course, bond the radio to the hull. Otherwise, connect the radio to the engine block, through-hull fittings, or other conductive path to surrounding seawater.

VHF Antenna Cable

A little extra effort can prevent aggravating noise caused by loose VHF antenna cables rattling inside the mast. Some of the newer sailboat masts have PVC conduit inside to hold the wires running to the masthead. Some riggers string a stout cord through the mast to serve as a fish. Use the fish to pull a new fish each time you run a wire through the conduit, and you'll always have a fish when you need it.

If your mast isn't fitted with PVC conduit, you can reduce the noise of a slapping cable inside by taping a hunk of foam rubber to the cable at intervals of three feet or so. Each hunk of foam should be just large enough to offer a slight resistance as the cable is pulled up the mast. Use duct tape or sail repair tape to hold the hunks of foam to the cable.

This mast has a built-in channel to protect cables and keep them from banging around inside.

Another highly recommended practice is using a support cord inside the mast to take the strain of the cable's own weight. If a support cord is not used, the cable's weight tends to stretch the wire and may damage fittings at the top of the mast. If your mast is relatively tall, the weight of antenna cable can be quite great. Inevitably, the cable or its fittings will be damaged. Nylon webbing, about ½" wide, makes a good support cord be-

Two views of coaxial cable.

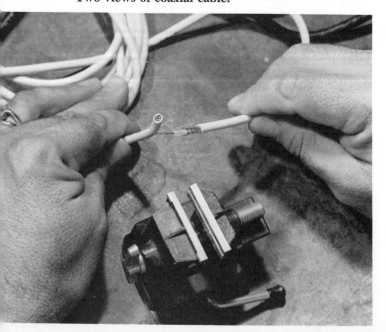

cause it doesn't cut into the insulation or distort the outer braid the way a round cord would do. Use a clove, timber, or rolling hitch at three foot intervals. These hitches tend not to cut into cable. For extra security, a wrap of duct or sail repair tape at each hitch may help keep the cable from slipping.

Coaxial Cable

VHF antenna wire is coaxial, i.e., one conductor runs inside the other conductor. The inner conductor is either solid or stranded wire, separated from the outer conductor by a layer of insulation. The outer conductor is copper braid, made of fine wires interwoven to form a hollow tube similar to the outer casing of braided dacron line.

The inner and outer conductor must never touch!

When attaching coaxial connectors to coaxial cable, be especially careful with the fine wires of the braid. Even a tiny wisp of wire, bridging the gap between the outer and inner conductors, can

Six types of coax connectors. From top left 259 chassis socket, BNC chassis socket, 259-BNC converter, 259 plug, BNC plug, 259 barrel connector.

create a short circuit that can seriously damage the transmitter or prevent your receiver from hearing even the strongest incoming signals.

Crimp on solderless coaxial connectors are not recommended for marine work, no matter how tight the connector is pressed on. Some amount of corrosion is always possible between the surfaces. A small amount of corrosion is acceptable in circuits operating at 12 volts, but incoming radio signals are measured in millionths of volts. It doesn't take much corrosion to resist a few millionths of a volt!

Solder coaxial connectors to their cables. Solder excludes corrosion and provides a better mechanical fit at the same time.

Installing Loran

Loran-C equipment simply won't perform satisfactorily if not installed properly—and that includes proper locations for the receiver and antenna, proper routing of cables, proper ground, and proper noise suppression where needed.

Some units are advertised as water-resistant or

waterproof. Don't count on it! Dealers tell me they occasionally receive damp and rusty receivers from angry customers who can't understand why they can't use a power nozzle to wash down the flying bridge with the Loran-C receiver mounted on the console. Water has a nasty way of finding its way through tiny crevasses to ruin electronics equipment. Perhaps 90% of all repairs result from the damage wrought by water.

If you must mount your "waterproof" Loran-C receiver out in the open, protect it with a vinyl or waterproof canvas cover when it's not in use. *Never* hose it down!

Better yet, mount the receiver where it is not exposed to any dampness. Sailboat owners may mount the receiver below in the chartroom or just inside the companionway away from the full fury of the elements. If your companion is set to one side, as it often is on larger boats, you may be able to install the receiver behind a portlight in the aft bulkhead of the trunk cabin so it can be seen from the helmsman's position.

If you're mounting a receiver in a pilothouse, be careful to place it so the indicator lamps are not reflected in the windows. Don't mount the unit where it will be exposed to direct sunlight or unreasonable heat. Above all, don't mount it where it can be kicked or stepped on.

If you insist on having a display out where you can see it, mount a remote unit. Remotes contain only display electronics and cost far less than a complete receiver to repair *or* replace.

If vibration is a problem, use rubber grommets under the mounting screws.

The power leads and antenna cable should not be routed close to each other. The power leads are a source of interference that can be picked up by the antenna cable. If possible, keep these cables three feet apart along their entire length. Do not route the antenna cable or power leads near other sources of electrical interference—especially microcomputers, television sets, or fluorescent lights.

Mount the antenna as high as possible and clear of other antennas, rigging, or metal spars. Do not make your initial mounting permanent. Secure the antenna in some likely position with stainless steel hoseclamps or some other suitable tem-

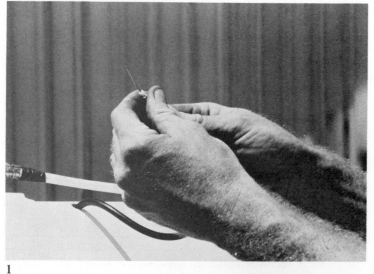

1

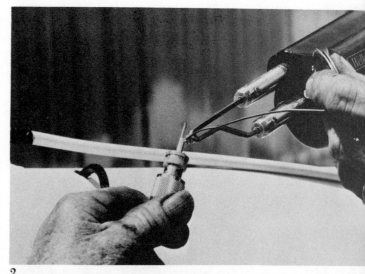

2

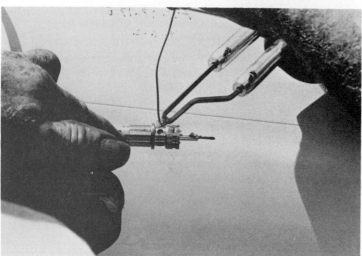

3

4

This series of photographs shows how to attach a
PL259 coaxial connector. If in doubt, let a
professional do it.

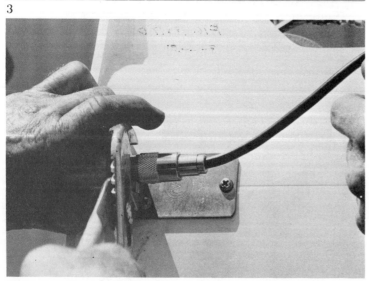

5

Loran-C antenna mounted to canopy support using stainless steel hose clamps—not necessarily a great method, but it does get the job done.

porary method. Try the Loran-C for a few days—in and out of harbor. Move the antenna a few feet and try it again. A slight change in antenna position can result in surprising improvements in performance.

Most manufacturers provide some method of measuring the quality of incoming signals. Today's units can acquire signals of unbelievably minute strength. A typical signal-to-noise ratio for signal acquisition may be as low as 1:10. That means the noise is ten times as strong as the signal. After acquisition is complete, a good Loran-C receiver should be able to track the signal with a SNR at 1:15 or even 1:20.

The manufacturer's literature should explain how to access the SNR displays for master and slave stations. With this display active, then, you can experiment with different antenna locations until you have found the optimum antenna location for best SNR's.

Be certain the antenna and its tuner are securely mounted. Use a good grade of marine sealant to prevent water from entering the connections. Do *not* use silicone sealant if it smells like vinegar while curing. Some sealants use acetic acid, a corrosive substance.

The Loran-C ground is as important as the ground on your SSB installation. In fact, if you have a properly installed SSB radio, you may connect the Loran-C ground to the SSB ground. If not, use the engine block, propeller shaft, metal tanks, through-hull fittings, or any other available

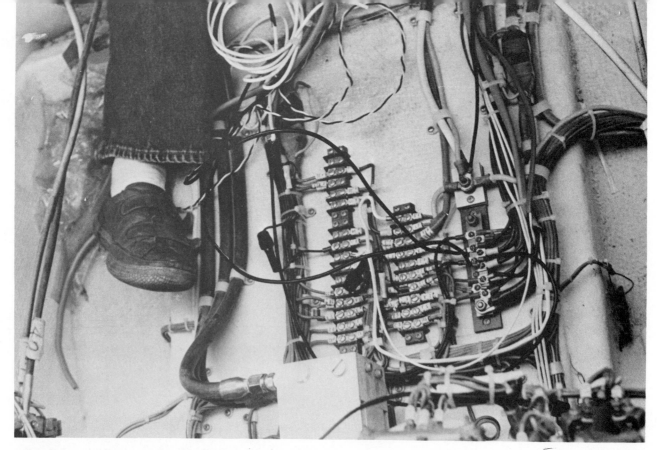

Behind the steering console of a modern motoryacht. Note extensive use of terminal strips to keep connections neat and permit instruments to be easily removed for servicing.

grounding points. Make all connections clean and tight. Seal with waterproofing.

Many installation manuals suggest running the power cables directly to the battery. This is good practice, but may not be necessary where a properly designed distribution panel is installed and supplied with heavy battery cables. The reason the installation manuals suggest routing the power leads to the battery is to make certain the Loran-C gets plenty of voltage without alternator noise or interference from other equipment connected to the distribution panel. If the wiring of your panel is questionable, route the Loran-C power leads to the battery. If the distribution panel is already connected to the battery with heavy cables, properly wired and protected with circuit breakers or appropriate fuses, a better choice may be to connect the Loran-C power leads to the switched side of one of the breakers on the distribution panel. Cut all leads as short as possible; leave only enough extra wire to remove the distribution panel or Loran-C from its mounting without disconnecting the power. (This is for servicing convenience.)

Alternator noise may be a problem. Alternator noise will be detected in the SNR readout when the engine is running. If you suspect alternator noise, attach noise suppression devices to the alternator.

Noise from other sources may be similarly discovered by watching the SNR display while turning on other devices one at a time. Televisions and fluorescent lighting are frequent culprits. Try to avoid locating the receiver, antenna, or cables near these or other sources of electronic interference.

Depth Sounder Installation

General points about locating and installing the transducer are covered in the chapter on depth sounders.

Manufacturer recommendations should be followed carefully. If a transducer cable is routed behind bunks and lockers, it should be protected from damage from shifting cargo or big feet. If the cable must be routed through the bilge, strap it up under the sole where it will be protected from bilge water. The rubber outer coating on wires and cables can only do so much to keep the damaging moisture out.

Transducer cables should not be subjected to kinks or sharp bends that could break the insulation.

Transducer cables should not be cut. Depth sounders are tuned to their transducers and the supplied length of cable. If you are left with an excess of cable after routing, flake it into a long bundle (not a round coil) and twist the bundle a half-turn so it will not pick up stray electrical fields. Secure the bundle where it can't be damaged. Select a location away from the engine alternator, generator, voltage regulator or other source of radio noise. When buying a new depth sounder, be certain the transducer cable is long enough to reach the display unit from the proposed transducer mounting location. If more cable is needed, additional cable can be added by a trained technician. The display unit may need to be re-tuned. Do not attempt this task. Improper tuning is certain to result in poor sounder performance.

Voltage supply is usually no problem. Most sounders draw one ampere or less. However, electrical interference picked up on the DC supply circuit can cause erratic soundings. Do not route power cables or transducer cables near equipment that might cause electrical interference, such as gasoline engine distributors or coils, alternators, generators, voltage regulators, etc. Stay away from radar circuits.

Do not run depth sounder power and transducer cables near each other. A power cable can pick up noise from the transducer cable, noise that can be amplified by the sounder and appear as false echoes. If the transducer cable must pass near the power cable, run the wires as nearly perpendicular to each other to limit induction coupling.

If a separate ground connection is provided on the display unit or transducer, bond tightly to the boat's grounding system. Grounding can reduce noise interference significantly.

Visibility of the readout is all-important. Location of the display is a critical consideration. Many manufacturers advertise their units as waterproof. If this is so, the display unit may be

The little box mounted on the firewall is a noise suppressor. Note wires from alternator. The noise suppressor itself must be securely grounded in order to work properly.

mounted on a flying bridge or in the aft end of a deckhouse where the readings are visible to the helmsman. Remember, however, that the power and transducer cable connections may not be absolutely waterproof. If possible, mount the display unit where it won't get doused.

Installing Depth Recorder

Chart recorders differ from depth sounders in that they are more susceptible to damage by vibration. Digital sounders have no moving parts. Rotating flasher type sounders have only the single rotating wheel. Chart recorders have a chart-driving mechanism and moving marker stylus that are far more susceptible to damage by bumps and constant shaking. The unit itself should be mounted to a solid bulkhead or other rigid surface where vibration is at a minimum. In heavy workboats or high-speed craft where vibration is unavoidable, the unit should be shock-mounted. A typewriter cushion or other heavy rubber mat can be secured under the mounting bracket. Thick rubber grommets can be used on the mounting bolts, between the mounting surface and the trunion bracket. Long life and trouble-free service require a vibration-free installation.

If the recorder must be mounted on an insubstantial bulkhead where vibration is a problem, bolt the trunion mount securely to a heavy steel or aluminum plate before bolting the plate itself to the flimsy bulkhead. Use the above described shock-reducing techniques. This method can lessen vibration damage considerably.

Power to chart recorders is more critical than with less current hungry depth sounders. A chart recorder may draw as much as 3 amperes—more than 10 times that required by the typical depth sounder. A wire resistance of only 1/10 ohm will cause a voltage drop of nearly 1 volt when 3 amperes are flowing. The same 1/10 ohm wire resistance connected to a depth sounder drawing only 0.3 amperes will cause a voltage drop of less than 1/100 volt! The more current a piece of gear draws, the more important are power connections. A tiny resistance can cause big voltage drops. Study the manufacturer's specifications. Some of the

newest gear uses voltage-sensitive IC chips that can shut themselves off if voltage levels drop too low.

Recorders are as sensitive to electrical noise as sounders. The noise reduction rules apply to both. Transducer cables should not be routed parallel to power cables. All connections should be clean and tight. Loose contacts can introduce unwanted electrical noise. Alternators or generators in need of service may introduce problems.

When a depth recorder is subjected to interference, it may interpret it as echoes returning from the bottom. The chart will mark the noise as false echoes.

How *not* to mount antennas. These are too many, too close to each other, and too close to the rigging. Mount your antennas in the clear when possible.

The principles of transducer installation are the same for recorders and depth sounders.

Installing Other Gear

The principles for installing other gear are pretty much the same as those for installing the equipment described in the preceding sections. SSB, VHF, Loran, and depth recorders give the most trouble. If you understand problems common to those items of gear, you should be able to install just about anything.

Remember: Adequate voltage is a must.

Keep your cables short and your connections clean and tight.

CHAPTER 19

Troubleshooting

It's been said, "Only two kinds of people repair their own watches—watchmakers and folks who don't care what time it is."

Similarly, those who try to repair their marine electronic gear should accept full responsibility if they fail. Most of the problems you encounter will be beyond your ability to correct.

There are a few exceptions, however, and this chapter may be an aid to help you fix the failures that aren't too severe.

The complexity of much of today's gadgetry is even beyond the competence of many professional marine electronic shops. They remove and replace complete circuit boards rather than attempting to isolate the problem. The faulty circuit board goes back to the factory. Test equipment required to analyze a computer circuit or measure the internal functions of an integrated circuit chip is simply too expensive for local shops to own. They use factory experts, swap circuit cards or send the entire device back to the wholesale supplier for repairs.

Clearly, then, the type of repairs possible with the limited tools and equipment found on most small craft is restricted to the most obvious situations. This chapter should give you a start toward being able to use a multimeter and simple hand tools to locate and correct the easiest problems. A special section offers some advice on preventing electrolysis and corrosion problems.

Do These Things First

When anything fails to work properly or at all, always check the supply voltage first. A frequent cause of equipment failure is improper or insufficient supply voltage. (Procedures for using multimeters to measure voltage and other electrical values appear later in this chapter.)

Check the fuse! It's surprising how many seemingly complex problems turn out to be nothing more than a blown fuse. Most gadgets have fuse holders mounted on the back or side of the chassis. Others use in-line fuses on the positive side of the power cable. Check the fuse first.

Always replace blown fuses with the same type and ampere rating as the fuse specified by the equipment literature. *Never* replace with a higher rating fuse, and *never* replace any fuse with a piece of wire, a coin, or aluminum foil. Manufacturers put fuses in their equipment to protect both your investment and your safety. If you replace a blown fuse with some cheater device or a bigger fuse, while an internal problem (short circuit, bad component, etc.) is causing the gear to draw excess current, the equipment may be permanently damaged. Or, heat from the excess current flow may cause a fire. In an emergency, you may temporarily replace a fuse with one having a lower rating. If the smaller fuse doesn't blow, you're safe. Replace the original fuse with the proper value at your earliest opportunity.

It is not always correct to replace the fuse with the same type and ampere rating as the fuse that you remove—since the last person to replace the fuse may not have used the correct rating. Refer to the literature.

Unfortunately, many serious failures are unnecessary. A simple problem caused a blown fuse. Someone replaced the bad fuse with a bigger fuse that permitted more current to flow through the faulty circuits—causing greater damage. So, never, replace a blown fuse with a higher rated fuse.

If the fuse is good, (Sometimes bad fuses look good, so see the tips on using a meter to check fuses later in this chapter.), make certain all cables are properly plugged in, all ground and antenna wires connected, and each plug is matched to the proper socket. Make certain the main battery switch is turned on and all necessary breakers and distribution panel switches are turned on.

Sometimes when one item of equipment won't work, it helps to turn all other equipment off, stop engines, disconnect everything except the faulty unit. Occasionally the problem exists outside the malfunctioning unit. Other equipment can steal voltage or cause interference that makes more sensitive equipment fail. By shutting everything down, that possibility is skirted.

Check for abnormal heat. Many units operate at elevated temperatures. Almost never should equipment be too hot to touch.

Sniff! If you smell acrid fumes, you have serious trouble. Disconnect the equipment and take it to a reputable repair shop.

Meters

Electricity can't be seen. Low voltages like those used on a boat can not be felt (except by the most sensitive individuals). Higher voltages, like shorepower, can be dangerous to the touch. Either way, direct contact with electrical circuits is not the recommended method for determining electrical conditions.

The only sensible way to measure electrical circuits is with a meter, and the most common meter found aboard today's boat is a multimeter, so-named because it is several meters in one package. Multimeters can measure AC voltage, DC voltage, DC current, and DC resistance. These are the primary electrical variables.

The two types of multimeter suitable for use on a boat are the digital readout and needle movement type. Digital multimeters are a bit more expensive with prices ranging from $50 to $200 or more. A simple needle movement type adequate for most uses can be found in discount electronic supply houses for as little as $20. Better needle movement meters cost from $40 to $100.

Both needle movement and digital readout multimeters are set to operate in their various modes and ranges by changing switches on the front panel or by plugging the test leads into appropriate panel jacks. Since all meters differ in the methods for selecting modes and ranges, study the instructions included with your meter for complete operating details.

All meters are delicate instruments that are incredibly easy to destroy and, if improperly used, can cause serious injuries or death. The following section explains some general principles and safety precautions pertaining to the use of multimeters. Read the warnings carefully. The remainder of the chapter treats each mode of operation, using typical applications by way of illustration.

Precautions

Don't take chances. Worn or cracked test probes with peeling insulation revealing bare spots on the probe wires is an outright invitation to injury or death. Replace faulty test probes at the first sign of deterioration.

Avoid testing live circuits unless absolutely necessary.

If you must measure live circuits where high voltages may be present, don't use both probes at the same time. Use one hand at a time. An alligator clip with a heavy, plastic insulating cover can be attached to the negative (black) probe. Clamp the clip to the negative (or neutral) side of the circuit (again using one hand) before touching the positive (red) probe to the other side of the circuit. Some experienced technicians automatically take a firm grip on their belt with one hand, keeping that one hand away from the high voltage. They work with only the other hand, moving the test probes cautiously, never removing that grip on the belt. If you do touch a high voltage source with only one hand, you may survive (unless you're standing on a steel deck with wet shoes or in a puddle of water with any kind of shoes or no shoes at all).

If you're working on a steel deck, wear dry rubber shoes. Don't take measurements if you're standing in a puddle of water.

Before touching the probes to any circuit, make certain the meter is set to the proper mode. If the meter is in current or resistance mode and the probes are touched to a live circuit, the meter will be destroyed unless its internal fuse blows first.

Return the meter to "OFF" when you are finished working. In the OFF position, the probe jacks are disconnected, and the meter is shunted internally so it can't be damaged by stray currents.

If your meter doesn't have an OFF setting, set the mode to "AC volts" and the range selector to its highest setting. This is the safest storage mode for a meter that has no OFF switch.

Finally, do not rely too heavily on meter accuracy.

Even digital meters are typically no more accurate than +/− 1% or +/− 1 digit in the least significant (rightmost) readout position, whichever is least accurate.

Needle movement meters are far less accurate than digital models, typically no better than +/−

3% of the full-scale reading in DC voltage and DC current modes, or +/− 4% in AC voltage mode. In other words, if you are measuring DC voltage on the 100–volt scale, readings can not be relied upon to better than +/− 3 volts at *any* point on the meter. A reading of 10 volts on the 100–volt scale, for example, may indicate an actual voltage anywhere from 7 to 13 volts. It's always more accurate, therefore, to select a scale that uses the top portion of the meter for any measurement.

To read a meter properly, your eyes should be directly in front of the meter. If you move your eyes to one side or the other, you'll find the meter reading differs by a small amount. This is called parallax error. A meter with a mirrored surface on the meter scale behind the needle gives the user a means to determine when he is viewing the meter from straight ahead, and not from one side or the other. The user positions himself and the meter so the reflection of the needle in the mirrored surface is hidden from view by the needle itself. At this position the observer's eye is perpendicular to the meter scale, and parallax error is eliminated.

One final point on accuracy. Needle movement type meters are sensitive to the position of the meter case and to magnetic field influences. If a meter is calibrated in its upright position, use it in that position, and do not rely on the accuracy of readings taken within strong magnetic fields.

Testing for AC Voltage

When measuring AC voltages, remember that carelessness can result in death or serious injury. Be careful.

Follow the precautions offered in the preceding section.

Always start with the multimeter set to its highest possible range first. If you inadvertently touch the probes to a 220 volt outlet, with the meter set to its 2 volt range, the meter may be damaged. Start at the highest range and step downward.

In the AC voltage mode, a multimeter can be used to test the shorepower connection *before* you plug in at the dock. At one dock visited a few years back, the dock owners had scrimped on cost by using ordinary house receptacles for both 110–volt and 220–volt outlets! We were tied up before dark, so we could read the little gizmo labels on the receptacles... but, if we had arrived later, when it was too dark to read the little labels, we might've tried to plug our 110–volt shore power cord into one of those deceptive 220–volt outlets. The results of applying 220 volts to equipment designed to operate at 110 is usually violent destruction—or worse.

Check AC power outlets at the dock *before* you plug in.

Many marina owners do their own electrical wiring. Though mistakes are rare, an occasional marina may cross the ground and neutral wires.

A properly wired 110–volt receptacle should show 110–volts between the hot side and ground, 110–volts between the hot side and neutral, and zero volts between the neutral side and ground. Any deviation from this pattern can result in damage to your on-board equipment.

A properly wired 220–volt receptacle should show 220 volts between the two hot sides, but only 110–volts between ground and either of the hot sides.

In both cases, if you touch one probe to the ground leg of a receptacle, and touch the other probe to the water under the dock or to a water pipe or other conductor that itself touches the water, there should be NO voltage at all. The ground socket of shore power receptacles should be exactly that: ground! Make a test before you plug in. Start with the highest AC voltage range, then step downward until you are measuring at the most sensitive, lowest AC voltage range of the meter. If any voltage appears between the ground socket of the dock receptacle and the water, do not plug in. A multi-million dollar yacht recently sank at the dock after being plugged in overnight to an improperly wired receptacle. The voltage incorrectly connected to the ground lug flowed through the boat and into the surrounding water by way of a through-hull fitting. Electrolysis destroyed the through-hull fitting in a matter of hours, sending the costly craft to the bottom.

Lethal voltages also exist when shore power ap-pliances are connected to an improperly grounded shore power receptacle. The voltage should return to ground via the ground conductor—not you!

Use your multimeter in its AC mode. Make certain AC voltages are at their proper levels and properly connected. Don't take any chances.

Testing for DC Voltage

The most obvious use of the multimeter in its DC mode is testing batteries or other DC voltage sources. Other uses may not be so obvious.

As always, start at the highest range setting when measuring DC voltages. Of course, if you're measuring the voltage across the terminals of a 12–volt storage battery, there is no need to begin with the meter set to its 1000–volt range. Make absolutely certain, however, that the meter is in DC volts mode. If by mistake the meter is in DC current mode, and the probes are touched to the terminals of a live DC voltage source such as a fully charged battery, unlimited current will flow through the meter. If the meter's fuse does not blow, the meter will undoubtedly be destroyed.

When measuring battery voltage, remember that voltage can be limited by internal resistance of the battery, and a dead battery may show full voltage when it is under no load. Begin to draw current from the battery through an external circuit, and the battery's internal resistance causes a voltage drop resulting in lower terminal voltage. In other words, test batteries under load and no-load conditions. With everything turned off, connect your multimeter to the battery and note the reading. Now begin to turn on circuits, one at a time. If the voltage does not drop appreciably as external circuits are added to its load, then the battery has little internal resistance. If the voltage drops rapidly as low-current devices such as running lights are switched on, the battery has high internal resistance and needs to be charged or replaced.

Another place to measure voltage is at the input terminals of a malfunctioning device. This may require partial disassembly of the power plug or part of the unit itself to gain access to the power leads at the unit. Be extremely cautious. Touch the meter probes *only* to the power leads—nothing else. Observe proper polarity (red is almost always positive). Observe the voltage when the unit is switched off. Again observe the voltage with the unit switched on. There should be no more than about 4% difference between the readings. If the difference is greater than 4%, several problems may exist: (1) the battery may be dead or dying and in need of recharging or replacement, (2) the power cable may be too long, causing unwanted voltage drop when current is drawn through its resistance, (3) the power cable may contain a wire gauge insufficient for its length, (4) the power cable may be corroded at some point, introducing unwanted resistance and consequent voltage drop, (5) a power cable connection may be loose or corroded, or (6) the unit itself may be faulty and drawing too much current, causing the voltage drop. If (1), check the battery and re-charge as necessary. If (2), shorten the cable run by re-routing to the source. If (3), replace with heavier wire. If (4), replace the cable. If (5), clean and tighten all connections. If (6), measure current drain (see next section).

Remember that current flowing through a resistance causes a voltage drop across the resistance. We can use this principle to locate a poor connection or corroded contact. If current flows through a switch in its "ON" position, for example, there should be no resistance between its terminals. A resistance inside will cause a voltage to appear across the switch terminals. You can measure this voltage using a multimeter.

Set the voltage range higher than the voltage applied to the circuit. Touch the red probe to the positive side of the switch (or wire splice, distribution panel tie-point, circuit component, etc.). Touch the black probe to the other side. Step the voltage selector to a lower range if required to obtain a reading. If the switch is good, there should be *no* internal resistance when the switch is turned "on", and *no* voltage should appear across the switch contacts when current is flowing through the switch. Any voltage reading indicates resistance between the switch contacts.

Use this process wherever you suspect unwanted resistance.

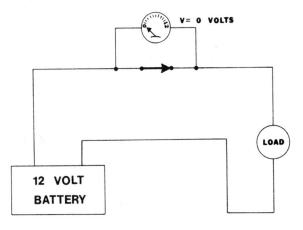

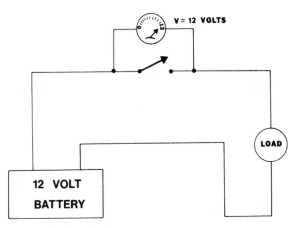

Using a multimeter in voltmeter mode to detect resistance in a switch.

Voltage across closed switch indicates internal resistance.

Testing for DC Current

As was mentioned in a previous section, a multimeter can be used in its DC current mode to determine whether an electronic device is pulling more juice from the battery than it should.

The rules for starting at the highest range must be obeyed. In addition, make certain the unit being tested is *in series* with the meter. If a meter in current mode is connected into a circuit with no series resistance (as would be the case if you touched both probes to the output terminals of a power cable), the meter may be damaged. Always

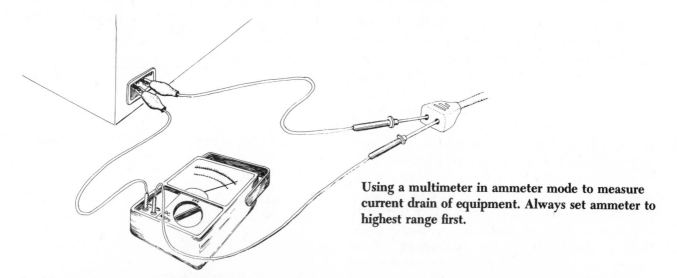

Using a multimeter in ammeter mode to measure current drain of equipment. Always set ammeter to highest range first.

use the meter in series with a resistance when measuring current. And, don't try to measure high currents, such as are drawn by an SSB radio while transmitting. If current drain exceeds the meter's setting or maximum capacity, the meter may be destroyed.

Suppose, for example, a digital depth sounder quits working. You check the cables and fuse. All is as it should be. Except for the depth sounder. It does nothing.

Remove the shield from the power cable connector, and check the voltage at the depth sounder end of the power cable. If no voltage, check the cable and its connections.

If 12.6 volts, or thereabouts, is available at the business end of the power cable plug, but the sounder doesn't work, it may be possible to proceed on your own just one step further. Put the meter *in series* with one lead of the power cable. This may require unsoldering one lead from the power cable plug and placing the meter between the disconnected points. Use of clip leads, short lengths of wire with alligator clips at each end, may help. To connect to female sockets, use stiff wire pushed carefully into the holes, and attach a clip lead between meter lead and stiff wire to make the circuit.

If the unit draws 3 amperes, when the specifications sheet says it should draw no more that 300 milliamperes (0.3 amperes), then you have a low resistance problem. Take it to the shop.

If, however, the unit draws zero amperes, no current at all, as measured on the lowest current scale (Be careful, this is the most sensitive range of the meter.), then you may have a faulty switch or an internal fuse that's blown. A few manufacturers put their fuses inside. Check—carefully.

Another possibility is reversed power cable polarity. Many manufacturers now protect their units with an internal diode that prevents current from flowing into the unit if the power cable is wired backwards. Check the cable. Make certain polarity is correct. Remember, some gear is *not* protected with diodes so, if you reverse the wires when they were correct to begin, you may damage an unprotected unit.

Keep in mind, however, *no* current can flow where there is no voltage. Check voltage first.

Testing for Resistance

Using a multimeter to measure resistance is a bit different from measuring voltage or current. Resistance is not an active force. It is a passive property of materials. In order to measure it, we apply voltage to the component being tested and measure the amount of current that flows through the component.

More current means less resistance.

Digital multimeters read resistance directly, displaying the value of resistance in ohms on the digital readout.

Needle movement type meters work somewhat

differently. The farther the meter needle moves to the right, the less resistance. If the meter needle moves all the way to the right, resistance is zero. If the needle doesn't move, resistance is infinite.

Needle meters must be zeroed before taking resistance measurements. Select the resistance range desired, touch the red and black probes together, and adjust the "zero ohms" control for a reading at the far right of the resistance scale.

Resistance mode is most often used to determine if a circuit is open or closed. Exact resistance values may be unimportant. If resistance is infinite, the circuit is open. If the resistance is something less than infinite (or maybe zero), we say there is continuity, that an electrical path exists between the test points. When testing for a perfect open circuit condition, i.e., infinite resistance, switch the meter to its highest range. When testing for continuity, switch to the lowest range.

One application of continuity testing has already been mentioned: testing fuses. Other applications include testing light bulbs, antenna coax cables and fittings, switches, or any circuit disconnected from its voltage source.

Do not test live circuits with meter in resistance mode!

To test an antenna cable, for example, disconnect both ends of the cable and use the meter in its resistance mode and highest range. There should be no continuity between the outer shield and the inner conductor. Any resistance less than infinite reveals an unwanted short. The lower the resistance, the more serious the problem.

Now, using a clip lead or short length of bare wire, connect outer shield to inner conductor at one end of the cable and test for continuity at the other end. Use the lowest resistance range. Resistance here should be quite low—only a few ohms at most. A higher resistance indicates worn or corroded wire somewhere between the ends of the cable.

Another application of the meter in current mode can quickly determine the condition of your lighting circuits. If you know how much current the masthead light or running lights should draw from your batteries, you can test

their operation by measuring current drain at the switch panel. A table of the more common 12-volt light bulbs and their current ratings appears below.

TABLE 19-1
LIGHT BULB CURRENT RATINGS

Bulb No.	Operating Voltage	Current Drain
67	13.5 volts	0.59 amps
89	13–14 volts	0.58 amps
90	13 volts	0.58 amps
93	12–12.8 volts	1.04 amps
1003	12.8 volts	.094 amps

Turn off the switch to the light(s) you want to test. With the meter in current mode and set to a safe range, touch the meter probes to each switch terminal. The current is now flowing through the meter rather than through the switch. The meter reading is the current drain. Since the current drain values given in the table above are dependent on voltage at the light bulb, current drain may differ somewhat from the tabulated values. By and large, however, they will be pretty close.

If more than the rated current flows through the circuit, an unwanted short circuit condition may exist. If less current flows, one or more bulbs may be burned out—or the contacts in the bulb sockets or at splices or other connections in the circuit may be corroded.

Note that the above described operations did not require a trip up the mast. Similar uses will occur to you as you become proficient with the various functions. Keep a record of your discoveries as you find new applications.

Testing for Electrolysis

If dissimilar metals are in contact with each other and with salty water or salty dampness (or other conducting fluid) a small electrical current may flow between the metals and through the liquid. As this current flows, a chemical reaction takes place. The less noble metal (see table below) dissolves.

The results can be catastrophic.

Don't mix metals!

Electrolysis can result in rapid and complete destruction of metallic parts in or around a boat. A serious electrolysis problem can cause through-hull fittings to fall out, propellers to disappear, or chainplates to disintegrate without warning.

Many electrolysis problems result from careless installation of marine electronic equipment. Others are the fault of the owner himself. A few are built into the boat by careless manufacturers. Electrical current can flow between the immersed metals by way of ground strapping, conductive bilge water (water solutions of salts are conductors), rigging or mooring cables. Any electrical path between the metals that permits electrons to flow from one metal to the other causes electrolytic decomposition to take place.

The atomic structure of metals creates the tendency to give up electrons. Metals with the greatest tendency to give up electrons are said to be the active metals. Metals less likely to give away electrons are called noble metals. The greater a metal's tendency to give away electrons, the more likely it is to be destroyed by electrolysis. The more noble metals are less affected by the ravages of electrolysis (and corrosion in general).

The following table lists a few of the metals you may expect to encounter on or around a boat. The most active are at the top. The most noble are at the bottom. Each is listed according to its tendency to give up electrons. Such a list is sometimes called anelectromotive series.

The list included here is not at all complete. Only generic boat materials are listed. There are far too many marine alloys to list them all here. For a more thorough electromotive series, consult a metallurgist's reference. This table should provide you with the relative activities of the most important metals so you can make tactical decisions in your battle against electrolysis.

The more diverse any two metals are, or the farther apart they appear in the electromotive series, the more likely are they to cause electrolysis problems on your boat.

Do not use diverse metals when you can avoid it.

Bronze and brass can be used together without much problem, but avoid using aluminum propellers on bronze propeller shafts. The aluminum propellers will be destroyed by electrolysis.

TABLE 19-2
ELECTROMOTIVE SERIES OF METALS

Most Active	Magnesium
	Zinc
	Aluminum
	Cadmium
	Mild steel
	Cast iron
	Stainless steel (active)
	Lead
	Tin
	Brass
	Copper
	Bronze
	Monel
	Stainless steel (passive)
	Titanium
Least Active	Graphite

Don't use stainless screws or bolts in aluminum if it can be avoided. The aluminum will disintegrate around the stainless. The aluminum threads will give way so the stainless screw or bolt can work free, or a mass of white aluminum salts will jamng resistance measurements. Select the resistance range desired, touch the red and black probes together, and adjust the "zero ohms" control for a reading at the far right of the resistance scale.

Resistance mode is most often used to determine if a circuit is open or closed. Exact resistance values may be unimportant. If resistance is infinite, the circuit is open. If the resistance is something less than infinite (or maybe zero), we say there is continuity, that an electricalmage.

The first is to apply a reverse voltage to each of the types of metals, according to its position in the electromotive series. Very little current is required to operate a properly-designed system. With an aluminum hull, this may be the only effective way to prevent serious damage. Installation should not be attempted without the assistance of an experienced and bonded professional. The potential for damages resulting from an improperly engineered reverse voltage electrolysis prevention system is great. If the job isn't done properly, the imposed voltage can work in reverse, enhancing electrolysis destruction!

The most common method of controlling electrolysis is with a sacrificial anode and ground strap bonding. The sacrificial anode most often used is made of zinc. Zinc anodes are available in dozens of shapes so they can be mounted to keel shoes, propeller and rudder shafts, through-hull fittings, struts, or to any metal surface that projects into the water beneath the hull. The zinc anode is consumed by the electrolytic action in place of the metals it is installed to protect. If all through-hulls are electrically bonded together and to the engine, negative battery terminals, grounding plates, keel bolts, etc., using heavy copper wire (or contact with aluminum or steel hull)—currents flowing between the dissimilar metals cancel with respect to each other. When all works well, the sacrificial zinc anodes disappear instead of the propeller shaft.

Zincs should be replaced at least once each season. When you suspect the presence of dissimilar metals below the waterline, an occasional check on the zincs may be in order. Some experts say a zinc should be replaced when 10% appears to have eroded. This may be a bit conservative, but better safe than sorry. Clearly, zincs that are heavily pitted are not effective simply because the pits represent where zinc used to be. Zinc anodes are alloys. The zinc may disappear and leave inert metal behind, metal that can't prevent electrolysis. Finally, badly pitted zinc anodes may suffer mechanical failure and fall off! Better to replace them early.

Remember: In the battle of electrolysis, it's the zinc or the metal the zinc was installed to protect. Sacrifice the zinc. They are extremely inexpensive—usually only a few dollars each, and they normally last an entire season. Always replace them at haul-outs.

In some fiberglass or wooden boats, where all through-hulls are bronze or stainless, bonding may not be required if zincs are placed strategically. If you suspect electrolytic action between any two metallic fittings—either under the hull or out on deck where they share a puddle of saltwater—you can check for the presence of a dangerous electromotive potential between them by using your multimeter in its DC volts mode. You may need to make an extension for one of the probes. Touch the probes to the two separate fit-

Zinc sacrificial anode collar around propeller shaft.

tings. If a voltage appears between them, you have located potential trouble. If your meter indicates more than a few hundredths of a volt, you could have *big* trouble. Install a zinc on the fitting showing a more positive potential. If you have any doubt, attach a sacrificial zinc to both.

Do not paint your zincs. Paint prevents them from working.

Preventing Corrosion

A great problem in shipboard installations of electronic equipment is corrosion. Salt air contains moisture and active ions that can combine with exposed metals to produce metallic salts. These salts, mostly chlorides, are not good conductors of electricity. When they form between connectors, on terminals, in light fixtures and sockets, the result is unwanted resistance.

Corrosion cannot be eliminated altogether, but it can be reduced.

The first step, of course, is to eliminate moisture. Contact points such as wire splices or cable connectors should not be exposed to spray or even damp night air. Corrosion can only be avoided by keeping connections clean and dry.

Careful planning goes a long way toward preventing corrosion problems. Screw contacts, splices, switches, light sockets, and other connections should be located where they are not exposed to moisture.

Some sprays are available to seal out moisture. Select one that remains flexible after application.

Simple varnish can work well. Fingernail polish or other lacquer can be applied judiciously to seal out corrosion. Tung oil can be sprayed on wires, when the wires are bone dry, to seal out dampness.

But do *not* spray electronic circuits with oil-based liquids. These sprays do not dry completely, causing cause dust to collect and form an insulating barrier. Components don't cool properly and fail prematurely.

Containers of dissicants, e.g., silica gel, can be placed inside "waterproof" or "not-so-waterproof" electronic equipment cabinets to absorb moisture. Some of these dessicant containers can be re-dried by placing them overnight in an oven set to 300. Consult the manufacturer's literature before oven-drying, however, since some may give off noxious or poisonous fumes when heated.

Gear that is not going to be regularly used (hand-held RDF, megaphone type loud-hailer, batteries, etc.) can be stored in plastic zip bags with a tiny sack of dessicant. Don't store where a wide range of temperatures may draw damp air into the bags.

When you aren't using your boat, take your electronic gear home. This affords the double protection of prevention against theft as well as corrosion. In some cases it's hard to tell which is the greater evil.

If you keep your boat in a slip where electrical shore power is available, leave a light turned on while you're away. Hang one in the engine room (a 40–watt droplight works nicely). Even a low wattage bulb can drive out moisture and stabilize the temperature changes that cause condensation.

Appendices

CONSTANTS

PHYSICAL CONSTANTS

horsepower	= 746 watts
speed of sound in air	= 1127 feet/second (@ sea level, 20° C.)
	= 331.45 meters/second
speed of sound in seawater	= 4945 feet/second (average)
speed of radio waves	= 299,800,000 meters/second
	= 186,280 miles/second
	= 984,000,000 feet/second
weight of pure water	= 62.43 pounds/cubic foot (@ 4° C.)

SPEED OF SOUND IN WATER AT VARIOUS TEMPERATURES

TEMP	SPEED
30	4717
40	4798
50	4870
60	4934
70	4987
80	5032
90	5068

ELECTRONICS TABLES

TABLE OF DECIBEL MULTIPLIERS

DB	ROUND POWER RATIO	POWER RATIO	VOLTS OR AMPERE RATIO
3	2	1.9953	1.4125
6	4	3.9811	1.9953
10	10	10.0000	3.1623
12	16	15.849	3.9811
16	40	39.811	6.3096
18	60	63.096	7.9433
20	100	100.000	10.0000
24	250	251.19	15.849
30	1000	1000.000	31.623
40	10000	10000.000	100.0000
50	100000	100000.000	316.23
60	1000000	1000000.000	1000.0000
70	10000000	10000000.000	3162.3

STANDARD RESISTOR COLOR CODE

COLOR	VALUE	MULTIPLIER
Black	0	10^0 = 1
Brown	1	10^1 = 10
Red	2	10^2 = 100
Orange	3	10^3 = 1000
Yellow	4	10^4 = 10,000
Green	5	10^5 = 100,000
Blue	6	10^6 = 1,000,000
Violet	7	10^7 = 10,000,000
Grey	8	10^8 = 100,000,000
White	9	10^9 = 1,000,000,000
Gold	—	10^{-1} = 0.1
Silver	—	10^{-2} = 0.01

RESISTOR TOLERANCES BY FOURTH BAND

No band	+/− 20%
Silver	+/− 10%
Gold	+/− 5%

WIRE SIZE V. OHMS PER 1000 FEET

Gauge (AWG)	Diameter (inches)	Ohms/1000'	Feet/Ohm
0000	.4600	.04901	20400
000	.4096	.06180	16180
00	.3648	.07793	12830
0	.3249	.09827	10180
1	.2893	.1239	8070
2	.2576	.1563	6400
3	.2294	.1970	5075
4	.2043	.2485	4025
5	.1819	.3133	3192
6	.1620	.3951	2531
7	.1443	.4982	2007
8	.1285	.6282	1592
9	.1144	.7921	1262
10	.1019	.9989	1001
11	.09074	1.260	794
12	.08081	1.588	629.6
13	.07196	2.003	499.3
14	.06408	2.525	396.0
15	.05707	3.184	314.0
16	.05082	4.016	249.0
17	.04526	5.064	197.5
18	.04030	6.385	156.5
19	.03589	8.051	124.2
20	.03196	10.15	98.5
21	.02846	12.80	78.11
22	.02535	16.14	61.95
23	.02257	20.36	49.13
24	.02010	25.67	38.96
25	.01790	32.37	30.90
26	.01594	40.81	24.50
27	.01420	51.47	19.43
28	.01264	64.90	15.41
29	.01126	81.83	12.22
30	.01003	103.2	9.691
31	.008928	130.1	7.685
32	.007950	164.1	6.095

RADIO TABLES

RDF CONVERSION TABLE

MID-LAT	DIFFERENCE IN LONGITUDE (D-LO)										
	2°	4°	6°	8°	10°	12°	14°	16°	18°	20°	22°
4°	.1	.1	.2	.3	.3	.4	.5	.6	.6	.7	.8
8°	.1	.3	.4	.5	.7	.8	1.0	1.1	1.3	1.4	1.6
12°	.2	.4	.6	.8	1.0	1.2	1.4	1.7	1.9	2.1	2.3
16°	.3	.5	.8	1.1	1.4	1.6	1.9	2.2	2.5	2.8	3.1
20°	.3	.7	1.0	1.3	1.7	2.0	2.4	2.7	3.1	3.5	3.8
24°	.4	.8	1.2	1.6	2.0	2.4	2.8	3.2	3.7	4.1	4.6
28°	.5	.9	1.4	1.8	2.3	2.8	3.2	3.7	4.2	4.7	5.3
32°	.5	1.0	1.5	2.1	2.6	3.1	3.7	4.2	4.8	5.3	5.9
36°	.6	1.1	1.7	2.3	2.9	3.5	4.1	4.7	5.3	5.9	6.6
40°	.6	1.2	1.9	2.5	3.1	3.8	4.4	5.1	5.8	6.5	7.2
44°	.7	1.3	2.0	2.7	3.4	4.1	4.8	5.5	6.2	7.0	7.7
48°	.7	1.4	2.2	2.9	3.6	4.4	5.1	5.9	6.7	7.5	8.3
52°	.8	1.5	2.3	3.1	3.9	4.6	5.4	6.3	7.1	7.9	8.8
56°	.8	1.6	2.4	3.2	4.1	4.9	5.7	6.6	7.4	8.3	9.2
60°	.8	1.7	2.5	3.4	4.2	5.1	6.0	6.9	7.8	8.7	9.6

Conversion is angle between great circle (RDF) bearing and the rhumbline bearing. Rhumbline is always toward the equator from great circle (RDF) bearing. Thus, if RDF bearing of station is 042°, and station longitude is 12° from ship longitude, while the mid-latitude between ship and station is 30° (ship at N40° and station at N20°) the RDF bearing corrected to rhumbline is 045°(T) measured from ship. Warning: Use cautiously near poles.

RADIO FREQUENCY SPECTRUM

3 – 30	kilohertz	VLF	Very Low Frequency	100000 – 10000 m.
30 – 300	kilohertz	LF	Low Frequency	10000 – 1000 m.
300 – 3000	kilohertz	MF	Medium Frequency	1000 – 100 m.
.3 – 3	megahertz	MF	Medium Frequency	1000 – 100 m.
3 – 30	megahertz	HF	High Frequency	100 – 10 m.
30 – 300	megahertz	VHF	Very High Frequency	10 – 1 m.
300 – 3000	megahertz	UHF	Ultra High Frequency	1 – .1 m.
.3 – 3	gigahertz	UHF	Ultra High Frequency	1 – .1 m.
3 – 30	gigahertz	SHF	Super High Frequency	.1 – .01 m.
30 – 300	gigahertz	EHF	Extremely High Frequency	.01 – .001 m.

STATIONS BROADCASTING STANDARD TIME

CALL	FREQUENCY (MHz)	LOCATION
WWV	2.5, 5, 10, 15, 20	Ft. Collins, Colorado
WWVH	2.5, 5, 10, 15	Kekaha, Kauai, Hawaii
CHU	3.33, 7.335, 14.670	Ottawa, Ontario, Canada
RID	5.004, 10.004, 15.004	Irkutsk, USSR
RWM	4.996, 9.996, 14.996	Novosibirsk, USSR
ZUO	2.5, 5	Pretoria, South Africa
VNG	7.5	Lyndhurst, Australia
BPV	5, 10, 15	Shanghai, China
JJY	2.5, 5, 10, 15	Tokyo, Japan
LOL	5, 10, 15	Buenos Aires, Argentina

VHF CHANNELS FOR U.S. RADIO USERS

DISTRESS, SAFETY & CALLING   16
    (Calling, Safety, and Distress)
INTERSHIP SAFETY   6
    (Intership Safety)
COAST GUARD COMMUNICATIONS   22A
    (Ship to CG Ship or Aircraft & Ship to CG Coast)
PORT OPERATIONS   1, 5, 12, 14, 20, 63, 65A, 66A, 73, 74, 77
    (Intership & Ship to Coast)
NAVIGATIONAL   13, 67
    (Intership & Ship to Coast)
NON-COMMERCIAL   9, 68, 69, 71, 72, 78A
    (Intership & Ship to Coast)
NON-COMMERCIAL   70, 72
    (Intership)
COMMERCIAL   1, 7A, 9, 10, 11, 18A, 19A, 63, 79A, 80A
    (Commercial Intership & Ship to Coast)
COMMERCIAL   8, 67, 77, 88A
    (Commercial Intership)
PUBLIC CORRESPONDENCE   24, 25, 26, 27, 28, 84, 85, 86, 87
    (Ship to Coast Marine Operator)

INTERNATIONAL MORSE CODE

A	didah	.-	N	dahdit	-.
B	dahdididit	-...	O	dahdahdah	---
C	dahdidahdit	-.-.	P	didahdahdit	.--.
D	dahdidit	-..	Q	dahdahdidah	--.-
E	dit	.	R	didahdit	.-.
F	dididahdit	..-.	S	dididit	...
G	dahdahdit	--.	T	dah	-
H	didididit	....	U	dididah	..-
I	didit	..	V	didididah	...-
J	didahdahdah	.---	W	didahdah	.--
K	dahdidah	-.-	X	dahdididah	-..-
L	didahdidit	.-..	Y	dahdidahdah	-.--
M	dahdah	--	Z	dahdahdidit	--..

1	didahdahdahdah	.----	6	dahdidididit	-....
2	dididahdahdah	..---	7	dahdahdididit	--...
3	didididahdah	...--	8	dahdahdahdidit	---..
4	dididididah	....-	9	dahdahdahdahdit	----.
5	didididit	.....	0	dahdahdahdahdah	-----

.	didahdidahdidah	.-.-.-
?	dididahdahdidit	..--..
/	dahdididahdit	-..-.
,	dahdahdididahdah	--..--
:	dahdahdahdididit	---...
;	dahdidahdidahdit	-.-.-.
-	dahdididididah	-....-
--	dahdidididah	-...-
(	dahdidahdahdit	-.--.
)	dahdidahdahdidah	-.--.-
'	didahdahdahdahdit	.----.

error	dididididididit	.... or more
wait	didahdididit	.-...-
end of message	didahdidahdit	.-.-.
invitation to transmit	dahdidah	-.-
end of work	didididahdidah	...-.-

AMATEUR RADIO

COMMON AMATEUR "Q" SIGNALS

QRA	What is the name of your station?
QRB	What is your distance from me?
QRL	Is this frequency busy?
QRM	There is interference from other stations.
QRN	There is interference from static.
QRO	Increase power.
QRP	Reduce power.
QRQ	Send faster.
QRS	Send more slowly.
QRT	Stop sending.
QRU	I have no traffic for you.
QRV	Ready.
QRX	I will call again at (give time) or (give frequency).
QRZ	You are being called by (give callsign) on (frequency).
QSB	Your signals are fading
QSL	I acknowledge receipt.
QSO	I can communicate with (give callsign).
QSY	Move to (give frequency).
QTH	My position is (give coordinates).

"TEN" SIGNALS

10-1	Your signals are weak.
10-2	Your signals are good.
10-3	Stop transmitting.
10-4	Received all ok, "roger".
10-6	Busy handling traffic, please stand by.
10-7	Unit going off the air, temporarily out of service.
10-8	Unit signing on, in service.
10-9	Please repeat your message.
10-10 ...	I have no further traffic, standing by.
10-11 ...	Please speak more slowly.
10-12 ...	There are visitors present at this end.
10-13 ...	Please advise your weather conditions.
10-18 ...	Do you have any message traffic for me?
10-19 ...	There is no traffic for you at this time.
10-20 ...	What is your location?
10-21 ...	Please call this station by landline.
10-27 ...	Please move to frequency (give frequency).
10-28 ...	What station is calling?
10-75 ...	You are causing interference.
10-99 ...	Task completed, all units secure.

NETS FOR MARITIME MOBILES

TIME	FREQ	NET NAME & AREA
0230	14.313	Seafarers' Net—Atlantic
0500	14.314	Pacific MM Net—S.E. Asia/Australia/S. Pacific
0630	14.320	South Africa MM Net—S. Atlantic/Indian
0700	14.313	International MM Net—Atlantic/Mediterranean/Caribbean
0715	3.820	Bay of Islands MM Net—S. Pacific/Australia/New Zealand
0800	14.303	United Kingdom MM Net—Atlantic/Mediterranean/Caribbean
0800	14.315	Pacific Interisland Net—S. Pacific/Indian/S.E. Asia
1130	14.320	South Africa MM Net—S. Atlantic
1130	3.815	Antilles Emergency Weather Net—Caribbean
1130	21.325	South Atlantic Roundtable—S. Atlantic/Indian
1200	14.320	Sea Net—S.E. Asia/Indonesia/Australia
1230	7.240	Caribbean MM Net—Caribbean
1300	7.268	Waterway Net—E. Coast of U.S./Caribbean
1600	14.313	Coast Guard MM Net—Atlantic/Caribbean/U.S. Inland
1700	14.313	International MM Net—Atlantic/Mediterranean/Caribbean
1800	14.303	United Kingdom MM Net—Atlantic/Mediterranean/Caribbean
1900	7.288	Friendly Net—Hawaiian Islands
2000	14.305	Confusion Net—S. Pacific
2330	7.190	Admirals' Net—U.S. West Coast
2400	14.320	Sea MM Net—Asia/Japan/Australia

Time in UTC (many 1 hour earlier during Daylight Savings Time)

SOUNDING

SONIC CONE DIAMETER VS. DEPTH

	BEAM ANGLE						
DEPTH	4	9	18	22	36	43	50
10	1	2	3	4	6	8	9
20	1	3	6	8	13	16	19
30	2	5	10	12	19	24	28
40	3	6	13	16	26	32	37
60	4	9	19	23	39	47	56
80	6	13	26	31	52	63	75
100	7	16	32	39	65	79	93
150	10	24	48	58	97	118	140
200	14	31	63	78	130	158	187
300	21	47	95	117	195	236	280
500	35	79	158	194	325	394	466
1000	70	157	317	389	650	788	933

RADAR

DISTANCE TO RADAR HORIZON

Ht.	Dist.	Ht.	Dist.	Ht.	Dist.	Ht.	Dist.
10	3.9	34	7.1	58	9.3	82	11.0
12	4.2	35	7.3	60	9.5	84	11.2
14	4.6	38	7.5	62	9.6	86	11.3
16	4.9	40	7.7	64	9.8	88	11.4
18	5.2	42	7.9	66	9.9	90	11.6
20	5.5	44	8.1	68	10.1	92	11.7
22	5.7	46	8.3	70	10.2	94	11.8
24	6.0	48	8.5	72	10.4	96	12.0
26	6.2	50	8.6	74	10.5	98	12.1
28	6.5	52	8.8	76	10.6	100	12.2
30	6.7	54	9.0	78	10.8	120	13.4
32	6.9	56	9.1	80	10.9	150	14.9

(Height is scanner distance from waterline. Distance is nautical miles)

BATTERIES

HYDROMETER TEMPERATURE CORRECTIONS

Fahrenheit	Celsius	Correction
160	71.1	+0.032
150	65.6	+0.028
140	60.0	+0.024
130	54.4	+0.020
120	48.9	+0.016
110	43.3	+0.012
100	37.8	+0.008
90	32.2	+0.004
80	26.7	none
70	21.1	−0.004
60	15.6	−0.008
50	10.0	−0.012
40	4.4	−0.016
30	−1.1	−0.020
20	−6.7	−0.024
10	−12.2	−0.028

RECOMMENDED CHARGING RATES AND TIMES

RESERVE MINUTES	SLOW CHARGE		QUICK CHARGE	
80 or less	10	hrs @ 5 amps	2.5	hrs @ 20 amps
	5	hrs @ 10 amps	1.5	hrs @ 30 amps
80–125	15	hrs @ 5 amps	3.75	hrs @ 20 amps
	7.5	hrs @ 10 amps	1.5	hrs @ 50 amps
125–170	20	hrs @ 5 amps	5	hrs @ 20 amps
	10	hrs @ 10 amps	2	hrs @ 50 amps
170–250	30	hrs @ 5 amps	7.5	hrs @ 20 amps
	15	hrs @ 10 amps	3	hrs @ 50 amps
over 250	24	hrs @ 10 amps	6	hrs @ 40 amps
			4	hrs @ 60 amps

Bibliography

BOOKS Azimov, Isaac, *Understanding Physics*, New American Library, Bergenfield, NJ, 1966.

Belt, Forest H., *Easi-Guide To Boat Radio*, Howard W. Sams & Co., 1973.

Brotherton, Miner, *12–Volt Bible for Boats*, Seven Seas Press, Newport, R.I., 1985.

Buchsbaum, Walter H., *Complete Handbook of Practical Electronic Reference Data, 2nd Edition*, Prentice-Hall, Inc., NJ, 1978.

French, John, *Electrical and Electronic Equipment for Yachts*, Dodd Mead & Company, 1974.

French, John, *Small Craft Radar*, Van Nostrand Reinhold Company, 1977.

Graves, Frederick, *Mariners Guide to Single Sideband*, Stephens Engineering Associates, Inc., Mountlake Terrace, WA, 1982.

Graves, Frederick, *Piloting*, International Marine Publishing Company, Camden, ME, 1981.

MacLean, David, *Marine Electrical Care And Repair*, Tab Books, 1978.

Miller, Conrad, *Your Boat's Electrical System*, Motor Boating & Sailing Books, 1973.

Sands, Leo G., *Marine Electronics Handbook*, Tab Books, 1973.

Stansell, Thomas A., *The Transit Navigation Satellite System*, Magnavox Company, 1978.

West, Jack, *Radar For Marine Navigation And Safety*, Van Nostrand Reinhold Company, 1978.

ARTICLES Bamford, D. A. "Electronics", *Cruising World*, vol. 2, no. 9, 1976.

Bingham, Bruce. "Basic Battery Care", *Cruising World*, vol. 9, no. 5, 1983.

Binns, Mary. "Understanding Electronic Corrosion", *Cruising World*, vol. 7, no. 2, 1981.

Burgess, Bob. "Picture This . . . The Morse Code", *Cruising World*, vol. 8, no. 7, 1982.

Dahl, Bonnie. "How To Use Loran-C", *Cruising World*, vol. 9, no. 5, 1983.

Dahl, Bonnie. "Adapting Loran-C To Everyday Navigation", *Cruising World*, vol. 9, no. 6, 1983.

Farnes, Quinn. "The Cruiser's Voice On The High Seas", *Cruising World*, vol. 6, no. 11, 1980.

Gilbert, Jim. "At Last, A Bona Fide Small-Boat Radar", *Cruising World*, vol. 9, no. 5, 1983.

Graves, Frederick. "Amateur Radio Goes To Sea", *Cruising World*, vol. 3, no. 10, 1977.

Graves, Frederick. "CB Radio Is Fun", *Cruising World*, vol. 6, no. 5, 1980.

Graves, Frederick. "Consumer's Pilot To SSB", *Cruising World*, vol. 9, no. 11, 1983.

Graves, Frederick. "Ham—A Consumer's Pilot", *Cruising World*, vol. 9, no. 12, 1983.

Graves, Frederick. "Instruments That Measure Up", *Cruising World*, vol. 11, no. 1, 1985.

Graves, Frederick. "Piloting With Depth Sounders", *Cruising World*, vol. 11, no. 2, 1985.

Graves, Frederick. "Piloting With Loran-C", *Cruising World*, vol. 11, no. 8, 1985.

Graves, Frederick. "Piloting With Radio Direction Finders", *Cruising World*, vol. 11, no. 3, 1985.

Graves, Frederick. "RDF Brings You Home In The Fog", *Cruising World*, vol. 4, no. 12, 1978.

Graves, Frederick. "VHF: A Consumer's Pilot", *Cruising World*, vol. 9, no. 10, 1983.

Greene, Danny. "Sailing With Self-Steering", *Cruising World*, vol. 10, no. 8, 1984.

Hamilton, Gene and Katie. "Radar Reflectors Can Show You're There", *Cruising World*, vol. 6, no. 10, 1980.

Hopkins, Mark. "Getting The News At Sea", *Cruising World*, vol. 8, no. 4, 1982.

Kirlin, Clyde. "How To Get Started In VHF", *Cruising World*, vol. 7, no. 5, 1981.

Kirlin, Clyde. "Radio Evolves To Synthesize SSB", *Cruising World*, vol. 6, no. 6, 1980.

Kirlin, Clyde. "Selecting An Autopilot Isn't Easy", *Cruising World*, vol. 8, no. 1, 1982.

Kirlin, Clyde. "Simple Electronic Tests You Can Do", *Cruising World*, vol. 6, no. 10, 1980.

Kuebler, Wolf and Sommers, Sharon. "A Critical Review Of The Fix Accuracy And Reliability Of Electronic Marine Navigation Systems", *Navigation*, vol. 29, no. 2, 1982.

Lush, Tony. "Setting Your Electrical Priorities", *Cruising World*, vol. 5, no. 3, 1979.

Lush, Tony. "The Ever Evolving Navstation", *Cruising World*, vol. 11, no.1, 1985.

Marken, Andy. "Self-Steering Systems Get An Informal Test", *Cruising World*, vol. 4, no. 11, 1978.

McDougle, Robert. "Space Technology To The Rescue!", *Cruising World*, vol. 8, no. 10, 1982.

Merriam, Robert. "Exposing The Myth Of The Great Floating Ground", *Cruising World*, vol. 10, no. 4, 1984.

Morrison, Bob. "A Mate That Won't Drink Your Whiskey", *Cruising World*, vol. 8, no. 3, 1982.

Norwalk, Jay. "On Choosing Between Navigational Wizards: Loran-C Or Sat-Nav?", *Cruising World*, vol. 10, no. 11, 1984.

Richardson, Cyrus. "Light Emitting Diodes Can Prevent Dead Batteries", *Cruising World*, vol. 4, no. 9, 1978.

Rudoff, Hyman. "The Pluses And Minuses Of Batteries", *Cruising World*, vol. 7, no. 10, 1981.

Rudoff, Hyman, "Fear The Big Ships But Talk To Them", *Cruising World*, vol. 8, no. 5, 1982.

Saunders, Mike. "Get The Best From Your RDF", *Cruising World*, vol. 5, no. 10, 1979.

Simon, Richard. "Sailing With Sat-Nav", *Cruising World*, vol. 8, no. 2, 1982.

Stanere, Bill. "Skipper's Choice: Radar or Loran?", vol. 10, no. 4, 1984.

Terman, Douglas. "The Coastal Connection", *Cruising World*, vol. 10, no. 1, 1984.

Viggiano, Rick. "The Able-Bodied Autopilot", *Cruising World*, vol. 11, no. 1, 1985.

Weseman, John F. "Loran-C: Present and Future", *Navigation*, vol. 29, no. 1, 1982.

Wood, Charles. "The Charge Of The Battery Brigade", *Cruising World*, vol. 5, no. 10, 1979.

GOVERNMENT PUBLICATIONS

American Practical Navigator, H.O. Pub. No. 9

Coast Guard Aids to Navigation, Coast Guard publication CG–193.

Loran-C User Handbook, Coast Guard publication COMDTINST M16562.3.

Mariners Weather Log, Environmental Data and Information Service, National Oceanic and Atmospheric Administration, U.S. Department of Commerce—all issues contain useful information.

Navigation Dictionary, H.O. Pub. No. 220

Radar Navigation Manual, Defense Mapping Agency Hydrographic Center publication Pub 1310.

Radio Aids to Navigation, H.O. Pub. No. 117–A and 117–B.

Index